COOKING WITH KURMA

COOKING
WITH
KURMA

MORE GREAT VEGETARIAN DISHES

BY KURMA DASA

CHAKRA PRESS

Chakra Press
10 Rochester St. Botany, NSW 2019 Australia

Chakra Press is an imprint of the Bhaktivedanta Book Trust, Australia

Publisher	Naresvara dasa
Photography	Peter Colville
Food Styling	Susan Whitter
Art Design and Direction	Phillip Little
Editor	Carol D'Costa
Food Preparation	Kurma dasa, Jagat Priya devi dasi
Colour Separations	Hitech Graphics, Melbourne

Cased Edition ISBN 0 947259 17 1

Limp Edition ISBN 0 9578345 2 7

Printed in Australia by McPherson's Printing Group

DEDICATION

This book is dedicated to my spiritual master, His Divine
Grace A.C. Bhaktivedanta Swami Prabhupada, who
encouraged me to cook by enjoying my *poories.*

ACKNOWLEDGMENTS

I am indebted to Naresvara dasa, the publisher, for bringing my second book to fruition. Peter Colville not only took the excellent photographs but was also good fun to be with. Susan Whitter's excellent food styling and cooking skills are evident in the abundant photos in this book. Her positive attitude and unpretentious manner was also very much appreciated.

The beauty of this book is due to Phillip Little's expertise as designer and art director. His level-headedness and good humour also kept the project on track.

Behind the scenes in the kitchen Jagat Priya and Dhara worked unrelentingly day after day. Their hard labour and wonderful attitude was an inspiration.

I would also like to thank the following persons for their assistance:
Tiani Kane for spending long hours keying-in the manuscript; Carol D'Costa for her expert editing; Howard Lyman for his *Foreword;* Drutakarma for the *Introduction,* and Trevor Absolom for the *Index.*

Thanks also goes to Aniruddha dasa, Kamsanasa dasa, Mandapa dasa, Sraddhavana dasa, Madhava Gouranga D'Costa, Gaura Jagannatha dasa, Navina-sakhi devi dasi, Privavrata dasa, Wanda and others whom I might have inadvertently forgotten.

A special thank you goes to my wife, Ananda Yukta, for her patience and understanding during the long months of recipe testing, and especially during my absence.

My special thanks to:
Ian & Elizabeth Hemphill of Herbies Spices, Rozelle, NSW;
Bertolli Australia Pty. Ltd.;
Basile Imports;
Oppenheimer Pty. Ltd., (importer of VICTORINOX professional cutlery and Chef Specialties Professional Pepper Mills); and
Villeroy and Boch Australia Pty. Ltd.

FOREWORD

Never before in the history of man have there been less trees, less fish, less clean air, less topsoil, less rainforest, less clean water; the list goes on and on. At the same time we are doubling the world's population every forty to fifty years. We are on a very slippery slope and the incline is getting greater every day.

On our chemically addicted farms in North America we are spending fourteen calories of energy for every calorie of grain we produce. In our factory feedlots we are spending up to seventy calories of energy for every calorie of beef we place on our plate. You don't need to be a rocket scientist to understand that this can't continue indefinitely.

The natural resources on planet Earth are limited and we should use them wisely. A person eating a plant-based diet treads much lighter on the Earth than one eating a meat-based diet. This book shows a practical way of doing your part to extend these resources to all the unborn generations.

Not only is the environment important, but our personal health should be a reason for change. Countless studies show that people eating a plant-based diet have had a longer and healthier existence.

I was raised during the Second World War on a small organic dairy in Montana. My parents couldn't hire help so they had to tend the cows themselves, while our grand-parents tended my brother, two sisters, and myself. Day care back then was much different than today. There weren't any swings, slides, or leggo blocks; day care was working in the garden. That's where I learned my love of the soil.

I thought working in the garden was as close to being in the Garden of Eden as was humanly possible. We had birds, trees, and living soil. To me it was heaven. The three most important things to humans are the air we breathe, the water we drink, and the food we eat, and I learned early on about growing food.

My parents owning a farm led me to believe that the rest of my life I would be involved in producing food to feed a hungry world. I received a degree in Agriculture from Montana State University after learning what was called "better living through chemistry". My great-grandfather was an organic farmer, my grandfather was an organic farmer, my father was an organic farmer — and I was a chemical junkie.

I took this new-found knowledge and turned our organic farm into a modern agri-business. I was using thousands of dollars a year of chemicals to attain my goal of a modern factory farm. The birds were dying, the trees were dying and the soil was beginning to resemble asbestos. I was the cause of the problem but I wouldn't admit it to myself until I was paralysed from the waist down with a tumor on my spinal cord. The doctor told me I had a one in a million chance of ever walking again if the tumor was on the inside of the cord. This condition finally got my attention, and I had to ask myself was I part of the problem or part of the solution?

Flat on my back in the hospital with odds of one in a million I made the commitment that the rest of my life, whether I walked or not, I would resolve to restore the birds, the trees, and the soil. I walked out of the hospital after a one in a million operation on a tumor on the inside of my spinal cord. I have never forgotten the promise that I made at a time when I didn't know if I would ever walk again.

Writing this *Foreword* recommending a book on good healthy eating is part of that commitment. Kurma has provided a great way to start the rest of your life. It is not about being perfect. It is about doing better tomorrow than you did today. This book will enable you to be part of the solution and less part of the problem. Read, prepare, and enjoy great food with Kurma's help. And, remember, starting with fresh organically-grown produce from local family farmers is always the first step toward recovery for both you and the planet.

Howard F. Lyman
President
International Vegetarian Union

CONTENTS

INTRODUCTION

In 1990, Kurma asked me to write the introduction to his first cookbook, *Great Vegetarian Dishes.* That work established his reputation as a master vegetarian chef and popular cooking teacher. Through television shows and personal appearances around the world, as well as through his cookbooks, he jovially introduced hundreds of millions of people to his special brand of elegant and eclectic cuisine. I am happy for his success and wish him more. And that is certain to come with *Cooking with Kurma.*

Cooking with Kurma is an invitation to embark on an exciting journey of culinary exploration. Each lucidly explained recipe is an adventure into new lands of international culture, taste, and nutrition. And Kurma is a master guide. He has travelled around the world, learning first-hand how to prepare a stunning variety of vegetarian dishes.

Whether you are looking to prepare a quick lunch or a twelve-course dinner, *Cooking with Kurma* will serve you well. The chapters are full of enticing soups, breads, salads, condiments, drinks, desserts and main courses.

You will notice that a good many of the recipes can be traced to India. There is a special reason for that. Kurma has a passion not only for cooking but also for *yoga.* Since 1970, Kurma has been practising the timeless system of *bhakti-yoga,* the *yoga* of devotion.

The *bhakti-yoga* practices were widely introduced to the Western world in the 1960s and 1970s by His Divine Grace A. C. Bhaktivedanta Swami Prabhupada, who founded the International Society for Krishna Consciousness, popularly known as the Hare Krishna Movement. Kurma became an initiated disciple of Prabhupada in 1971.

One of the main elements of *bhakti-yoga* is the preparation of sacred foods, foods fit for God. For thousands of years, priests in temples throughout India have prepared divine vegetarian offerings for the Supreme Being, known by names such as Krishna and Rama. These offerings are saturated with love and devotion.

Cooking thus becomes *yoga.*

The Sanskrit word *yoga* carries the meaning of "connection", specifically the connection between the individual soul and the Supreme Soul. This connection has now been broken, and *yoga* is the means for reestablishing it.

The connection between the soul and Supreme Soul is intimate and personal, and the techniques for reestablishing the connection are also intimate and personal. If we love someone, we want to do things for them, and a very common thing that people do for people they love is to cook for them.

Practitioners of *bhakti-yoga* prepare offerings for Krishna in this same spirit of love. This love is manifested at every stage of the cooking process — from the purchasing of the ingredients to the final offering of the sacred meal to the object of one's devotion.

In the *Bhagavad-gita,* the Supreme Lord says He is very pleased to accept such offerings. The text specifically says that such offerings should be vegetarian. This is the main reason why a practitioner of *bhakti-yoga* is a vegetarian.

When delicious vegetarian dishes are offered to the Lord with love and devotion and the Lord accepts them, the offerings are infused with the spiritual energies of God. By tasting such foods, the practitioner of *bhakti-yoga* experiences divine pleasure. Vegetarian food offered to the Lord is called *prasadam,* or mercy. Many spiritual truths are automatically revealed to one who simply eats *prasadam. Prasadam* also has the power to cleanse the heart of the negative effects of *karma.* On the other hand, consuming food saturated with violence and selfishness increases the negative effects of *karma.*

Shri Shri Radha-Krishna

The *bhakti-yoga* diet is thus spiritually elevating. If something is good for you spiritually, it is generally also good for you materially. Medical studies have shown that vegetarians tend to suffer less than others from various heart diseases and cancers. As far as the planet is concerned, the meat industry is one of the most wasteful of natural resources and the most destructive of the environment. A spiritual vegetarian diet of food offered to Krishna is good not only for your soul but also for your body and our planet.

If you have some hesitation about offering your food specifically to Krishna, then you can offer it to God according to your own understanding.

But if you do want to offer your food to Krishna, here is how you can go about it. Somewhere in your home or kitchen you can make a small altar. On this altar you can place three pictures: one of the spiritual master, one of Krishna, and one of Lord Caitanya. Such pictures are also available from the publisher of this book.

The spiritual master, or *guru*, serves as Krishna's representative, and it is through the spiritual master that Krishna receives offerings. If you seriously take up the practice of *bhakti-yoga*, you will eventually want to connect yourself with a living spiritual master through initiation. In that case, you will use a picture of your personal spiritual master for offering food. But until that time one may make offerings using a picture of Srila Prabhupada, along with pictures of Lord Krishna and Lord Caitanya.

For the purpose of offering, it is best to reserve a special plate that is not used for anything else. After you have finished cooking, place a little of each preparation on the plate for offering. Soups and drinks can, of course, go in special cups and bowls reserved for making offerings.

The simplest kind of offerings you can make is to place the offering before the pictures of Srila Prabhupada, Krishna, and Lord Caitanya and simply ask them to please accept it. But the usual procedure is to say some additional Sanskrit prayers, or *mantras*. Each of the following four *mantras* should be softly repeated three times. The English translations do not have to be spoken. I have provided them simply so you will know what the Sanskrit *mantras* mean.

Lord Caitanya (the Panchatattva)

1) *nama om vishnu-padaya
krishna-presthaya bhutale
srimate bhaktivedanta-
svamin iti namine*

"I offer my respectful obeisances unto His Divine Grace A.C. Bhaktivedanta Swami Prabhupada, who is very dear to Lord Krishna, having taken shelter at His lotus feet."

2) *namas te sarasvate devam
gaura-vani-pracharine
nirvishesha-shunyavadi-
paschatya-desha tarine*

"Our respectful obeisances unto you, O spiritual master, servant of Sarasvati Goswami. You are kindly preaching the message of Lord Caitanya and delivering the Western countries, which are filled with impersonalism and voidism."

3) *namo maha-vadanyaya*
krishna-prema-pradaya te
krishnaya krishna-caitanya
namne gaura-tvishe namaha

"I offer my respectful obeisances unto the Supreme Lord Sri Krishna Caitanya, who is more magnanimous than any other incarnation, even Krishna Himself, because He is bestowing freely what no one else has ever given — pure love of Krishna."

4) *namo-brahmanya-devaya*
go brahmana hitaya cha
jagad-hitaya krishnaya
govindaya namo namaha

"I offer my respectful obeisances to the Supreme Absolute Truth, Krishna, who is the well-wisher of the cows and the *brahmanas* as well as the living entities in general. I offer my repeated obeisances to Govinda [Krishna], who is the pleasure reservoir for all the senses."

After chanting these four *mantras* three times each, you can chant the following *mantra*, called the *maha-mantra*, or great *mantra*, several times:

Hare Krishna, Hare Krishna
Krishna Krishna, Hare Hare
Hare Rama, Hare Rama
Rama Rama, Hare Hare

When the offering is completed, you and your family or guests can enjoy your meal. Be prepared for a nourishing and satisfying taste experience.

Michael A. Cremo (Drutakarma Dasa),
co-author of *The Higher Taste: A Guide to Gourmet Vegetarian Cooking and a Karma-Free Diet;*
Divine Nature: A Spiritual Perspective on the Environmental Crisis;
and *Forbidden Archaeology: The Hidden History of the Human Race.*
Los Angeles, December 25, 1997

Suggested reading:

Great Vegetarian Dishes, by Kurma dasa.

Lord Krishna's Cuisine: The Art of Indian Vegetarian Cooking and *Yamuna's Table*, by Yamuna Devi.

The Higher Taste: A guide to Gourmet Vegetarian Cooking and a Karma-Free Diet.

The Hare Krishna Book of Vegetarian Cooking, by Adiraja dasa.

Food for the Spirit: Vegetarianism and World Religions, by Satayaraja dasa

Prabhupada, by Satsvarupa dasa Goswami.

Bhagavad-gita As It Is, by A. C. Bhaktivedanta Swami Prabhupada

HOW TO MEASURE AND USE THE RECIPES

MEASUREMENT OF VOLUME

Because there is some difference between the Australian, American and British cup and spoon measurements, this book gives quantities for most ingredients in Australian cups and spoons with the metric volume equivalent (litres or parts thereof) in parentheses. This avoids the troublesome business of looking up conversion charts or using kitchen scales to weigh ingredients.

To conveniently use these recipes, you will require a set of graduated spoons (¼ teaspoon, ½ teaspoon, 1 teaspoon and 1 tablespoon) and a set of graduated cups (¼ cup, ⅓ cup, ½ cup and 1 cup) and perhaps a glass or plastic liquid measuring container, usually containing both cup and litre markings.

TEASPOONS

The Australian, American and British teaspoons all hold approximately 5ml. I have rounded off fractions of teaspoons to the nearest ml. Thus:

½ teaspoon (2ml) salt
¼ teaspoon (1ml) black pepper

TABLESPOONS

Tablespoon measurements given in this book are standard Australian tablespoons, holding 20ml. The American standard tablespoon holds 14.2ml and the British standard tablespoon holds 17.7ml. Thus American readers should heap their tablespoons, and British readers should slightly heap their tablespoons.

CUPS

Cup measurements given in this book are standard Australian cups, which hold 250ml. The American and British standard cups hold 240ml. Thus American and British readers should generously fill their standard measurement cups, or, in the case of liquids, should add 2 teaspoons extra for every cup required.

MEASUREMENT OF WEIGHT

Measurement for items which cannot be conveniently measured by volume, such as unmelted butter, pastry, spaghetti, ungrated cheese, and so on have been given in grams. Thus:

60g butter
400g filo pastry

MEASUREMENT OF TEMPERATURE

Accurate temperatures are indicated for baking, some deep-frying and for confectionery making. In this book, measurements are given first in Celsius, then in Fahrenheit. Thus: 185C/365F.

A cooking thermometer is a useful accessory.

MEASUREMENT OF LENGTH

Measurements are given in centimetres with inches in parentheses. Thus:

1.25cm (½-inch)
25cm (10 inches)

IN CONCLUSION

Take note of the following suggestions to get the best out of these recipes:

1. Read the entire recipe first and obtain all the ingredients before commencing to cook. Measure all the spices and ingredients beforehand and place them where they can be easily reached.
2. All measurements for the spoons and cups are level unless otherwise specified.
3. Pan size is specified whenever important. For example, 3-litre/quart pan.
4. "PREPARATION TIME: 15 Minutes" does not include the time needed to gather the ingredients. Some ingredients, when indicated, are pre-cooked and the assembling and chopping time of most vegetables, fruits and herbs is not included in the preparation time.
5. "COOKING TIME: 25 Minutes" is based on the time it took me to cook the dish over a household gas stove. This should serve only as a guideline. Adjust cooking time according to the capabilities and liabilities of your heat source. For instance, keep in mind that compared to gas, electric cooking elements are slow to heat up and cool down.
6. For information about unfamiliar ingredients, see *Glossary*.

SPECIAL NOTES FOR AMERICAN COOKS

The following list will clarify any confusion that may arise because of the different cooking terms and ingredient names used in Australia and America.

AUSTRALIAN	AMERICAN
baking tray	baking sheet
beetroot	beet
bicarbonate of soda	baking soda
biscuit	cookie
bulgur wheat	cracked wheat
butternut pumpkin	butternut squash
cake tin	cake/baking pan
capsicums	peppers
caster sugar	fine granulated sugar
chickpeas	garbanzo beans
continental parsley	flat-leaf parsley
cornflour	corn starch
double cream	heavy cream
frying pan	skillet
glacé fruit	candied fruit
grill	broil
icing sugar	confectioner's sugar
plain flour	all-purpose flour
raw sugar	turbinado sugar
self-raising flour	self-rising flour
semolina	farina
sultanas	golden raisins
unsalted butter	sweet butter
wholemeal flour	wholewheat or graham flour

SPECIAL INGREDIENTS

Fresh produce is of primary importance to the serious cook, and, as a rule, the freshest ingredients are those prepared at home. Here are a few homemade items to get you started: vegetable stocks, *panir* cheese, sour cream, gluten, cottage cheese, coconut milk, and various spice blends.

VEGETABLE STOCKS

There is a Vedic axiom *Annam Brahma* — "Food is God". The Western counterpart may be "waste not, want not". If you subscribe to either, or both of these mottos, you'll be aware of the goodness of vegetable stock. It's natural to save trimmings, outer leaves and stalks of vegetables to be simmered with seasonings into a pot of liquid nutrition. Don't think of the stockpot as a reject pot, however. Only fresh and sound trimmings should be used.

Some of the recipes in this book call for vegetable stock; most of those stocks should resemble Italian *brodo* rather than what comes out of French stockpots. For a start, they will be vegetable-based; they need only be light, and are generally made fairly quickly — no longer than two hours. The stock will thus be a delicate base, a reservoir of subtle flavours, or a background to other more prominent flavours in the dish.

The basic method of stock making is to put the ingredients into cold water and simmer very gently until all the flavours are extracted. The flavour can be adjusted and enriched by the addition of aromatic herbs. There are a few standard guidelines for making a good stock:

1. Choose a suitably large stockpot. It should be heavy-bottomed with a tight-fitting lid. Traditionally, pots for cooking stock are tall and narrow to avoid evaporation.
2. Your stock ingredients should be fresh — a stock will only be as good as the quality of the ingredients.
3. Chop your stock ingredients into similarly sized small pieces — the smaller the pieces, the faster they will flavour the water.
4. Remember that a stock's flavour can be enhanced if the vegetables are first softened in butter or oil. Such cooking releases their natural sugars and allows their full flavour to be realised.
5. As a rule, although the proportion of water to ingredients is never exact, the closely packed ingredients should be covered by about 5cm (2 inches) of water.
6. Root vegetables should be peeled or scraped. Bring the water to the boil slowly. Once the stock is boiling, reduce it to a very gentle simmer. Vigorous boiling causes the ingredients to disintegrate.
7. Be careful with salt and pepper. Some cooks prefer to season after cooking because reduction in a stock that is pre-salted intensifies the salty flavour. It's up to you. And keep in mind that peppercorns contribute to a cloudy stock. Cook the stock without stirring — this reduces clouding.
8. Strain your stock at the end of cooking, but avoid forcing the ingredients through a sieve. A stock should last, covered, in a fridge for a few days.

   Here's a list of suitable herbs, aromatics, and vegetables suitable for a vegetarian stockpot, and specifically for the recipes requiring stocks in this book. Note that "discretion is the better part of valour" — don't be heavy-handed with strong-flavoured herbs.

Herbs and aromatics: parsley, rosemary, thyme, basil, marjoram, oregano, dill, curry leaves, lime leaves, fennel fronds, bay leaves.
Vegetables: carrots, green beans, corn, celery, potatoes, cauliflower, broccoli, lettuce, eggplant, asparagus, pumpkin, fennel root, tomatoes, green leafy vegetables, cabbage, pea pods, squash.

Here are a few stock recipes:

Quick Vegetable Stock
COOKING TIME: 35 minutes
YIELD: about 3–4 cups (750ml–1 litre)

2 tablespoons (40ml) butter
¼ teaspoon (1ml) yellow asafetida powder
2 carrots, peeled and diced
2 celery sticks with leaves, chopped
2 cups (500ml) trimmings from the following: broccoli, asparagus, green beans, fennel and lettuce
3 or 4 stalks parsley
a few sprigs aromatic herbs
1–2 teaspoons (5–10ml) salt
4 cups (1 litre) water

Melt the butter in a heavy 5-litre/quart saucepan or stockpot, and stir in the yellow asafetida powder and the vegetables. "Sweat" the vegetables over low heat for 10 minutes. Add the herbs, the salt and the water. Bring to the boil, partially cover and simmer for 15 minutes. Strain and use as needed.

Green Vegetable Stock
COOKING TIME: 2 hours
YIELD: 3–4 cups (750ml–1 litre)

2 tablespoons (40ml) butter
6 cups (1.5 litres) chopped fresh green vegetables
¼ teaspoon (1ml) yellow asafetida powder
8 cups (2 litres) water
1½ cups (375ml) chopped fresh herbs, chopped celery stalks, beans, pea pods, etc.
1–2 teaspoons (5–10ml) salt
1 or 2 bay leaves
1 or 2 cloves

Melt the butter in a heavy 5-litre/quart saucepan or stockpot. Sauté the vegetables and yellow asafetida powder for 20 minutes over low heat. Turn off the heat and allow the vegetables to "sweat" with the lid on for 10 minutes. Add the water and remaining ingredients and bring to a boil, then simmer for 1½ hours with a tight-fitting lid. Strain. Refrigerate the stock and use as required.

Hearty Brown Stock
BEAN SOAKING TIME: overnight
COOKING TIME: 2 hours
YIELD: about 2 litres/quarts

2 cups (500ml) lentils, kidney beans, chickpeas, or any dried beans soaked in water overnight
3 litres/quarts water
3 tablespoons (60ml) butter
2 celery stalks with leaves, chopped
1 cup (250ml) squash or pumpkin
1 large carrot, chopped
½ teaspoon (2ml) yellow asafetida powder
2 cloves
1 teaspoon (5ml) shredded fresh ginger
1 bay leaf
2–3 teaspoons (10–15ml) salt

1. Drain the water from the soaking beans. Place the beans in a large heavy saucepan with 2 litres/quarts water. Bring to the boil, and simmer for 1 hour or until the beans are soft.

2. Melt the butter in a heavy 5-litre/quart saucepan or stockpot over low heat. Sauté the vegetables along with the yellow asafetida powder for 10 minutes. Remove the saucepan from the heat, cover, and allow the vegetables to "sweat" for 10 minutes.

3. Pour the cooked beans and their cooking water along with another 1 litre/quart water into the pot with the vegetables. Add the remaining ingredients, bring to the boil, then simmer for another hour. Strain, refrigerate and use as needed.

HOMEMADE WHITE CURD CHEESE (PANIR)

When it comes to milk products, one cannot overstate the merits of freshness. The fresher the ingredients, the more vibrant and exciting your cooking will be.

Panir cheese is the simplest kind of protein-rich unripened cheese used by millions of vegetarians in India. When milk is heated and an acid reagent added, the milk protein coagulates to form a soft curd of casein. When drained of its whey and then compacted, it has a texture vaguely resembling firm tofu, but with a delicious creamy taste.

Panir is a versatile ingredient in a vegetarian's kitchen — there are hundreds of ways to use *panir*. Since it is quick and easy to prepare, and since it generally cannot be purchased in shops outside of India, I have included the master recipe here.

Panir cheese can be pan-fried into *Juicy Curd Steaks*, or added to other dishes such as *Festive Nine-jewels Rice* or *Succulent Satay Sticks*. It can be kneaded and rolled into balls as in *Malai Kofta*. It is also delicious crumbled into salads, stuffed into breads and pastries, and creamed into dips. It also makes a good substitute for ricotta cheese such as in *Sweet Cheese-Filled Pancakes*, and *Apricot and Walnut Crescents*.

PREPARATION AND COOKING TIME:
about 15 minutes
CHEESE RESTING TIME: about 30 minutes
YIELD: about 3 cups (750ml)

16 cups (4 litres) whole fresh milk
6 tablespoons (120ml) strained fresh lemon juice

1. Place the milk in a large, heavy-bottomed saucepan. Bring to a rolling boil, stirring frequently. Remove from the heat and gently stir in the lemon juice. If the milk does not immediately separate into curds and whey, place it momentarily over the heat. The liquid should be a pale greenish colour.

2. Drape a double thickness of cheesecloth over a colander resting in the sink. Using a slotted spoon, transfer the large curds into the colander. Pour the whey and remaining bits of cheese into the colander. Gather the ends of the cloth and hold the "bag" of cheese under warm running water for 30 seconds. Place a heavy weight over the wrapped cheese and press for 30 minutes on a slanted board, to allow drainage. Use as directed in any recipes calling for *panir* cheese in this book. *Panir* cheese can be refrigerated, tightly covered, for up to 1 week.

HOMEMADE SOUR CREAM

This ambrosial-tasting cultured dairy product can be easily made at home, and is significantly cheaper than shop-bought sour cream. Success depends on the freshness of your ingredients, as well as controlled incubation. Use *Homemade Sour Cream* in any recipe calling for sour cream in this book.

PREPARATION TIME: a few minutes
CULTURING TIME: 24 hours
YIELD: 2 cups (500ml)

2 cups (500ml) light cream (no more than 30 per cent butter fat), at room temperature
2 tablespoons (40ml) cultured buttermilk at room temperature

Place the cream in a glass or ceramic bowl, or better still in a glass-lined thermos flask, or an electric yogurt maker. Stir the buttermilk into the cream, and tightly cover it. Leave it in a warm place for twenty-four hours. Stir to blend, and refrigerate.

HOMEMADE GLUTEN

Gluten is a mixture of proteins which occur in wheat. When mixed with water, gluten becomes sticky, holding wheat flour doughs together and giving them strength. When gluten is isolated from wheat flour, it forms a chewy, almost meaty-textured, product.

Here are two methods of preparing gluten at home. The traditional method is made by kneading a wheat flour dough under water, effectively separating the water-soluble ingredients from the insoluble gum-like elastic gluten mass. The quick method uses shop-bought gluten flour simply mixed with water. The results of both methods are practically identical.

Traditional Gluten

SOAKING TIME: 2 hours
PREPARATION TIME: about 30 minutes
YIELD: 250g gluten

---
5 cups (1250ml) unbleached plain flour
---
a little under 2 cups (500ml) lukewarm water
---

1. Combine the flour and water to make a fairly stiff dough. Submerge the dough in a large bowl of cold water for 2 hours.

2. Place the bowl of submerged gluten in the sink, and, still keeping the dough under-water, knead it to work out the starch. Pour off the starchy water and replace several times, kneading the ball until the water is almost clear.

3. The remaining lump of spongy matter is called raw gluten. This can be cooked either by boiling it in water or flavoured broth, then deep-frying, pan-frying, or baking as per the recipe requiring it.

Quick Gluten

PREPARATION TIME: a few minutes
GLUTEN RESTING TIME: one hour
YIELD: 300g gluten

---
1 cup (250ml) water
---
1 cup (250ml) gluten flour

Pour the water into a fairly large bowl. Sprinkle in the gluten flour while mixing with the other hand. Combine the flour and water mixture into a lump. Knead it briefly. Set the lump aside for 1 hour. Use as required.

QUICK AND EASY HOMEMADE COTTAGE CHEESE

Although cottage cheese is easily available in the shops, it always seems to taste better when prepared at home. The big "plus" with this recipe is that it is outrageously simple.

PREPARATION TIME: a few minutes
CHEESE RESTING TIME: 12–18 hours
YIELD: 200g cottage cheese, about ⅚ cup (210ml)

---
one 600ml carton of buttermilk
---

1. Place the whole, unopened carton of buttermilk in a large, deep saucepan and fill the saucepan with water.

2. Bring the water to the boil, and boil gently for 30 minutes. Remove the saucepan from the heat and move it to a quiet, undisturbed corner of the kitchen. Put a lid on it and leave it for 12–18 hours.

3. Carefully remove the carton from the water, open it and pour the contents through a colander. Clear whey will drain off leaving the cottage cheese. *Voîla!* Drain for a few minutes, then transfer the cottage cheese to a refrigerator. Consume within a few days.

Homemade Coconut Milk (Santan)

The coconut palm is one of the oldest food plants, its name being recorded in ancient Sanskrit literature. Today it remains as one of the world's most important food sources. The coconut palm grows successfully on poor uncultivated soil, and its fruit provides not only coconut flesh and coconut oil, but also cooling waters to quench one's thirst. The tree itself also provides fibre, lumber and charcoal.

Creamy coconut milk (not the liquid inside the coconut) is extracted from the flesh of ripe coconuts. This product gives many South-East Asian dishes their characteristic richness. It can be readily purchased in cans, but fresh is best. If you have access to fresh coconuts, give this recipe a try.

PREPARATION TIME: about 30 minutes
YIELD: about 1½ cups (375ml)

1 coconut
1¼ cups (310ml) hot water

1. Drill or pierce the two "eyes" of the coconut. Drain off the liquid inside (you can drink it). Crack open the coconut and lever out the flesh. If it smells "off", or looks any colour other than snowy white, throw it away — it's bad.

2. Cut the flesh, which will still be joined to a smooth brown skin, into pieces. Place the pieces in a food processor and process to a pulp. Add the hot water and process for 2 minutes. Let the machine rest for a minute, then process for another 2 minutes.

3. Remove all the pulp, place in a large bowl and knead and squeeze the mixture with your hands. Place the pulp in a cloth, tie it into a bundle and squeeze out as much liquid as you can. This liquid is thick coconut milk. Use immediately as per your recipe, or refrigerate, or pour into an ice-cube tray and freeze until required.

Homemade Spice Blends (Masalas)

Ayurveda, India's *yoga* science of healthy lifestyle, explains the preventative and curative properties of hundreds of herbs and spices. Used correctly, spices not only add a myriad wonderful flavours, but can also promote well-being and good health by allowing food to be digested more easily. For instance, turmeric is a blood purifier, black pepper and chilies are digestive stimulants, and ginger is a respiratory tonic. Toasted cumin, fennel and mustard seeds help make foods lighter on the stomach, cinnamon aids in the absorption of nutrients, and fragrant cardamom added to hot milk helps neutralise its mucus-forming properties.

As well as using spices individually, they can be combined in what is known as a *masala*. A *masala* is a term referring to any number of spice, herb, or seasoning combinations, containing anything from two to 20 ingredients. Its contents, proportions and applications are limitless. For instance, *garam masala* is an aromatic blend of "warm" spices, and, unless otherwise specified, is added towards the end of cooking.

Some spices are used "raw" and others toasted. Spices can be successfully toasted in a heavy pan over low heat for 15 minutes, and stirred every 5 minutes, or toasted on a cookie sheet or baking tray in a pre-heated 90°C/195°F oven for about 30 minutes. Homemade spice blends can be ground to a powder in a spice mill or a coffee grinder, finely sieved, then stored well sealed away from light or heat. They're great to have in the kitchen and can add fascinating depth to your cooking.

Delhi-style Garam Masala

PREPARATION AND COOKING TIME:
15 minutes in a pan or 30 minutes in the oven
YIELD: about ⅔ cup (100ml)

1½ tablespoons (30ml) coriander seeds
2 tablespoons (40ml) cumin seeds
1 tablespoon (20ml) green cardamom pods
one 7.5cm (3-inch) cinnamon stick
2½ teaspoons (12ml) whole cloves

Toast and grind all the spices as described
above.

Punjabi-style Garam Masala

PREPARATION AND COOKING TIME:
15 minutes in a pan or 30 minutes in the oven
YIELD: about 1 cup (250ml)

2½ tablespoons (50ml) cumin seeds
3 tablespoons (60ml) coriander seeds
2½ tablespoons (50ml) ajowan seeds
1½ tablespoons (30ml) green cardamom pods
5 teaspoons (25ml) black peppercorns
5 teaspoons (25ml) whole cloves
one 10cm (4-inch) cinnamon stick
1 bay leaf
3 teaspoons (15ml) ground nutmeg
½ teaspoon (2ml) ground ginger

Toast and grind the first eight ingredients as
described above. Combine with the last two
ingredients.

North African Spice Blend (Ras el hanout)

PREPARATION AND COOKING TIME:
15 minutes in a pan or 30 minutes in the oven
YIELD: about ¾ cup (185ml)

1 tablespoon (20ml) cumin seeds
1 tablespoon (20ml) allspice berries
2 teaspoons (10ml) green cardamom pods
1 tablespoon (20ml) coriander seeds
2 tablespoons (40ml) black peppercorns
two 10cm (4-inch) cinnamon sticks
2 teaspoons (10ml) whole cloves
1 tablespoon (20ml) ground ginger
2 teaspoons (10ml) cayenne pepper
1 teaspoon (5ml) freshly grated nutmeg
4 tablespoons (80ml) crumbled dried rose petals (optional)

Lightly toast and grind the first seven
ingredients. Combine with the remaining four
ingredients.

Sambar Masala

A hot spice blend used for preparing South Indian dishes.

PREPARATION TIME: a few minutes
YIELD: about 1¼ cups (310ml)

1 tablespoon (20ml) urad dal
1 tablespoon (20ml) chana dal
⅔ cup (165ml) coriander seeds
1 tablespoon (20ml) cumin seeds
2 tablespoons (40ml) whole black peppercorns
1 tablespoon (20ml) fenugreek seeds
40 dried red chilies

Toast the first two ingredients for 5–8 minutes, or until golden. Set aside. Toast the remaining five ingredients. Grind and store as described above.

Chat Masala

Great sprinkled on freshly-cut fruit, or added to bean dishes, according to the recipe.

PREPARATION AND COOKING TIME:
15 minutes in a pan or 30 minutes in the oven
YIELD: about ¾ cup (185ml)

one large cassia leaf, or bay leaf
3 tablespoons (60ml) coriander seeds
1½ tablespoons (30ml) cumin seeds
1¼ teaspoons (6ml) whole cloves
1 teaspoon (5ml) cardamom seeds
1¼ teaspoons (6ml) red chili powder
1 teaspoon (5ml) turmeric
¼ cup (60ml) mango powder
1 tablespoon (20ml) ginger powder
2 tablespoons (40ml) finely-ground black salt

Toast and grind the first five ingredients. Combine with the remaining five ingredients.

Cajun Spice Blend

PREPARATION TIME: a few minutes
YIELD: about ¼ cup (60ml)

1½ teaspoons (7ml) yellow asafetida powder
1 teaspoon (5ml) oregano powder
½ teaspoon (2ml) nutmeg powder
2 tablespoons (40ml) sweet paprika
1 teaspoon (5ml) fine sugar
1 teaspoon (5ml) cayenne pepper
1 teaspoon (5ml) ground black pepper
1 teaspoon (5ml) turmeric
1 teaspoon (5ml) salt

Combine all of the above ingredients.

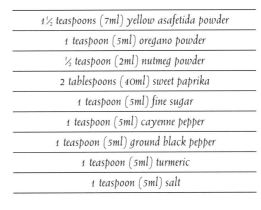

RICE DISHES

Fragrant Basmati Rice

Seasoned Eggplant Rice

Azerbaijan-style Savoury Rice with Broad Beans and Fresh Dill

Italian Rice with Peas (Risi E Bisi)

Asparagus Risotto

Mexican Green Chili Rice (Arroz Verde)

Thai-style Fragrant Rice Balls

Bengali Flat Rice Pulao (Chira Pulao)

Festive Nine-jewels Rice (Navaratnam Pulao)

Pecan and Orange Wild Rice Pilaf

Saffron Flavoured Sweet Fruit and Nut Rice (Keshari Bhat)

Hot and Spicy South Indian Tomato Rice

Turkish Pilaf with Currants and Pine Nuts

Hearty Rice and Mung Bean Hotpot (Khichari)

FRAGRANT BASMATI RICE

Basmati rice is a long-grain scented rice that has been cultivated in the Himalayan foothills for thousands of years. The pointed, milk-white grains are four or five times as long as they are wide, and cook to an aromatic delight — literally translated, *basmati* means "queen of fragrance". The best *basmati* rice comes from Dehradun and Patna in northern India, and Pakistan. *Basmati* rice now enjoys extensive popularity worldwide and is available from well-stocked supermarkets and grocers everywhere.

Here's an ultra-simple "foolproof" recipe for *basmati* rice that is first gently sautéed in a little butter or ghee, then boiled to flaky perfection in lightly salted water. This basic cooking method can be used for any long-grain white rice. You may omit the sautéing if you wish, and add the butter or ghee to the rice after it's cooked, or miss it out altogether.

PREPARATION TIME: 5 minutes
COOKING TIME: 25–35 minutes
YIELD: enough for 3 or 4 persons

1 cup (250ml) basmati rice
1 tablespoon (20ml) unsalted butter or ghee
1⅔–2 cups (415–500ml) water
¾ teaspoon (3ml) salt

1. Wash and drain the *basmati* rice.
2. Heat the butter or ghee in a heavy 1½-litre/quart non-stick saucepan over moderate heat. When the butter is frothy or the ghee is hot, pour in the rice and gently stir-fry it for about 2 minutes.
3. Meanwhile, bring the water and salt to the boil in another saucepan over moderate heat. Pour the boiling water into the sautéed rice, increase the heat, and allow the rice to boil for a few seconds. Immediately reduce the heat to very low, cover with a tight-fitting lid, and gently simmer for 20–25 minutes or until the rice is tender and the water is fully absorbed. Remove the rice from the heat, and let it sit, covered, for another 5 minutes to allow the fragile grains to firm up. Serve piping hot.

SEASONED EGGPLANT RICE

Despite sixteenth-century English herbalist John Gerard's warnings of their "mischievous quality", eggplants today have many devotees worldwide. Southern Italians love them; Middle Eastern cooks know them as "poor man's caviar". They're relished in Turkey and Greece and are prepared with much enthusiasm and ingenuity all over India, especially in Bengal where they are called *baigun* — which means "having no good qualities" — strictly "tongue-in-cheek", considering that Bengalis love them so much.

This flavoursome eggplant-laced rice dish from the state of Gujarat in western India is an ideal main dish rice for any lunch or dinner menu.

PREPARATION TIME: 15 minutes
COOKING TIME: 35–40 minutes
YIELD: enough for 4–6 persons

3 tablespoons (60ml) sesame seeds
2½ cups (625ml) water
4 tablespoons (80ml) oil or ghee
4 tablespoons (80ml) peanuts
1 teaspoon (5ml) cumin seeds
4 green chilies, seeded and chopped
1 tablespoon (20ml) grated fresh ginger
1 small eggplant, about 250g, cut into 1.25cm (½-inch) cubes
2 teaspoons (10ml) salt
1¼ cups (310ml) basmati rice, or other long-grain white rice
1 tablespoon (20ml) sugar
1 tablespoon (20ml) lemon juice
1 teaspoon (5ml) coarsely-ground black pepper

1. Pour the sesame seeds into a 2-litre/quart saucepan over low heat. Dry-roast swirling the pan and stirring occasionally, until the sesame seeds are golden brown and fragrant. Transfer the roasted sesame to a spice mill and grind it to a powder. Remove the powder and set it aside.

2. Place the water in a small saucepan and bring it to the boil. Meanwhile, return the 2-litre/quart saucepan to moderate heat and add the oil. When fairly hot, drop in the peanuts. Stirring, fry the nuts until light golden-brown. Remove with a slotted spoon and set aside.

3. Sprinkle the cumin seeds into the hot oil that remains in the saucepan, still over moderate heat. When the seeds darken a few shades, add the chilies and ginger. Fry for 1–2 minutes, or until fragrant. Add the eggplants and salt, and sauté, stirring for 2–3 minutes, or until the eggplants have absorbed all the flavoured oil and are semi-translucent. Pour in the rice and stir with the eggplants and spices until the rice goes a little whitish in colour.

4. Add the boiling water, sugar, lemon juice and black pepper. Raise the heat to high and quickly bring to a full boil. Immediately reduce the heat to very low, cover with a tight-fitting lid, and gently simmer, without stirring, for 20–25 minutes or until the liquid is absorbed and the rice is tender and fluffy. Turn off the heat and let the rice sit, covered for 5 minutes, to allow the rice grains to firm up.

5. Chop the peanuts coarsely and combine them with the ground sesame seeds. Just before serving, evenly fold the sesame-nut mixture into the piping hot rice.

AZERBAIJAN-STYLE SAVOURY RICE WITH BROAD BEANS AND FRESH DILL

Because of its geographical location at the juncture of Europe and Asia, Azerbaijan has been dominated either by Turkey or Iran for much of its history. Its cuisine therefore imbibes Turkish and Persian influences, as shown by this rice *pilaf*, studded with tender bright-green broad beans and flavoured with fresh dill.

PREPARATION TIME: 10 minutes
FRESH BROAD BEAN COOKING TIME:
30–40 minutes
RICE COOKING TIME: 25 minutes
YIELD: enough for 6 persons

350g fresh broad beans, weighed after removing the beans from their long green pods, or 400g frozen broad beans
3 cups (750ml) vegetable stock or water
1½ teaspoons (7ml) salt
1 tablespoon (20ml) lemon juice
2 tablespoons (40ml) butter
1½ cups (375ml) basmati rice or other good quality, long-grain white rice
1 cup (250ml) fresh chopped dill leaves and slender stalks

1. Remove the thick skins from the broad beans, revealing the tender green beans inside. Discard the skins. If the broad beans were frozen, set the beans aside. If using unfrozen beans, place them in a small saucepan along with 1½ cups (375ml) lightly salted water. Boil the beans for 30–40 minutes or until almost tender. Remove and drain. You'll need about 1½ cups (375ml) broad beans measured after removing their skins.

2. Pour the vegetable stock into a small saucepan. Add the salt and lemon juice, and bring it to the boil.

3. Meanwhile, place the butter in a heavy 3-litre/quart saucepan and melt it over moderate heat. Add the rice and stir-fry it for 3–5 minutes or until the grains go whitish. Pour the boiling stock into the rice. Add the broad beans, raise the heat to high and quickly bring the rice to a full boil. Immediately reduce the heat to very low, cover with a tight-fitting lid, and gently simmer, without stirring, for 20–25 minutes or until the liquid is fully absorbed and the rice is tender and fluffy. Set the rice aside for 5 minutes to firm up the tender grains. Finally, carefully fold in the fresh dill and serve the rice hot.

Azerbaijan-style Savoury Rice with Broad Beans and Fresh Dill

ITALIAN RICE WITH PEAS
(RISI E BISI)

This is my vegetarian version of the classic rice dish from Venice. It is especially served in spring when tiny, tender, young peas are in season. Traditionally, *risi e bisi* is moist, something between a *minestra* (soup), and a *risotto*. (See *Asparagus Risotto* for more information on *risotto* cooking.) Whereas traditional *risi e bisi* would be served as a first course, my version is drier, cooked in the style of an Indian *pulao* and can be served any time a tasty rice dish is required. If you can't get new season baby peas, I suggest you use frozen *petit pois* as an alternative. Thaw them and stir them in when the rice is almost cooked.

PREPARATION AND COOKING TIME:
about 50 minutes
YIELD: enough for 4–6 persons

4 cups (1 litre) vegetable stock (a stock made from the pea pods is delicious)
2 tablespoons (40ml) butter
1 tablespoon (20ml) olive oil
½ teaspoon (2ml) yellow asafetida powder
1 stalk celery, finely sliced, about ½ cup (125ml)
350g shelled baby peas, about 2 cups (500ml), (approximately 1kg of pods)
1¼ cups (310ml) arborio rice, or other Italian superfino rice
1 teaspoon (5ml) salt
¼–½ teaspoon (1–2ml) black pepper
1 teaspoon (5ml) sugar
⅓ cup (85ml) parsley, finely chopped
½ –¾ cup (125–185ml) freshly-grated parmesan cheese

1. Pour the vegetable stock into a small saucepan and bring it to the boil over moderate heat.

2. Meanwhile, melt half the butter over moderate heat in a heavy non-stick 3-litre/quart saucepan. Add the olive oil, the yellow asafetida powder and the celery. Sauté the celery for about 2–3 minutes or until tender. Add the peas, cover, reduce the heat, and braise for 2–3 minutes, stirring occasionally.

3. Remove the lid, add the rice and cook for 2–3 minutes, stirring to coat all the grains with the butter and oil. Add the boiling vegetable stock, salt, pepper and sugar, bring to the boil, cover, and reduce the heat to a simmer. Cook very slowly for 35–40 minutes, or until the rice and peas are soft. Finally, stir in the remaining butter, parsley and parmesan cheese, and serve hot.

ASPARAGUS RISOTTO

Risotto is the rice eaten throughout northern Italy, and can be flavoured with a variety of ingredients. My version of this light, delicious and fresh-tasting *risotto* features tender asparagus which marries well with the parmesan cheese. Rice purists, please note — unlike *pilaf* and *pulao*, *risotto* is not left to slowly steam with a lid, but is stirred continuously with a wooden spoon to form a texture which is neither dry nor soupy, but rather moist and creamy smooth — a texture the Venetians describe as *all'onda* — "with waves".

Authentic *risotto* should be prepared only with Italian *superfino* rice. The most widely available is *arborio*, a highly glutinous rice that easily survives the long, slow-stirring ordeal. This *risotto* follows the age-old formula. The rice is first coated in butter, then cooked slowly with the gradual addition of stock, and stirred continuously until the stock is absorbed and the rice is soft with a gentle coating of sauce, but still firm — *al dente*. The recipe yields a drier *risotto* in the Milanese style.

PREPARATION AND COOKING TIME:
about 50 minutes
YIELD: enough for 4–6 persons

500g asparagus spears
6–7 cups (1500–1750ml) light vegetable stock
3 tablespoons (60ml) butter
½ teaspoon (2ml) yellow asafetida powder
2 cups (500ml) arborio rice
1 teaspoon (5ml) salt (or to taste — take care that your stock is not very salty)
¼ teaspoon (1ml) freshly-ground black pepper
1 cup (250ml) freshly-grated parmesan cheese (reserve some for sprinkling on individual serves)

1. Steam the asparagus in an asparagus cooker or saucepan until just tender. Remove, cut into 3cm (1¼-inch) lengths, reserving some tips for garnish. Set the asparagus aside.

2. Place the vegetable stock in a 3-litre/quart saucepan, bring to the boil and reduce to a gentle simmer.

3. Melt 2 tablespoons (40ml) of the butter in a heavy-bottomed saucepan — at least 3-litres/quart capacity — over low to medium heat. Sprinkle in the yellow asafetida powder. Stir momentarily, and add the rice. Stir the rice in the flavoured butter to coat it well. After 2 or 3 minutes, when the rice makes a crackling sound, ladle in ½ cup (125ml) hot stock. As you gently stir, the liquid will bubble, reduce in volume and gradually absorb into the rice. When the stock is fully absorbed, add another ½ cup (125ml) to the rice. Keep stirring. When it is absorbed, add another. Continue the process, adding stock and stirring for another 20 minutes or until the rice is soft but still slightly firm. You may not need to add all the stock, but there should be a general creaminess to the sauce — neither soupy, nor dry.

4. Finally, fold in the asparagus, salt, pepper, the remaining butter and the parmesan cheese, and stir through. Adjust the consistency with a little extra stock if necessary. Cover for 2–3 minutes. Serve the *risotto* hot with a garnish of the reserved asparagus tips and parmesan cheese.

MEXICAN GREEN CHILI RICE (ARROZ VERDE)

Arroz verde (literally "green rice") is coloured with spinach, fresh parsley and coriander leaves, and flavoured with fresh, very mild, large green chilies, such as *poblano* or *anaheim*. If these chili varieties are unavailable, use any large, mild green chilies that you can find.

PREPARATION AND COOKING TIME:
about 40 minutes
YIELD: enough for 4–6 persons

3 large mild fresh green chilies
3 or 4 large spinach leaves
1 cup (250ml) chopped parsley
½ cup (125ml) chopped fresh coriander leaves
3 cups (750ml) vegetable broth or stock
1½ teaspoons (7ml) salt
2–3 tablespoons (40–60ml) olive oil
½ teaspoon (2ml) yellow asafetida powder
1½ cups (375ml) long-grain white rice
¼ teaspoon (1ml) coarsely-ground black pepper

1. Hold the chilies over a burning gas jet on your stove with a pair of kitchen tongs, or place under the griller. Roast the chilies until they brown a little. Transfer them to a plastic bag. Seal the bag. When cool, carefully remove the chilies, peel them, remove the seeds and cut them into thin strips. Put aside in a small bowl.

2. Place the spinach leaves and half the herbs in a food processor with a little of the vegetable stock. Blend to a purée. Add this purée, along with the remaining stock and the salt to a 2-litre/quart saucepan. Place it over moderate heat and bring it to the boil.

3. Meanwhile, heat the oil in another 2-litre/quart saucepan over moderate heat. When hot, sprinkle in the yellow asafetida powder, stir momentarily, then add the rice and sauté for 2 or 3 minutes, or until translucent.

4. Pour in the boiling vegetable stock. Increase the heat to full, bring to the boil, cover with a lid, and reduce the heat to a gentle simmer. Cook the rice without stirring for 15–20 minutes, or until the grains are soft, dry and tender. Remove the pan from the heat and set aside for 5 minutes. Remove the lid, stir in the remaining herbs and black pepper. Serve hot, garnishing each serve with strips of roasted chilies.

THAI-STYLE FRAGRANT RICE BALLS

This is a recipe I've developed over the years, incorporating some of my favourite South-East Asian flavours. Obtain fragrant Thai basil at well-stocked Asian greengrocers.

PREPARATION AND COOKING TIME:
about 45 minutes
YIELD: 12 rice balls

1½ cups (375ml) *Thai jasmine rice*
1½ cups (375ml) *water*
1½ cups (375ml) *thick coconut milk*
2 teaspoons (10ml) *minced fresh ginger*
1½ tablespoons (30ml) *soy sauce*
one 12.5cm (5-inch) *stem lemon grass, bruised with a wooden mallet and cut into 5 pieces*
15 *fresh curry leaves*
16 large whole *Thai basil leaves, cut into julienne strips*

1. Pour the rice into a sieve and rinse it under cold running water until the water runs clear. Drain well. Place the rice, water, coconut milk, ginger, soy sauce, lemon grass and curry leaves in a heavy-based non-stick 2-litre/quart saucepan. Bring to a boil over moderate heat. Reduce the heat to low and simmer for 10 minutes, uncovered. Cover the pan and cook for another 10 minutes or until the rice is fully cooked and the liquid has disappeared.

2. Remove the saucepan from the heat and allow the rice to steam for another 10 minutes. Fold in the basil leaves and turn the rice out of the pot into a bowl to cool.

3. When cool enough to handle, remove the lemon grass and form the rice into 12 lumps. Roll each into a ball and serve warm or at room temperature. As an alternative serving suggestion, serve the rice hot as an accompaniment to any Asian-style meal.

BENGALI FLAT RICE PULAO (CHIRA PULAO)

Flat rice, *chira*, also known as flaked rice or pressed rice, is a partially cooked rice product that has been prepared in India for millennia. Unhusked rice is first soaked, boiled briefly, then drained, heated until it puffs, then flattened into thin flakes. It can be stored for months without deterioration, then simply reconstituted by soaking, rinsing in boiling water, or deep-frying.

This dish is a comforting combination of flat rice and seasoned vegetables. You may wish to deep-fry the vegetables instead of pan-frying them. It's important to note that two grades of flat rice are commonly sold in Indian grocers — thick and thin. The thick variety, *poha*, is used for deep-frying and adding to crunchy *chidwa* snacks, but is unsuitable for this recipe. Instead, make sure you ask for the thin variety.

Bengali Flat Rice Pulao is delicious served at breakfast time with fruits and yogurt accompanied by a simple chutney such as *Bush Tomato Chutney* or *Hot Chili Relish*.

PREPARATION AND COOKING TIME:
about 25 minutes
YIELD: enough for 4 persons

6 litres water
2¾ cups (685ml) fine flat rice, about 250g
3 tablespoons (60ml) ghee or oil
2 medium potatoes, diced 0.5cm (¼-inch), about 1 cup (250ml)
1 small cauliflower, cut into tiny florets, about 2 cups (500ml)
one 5cm (2-inch) cinnamon stick
3 bruised cardamom pods
3 whole cloves
2 or 3 green chilies, seeded and sliced into long julienne strips
1 teaspoon (5ml) turmeric
1 cup (250ml) cooked green peas
1½ teaspoons (7ml) salt

1. Set the water in a large saucepan over full heat, and bring it to the boil. Place the flat rice in a colander in the sink, and rinse it under the cold tap until the water runs clear.

2. Pour the boiling water slowly over the colander of rinsed flat rice to soften it. Remove the colander from the sink and set it aside for the rice to fluff up and dry.

3. Heat the ghee or oil in a wok or non-stick saucepan over moderate heat. When the oil is hot, drop in the potato and cauliflower pieces. Stir-fry them for three or four minutes or until they are golden brown and they yield easily to a knife point. Remove the vegetables with a slotted spoon, and set them aside covered, allowing the ghee to remain in the pan.

4. Drop the cinnamon, cardamom and cloves into the hot ghee, and fry them for one or two minutes, or until they are slightly darker and fragrant. Drop in the chilies and fry them for another minute. Sprinkle in the turmeric, then add the flat rice, cooked peas, cauliflower and potatoes, and the salt. Reduce the heat to low and gently sauté for 5–10 minutes, stirring occasionally. Remove the cinnamon stick, cardamom pods and cloves, and serve the *pulao* hot.

FESTIVE NINE-JEWELS RICE (NAVARATNAM PULAO)

This rich and opulent rice from Bengal is so-named because it is studded with a large assortment of colourful ingredients. It is flavoured with a traditional homemade spice stock called *akhnir jhol*. Serve *Navaratnam Pulao* for special occasions like weddings, special holiday feasts or important dinners.

PREPARATION TIME: 30 minutes
STOCK COOKING TIME: 1 hour
REMAINING COOKING TIME: 30 minutes
YIELD: enough for 6 persons

For akhnir jhol stock:

one 2.5cm (1-inch) chunk of ginger, shredded
2 teaspoons (10ml) chana dal
2 teaspoons (10ml) cumin seeds
2 teaspoons (10ml) coriander seeds
3 whole dried red chilies
one 3.75cm (1½-inch) cinnamon stick
3 cardamom pods, bruised with a kitchen mallet
2 bay leaves
6 cups (1.5 litre) water

Remaining ingredients:

⅓ cup (85ml) ghee
¼ cup (60ml) cashew halves
¼ cup (60ml) slivered almonds
2 tablespoons (40ml) raisins
¾ cup (185ml) panir cheese, cut into 0.5cm (¼-inch) cubes
½ cup (125ml) tiny cauliflower florets
½ cup (125ml) carrots, cut into 1.25cm (½-inch) cubes
1 cup (250ml) evaporated milk
1 small, whole nutmeg, grated finely
2 teaspoons (10ml) sugar
1½ teaspoons (7ml) salt
½ teaspoon (2ml) turmeric
one 5cm (2-inch) cinnamon stick
6 whole cardamom pods, bruised
2 bay leaves
1 teaspoon (5ml) grated fresh ginger
2 medium-sized fresh red chilies, seeded and sliced into strips
1 teaspoon (5ml) yellow asafetida powder
1½ cups (375ml) basmati rice, or other long-grain white rice
¼ cup (60ml) cooked green peas

To prepare akhnir jhol stock:

Combine all the ingredients in a large saucepan. Bring to a rolling boil and cook uncovered for 1 hour, or until the liquid is reduced to about half. Strain, reserving the liquid.

To prepare the other ingredients for the dish:

1. Warm the ghee in a 1-litre/quart saucepan over moderate heat. When hot, drop in the cashews and fry them until they turn a light golden colour.

Remove them with a slotted spoon and drain them in a colander, being careful to allow the ghee to remain in the saucepan. Fry and drain the almond slivers in a similar fashion. Drop in the raisins and fry them briefly until they puff up. Remove and drain them.

2. Fry the *panir* cheese cubes, stirring occasionally, until richly browned. Remove and drain. Fry the cauliflower until just tender to the point of a knife. Remove and drain. Fry the carrots until tender. Remove and drain them. Remove the saucepan from the heat.

To prepare the rice and assemble the dish:

1. Combine the evaporated milk with 2 cups (500ml) of the strained stock in a 2-litre/quart saucepan over moderate heat. Add the nutmeg powder, sugar, salt and turmeric. Cover well and bring to the boil, then reduce it to barely simmering, taking care not to lose any liquid through evaporation.

2. Transfer the remaining ghee to a 3-litre/quart saucepan over moderate heat. When fairly hot, drop in the cinnamon stick, cardamom pods and the bay leaves. Stir them until they darken a few shades and become fragrant. Drop in the shredded ginger and the chilies, stir for 1 or 2 minutes. Sprinkle in the yellow asafetida powder, stir momentarily, add the rice and stir-fry for 1 or 2 minutes, or until the grains become translucent. Pour the boiling liquid into the sautéed rice and spices. Raise the heat and quickly bring to a full boil. Immediately reduce the heat to very low, cover with a tight-fitting lid and gently simmer the rice without stirring for 20 minutes, or until the liquid is absorbed and the rice is tender and fluffy. Remove the saucepan from the heat and allow the rice to sit, covered, for 5 minutes more to allow the grains to firm up.

3. Finally, fold in the cashews, almonds, raisins, carrots, cauliflower, *panir* cheese cubes and cooked green peas to the rice. Mix well to combine, and serve the rice hot.

PECAN AND ORANGE WILD RICE PILAF

Wild rice is the seed of an aquatic grass that grows in ponds, lakes and waterways of the United States and Canada. It is not actually a grain, but it is treated as such. Its long, thin, ash-brown to blackish grains cook to a chewy texture, with a slightly smoky flavour. Wild rice teams up very well with *basmati* rice, and in this recipe is joined by continental parsley, slivered toasted pecans, currants and orange zest. Serve as a side dish.

PREPARATION AND COOKING TIME:
about 40 minutes
YIELD: enough for 6 persons

3¼ cups (935ml) water
½ cup (125ml) wild rice
1 cup (250ml) basmati rice
1 tablespoon (20ml) extra virgin olive oil
⅓ cup (85ml) dried currants
1 teaspoon (5ml) salt
2 tablespoons (40ml) fresh orange juice
¼ teaspoon (1ml) black pepper
2 teaspoons (10ml) grated orange zest
3 tablespoons (60ml) chopped, fresh continental parsley
⅓ cup (85ml) pecan nuts, slivered lengthwise into thirds and pan-toasted
2 small green chilies, seeded and finely slivered
sprigs of continental parsley

1. Bring 2 cups (500ml) water to the boil in a 1-litre/quart saucepan over full heat. Stir in the wild rice, reduce the heat, cover the pan and simmer for about 40 minutes, or until the grains are tender. Do not allow the grains to split. Transfer the rice to a sieve and drain off the liquid. Set the rice aside.

2. Meanwhile, wash the *basmati* rice, and soak it in water for 10 minutes. Drain the rice, and allow to dry thoroughly. Heat the olive oil in a 2-litre/quart saucepan over moderate heat. Add the *basmati* rice and currants, and gently stir-fry for 2–3 minutes, being careful not to break up the rice grains. Add the remaining 1¾ cups (435ml) water to the saucepan and bring it to the boil. Add the salt, orange juice, black pepper and orange zest. Reduce the heat to a simmer, and cook, covered, for about 18 minutes or until the rice is soft and dry. Remove from the heat and set aside for 10 minutes.

3. Fluff the rice gently with a fork. Add the wild rice, the chopped parsley, the pecan nuts and chilies, and gently mix. Serve immediately, garnished with the sprigs of continental parsley.

PREPARATION AND COOKING TIME: 45–50 minutes
YIELD: enough for 6–8 persons

Ingredients
½ teaspoon (2ml) saffron threads
4½ cups (1125ml) milk
4 tablespoons (80ml) ghee
¼ cup (60ml) slivered raw almonds
¼ cup (60ml) whole raw pistachios
¼ cup (60ml) sultanas or raisins
2 cups (500ml) high-quality basmati rice
1 tablespoon (20ml) cardamom seeds, powdered
1 ripe mango, cut into 0.5cm (¼-inch) cubes, about 1 cup (250ml)
1 cup (250ml) fine sugar
2 rings preserved or dried pineapple, cut into 0.5cm (¼-inch) cubes, about 1 cup (250ml)

SAFFRON FLAVOURED SWEET FRUIT AND NUT RICE (KESHARI BHAT)

Saffron has enjoyed great popularity the world over as a dye, a drug, a perfume and a kitchen flavour.

In ancient Greece, cloth dyed with saffron was considered appropriate for women of the Court. In India, it has always enjoyed a great reputation as a drug that strengthens the functioning of the stomach, and as a treatment for digestive disorders and various female ailments.

Saffron is mentioned in the *Song of Solomon* as a perfume; and as far as the flavouring in the kitchen is concerned, it was so popular in England in the Middle Ages that it is said to be called for in nearly one-third of all the recipes of the time. Apparently, Henry VIII was so fond of it in his food that he is said to have prohibited court ladies from using it as a hair dye.

Despite being somewhat out of fashion in English cooking, and despite now being the world's most expensive spice, saffron is still very popular. It is a vital ingredient in many superb rice dishes from the Indian subcontinent, like the following recipe. (*Keshar* means saffron, and *bhat* means rice.) *Keshari Bhat* can be served as a delightful sweet foil alongside savoury dishes in special feasts or banquets, or as a dessert, alone or with whipped cream. The success of this dish rests on the choice of a high-quality rice. I recommend a top-grade *basmati* like *Debradun*.

Other recipes featuring saffron in this book include *Old English Saffron Bread*, *Flaked Almond and Saffron Semolina Halava*, and *Crispy Fried Batter Spirals in Saffron Syrup*.

1. Place the saffron threads in a small saucepan along with 1 tablespoon (20ml) milk and 2 tablespoons (40ml) water over moderate heat. Bring to the boil and then reduce to a simmer over very low heat, covered, for about 10 minutes in order to extract the full colour and fragrance of the saffron. Remove the pan from the heat and set it aside.

2. Heat the ghee in a 2-litre/quart saucepan over moderate heat. Add the almonds and the pistachios and fry them for 1 or 2 minutes, or until light golden brown. Add the sultanas or raisins and fry them until they puff up. Remove the pan from the heat and spoon out the nuts and raisins from the pan with a slotted spoon, allowing the ghee to remain in the saucepan. Set the nuts and dried fruits aside, separating ¼ cup (60ml) for garnish.

3. Return the ghee to moderate heat. Add the rice and cardamom, and stir the rice for about 2 minutes, or until it is well-coated and translucent. Add the milk, and the saffron milk infusion, to the rice. Stir constantly until it boils, then reduce the heat to very low, place a tight-fitting lid on the pan and cook the rice without stirring for 25 minutes, or until the grains are soft and tender.

4. Remove the saucepan from the heat and allow the rice to firm up for 10 minutes. When ready to serve, spoon out the rice into a serving dish, fold in the mango, sugar, nuts and dried fruits. Sprinkle on the reserved garnish and serve as is, or with whipped cream.

HOT AND SPICY SOUTH INDIAN TOMATO RICE

No self-respecting chef should ever use boring packaged commercial curry powder! As an alternative, homemade spice blends, or *masalas*, add vibrant, multi-dimensional flavours to your cooking, and can be easily prepared in your kitchen. Several spice blends are listed in the *Special Ingredients* section; others are scattered throughout the book, such as in this delectable, chili-hot, moist and spicy rice that I tasted on my first trip to Tamil Nadu, India.

PREPARATION TIME: 15 minutes
COOKING TIME: 35–40 minutes
YIELD: enough for 4 persons

The spice masala:

1½ teaspoons (7ml) oil
3 large dried red chilies
1 teaspoon (5ml) coriander seeds
3 teaspoons (15ml) chana dal or yellow split peas
1 teaspoon (5ml) urad dal
¼ teaspoon (1ml) fenugreek seeds
1 tablespoon (20ml) desiccated coconut

Remaining ingredients:

1 tablespoon (20ml) oil
2 cups (500ml) water
1 teaspoon (5ml) salt
1 tablespoon (20ml) ghee
1 cup (250ml) basmati rice or other long-grain white rice
1 teaspoon (5ml) mustard seeds
10 fresh curry leaves
2 large red chilies, sliced in rings
½ teaspoon (2ml) yellow asafetida powder
4 large firm ripe tomatoes, blanched, peeled and chopped

To prepare the spice masala:

Heat 1½ teaspoons (7ml) oil in a wok or heavy pan over moderate heat. Drop in the red chilies, coriander, *chana dal* and *urad dal*. Toast, stirring occasionally, for 3–5 minutes or until they darken in colour and become fragrant. Towards the end, drop in the fenugreek and coconut, and stir until the coconut becomes golden brown. Remove the spices and coconut and transfer to a spice mill. Grind the spices to a powder. Remove and set aside.

To prepare the rice:

1. Slowly bring the water and salt to the boil in a 1-litre/quart covered saucepan.

2. Warm 1 teaspoon (5ml) ghee or oil in a 2-litre/quart saucepan over moderate heat. Pour in the rice and stir-fry for 2 minutes or until the grains glisten and turn whitish. Add the boiling water, raise the heat and quickly bring to a full boil. Immediately reduce the heat to very low, cover with a tight-fitting lid and gently simmer, without stirring, for 20–25 minutes, or until the

liquid is absorbed and the rice is tender and fluffy.
Remove the pan from the heat and let the rice sit,
covered, for 5 minutes to allow the grains to firm up.

To prepare the tomatoes and complete the dish:

1. While the rice is cooking, place the remaining ghee
   and oil in a wok or heavy frying pan over moderate
   heat. When the oil is hot, drop in the mustard
   seeds. They will crackle, splutter, and start to turn
   grey. Add the curry leaves, stir briefly, then add the
   chilies and fry them for 1 or 2 minutes, or until
   they turn translucent. Sprinkle in the yellow
   asafetida powder, sauté momentarily and add the

chopped tomatoes. Cook for about 5 minutes or
until the tomatoes soften and break down. Stir the
spice *masala* into the tomatoes and cook for an
additional one minute. Remove from the heat.

2. When the rice is fully cooked and firm, stir in the
   spicy tomatoes, fluffing the rice and tomatoes
   gently with a fork to mix evenly. Serve piping hot.

TURKISH PILAF WITH CURRANTS AND PINE NUTS

Pine nuts are the kernels or seeds that are shed as the pine cones dry, open out and mature in the summer months. These little cream-coloured nuts can be toasted lightly in a dry frying pan, or with a little olive oil, to release a deeper nuttier flavour. Coupled with flavoursome cloves, orange, ginger, thyme, and succulent currants, they add a tasty crunch to this exotic rice dish from Turkey.

PREPARATION TIME: 10 minutes
COOKING TIME: 30 minutes
YIELD: enough for 6 persons

3 cups (750ml) vegetable stock or water
3 tablespoons (60ml) extra virgin olive oil
½ cup (125ml) pine nuts
½ teaspoon (2ml) yellow asafetida powder
1½ cups (375ml) basmati rice or other good quality long-grain white rice
4 whole cloves
one 2.5cm (1-inch) cube ginger, sliced
2 bay leaves
2 whole 10cm (4-inch) stalks fresh thyme
three 3-inch strips orange zest
1½ teaspoons (7ml) salt
½ teaspoon (2ml) freshly-ground black pepper
⅓ cup (85ml) currants
3 tablespoons (60ml) chopped continental (flat-leaf) parsley

1. Place the vegetable stock in a small saucepan over moderate heat, cover and bring it to the boil.

2. Meanwhile, warm the olive oil in a 2-litre/quart saucepan over low to moderate heat. When slightly hot, add the pine nuts. Stir-fry them for a minute, or until they turn a light golden brown and smell fragrant. Remove the saucepan from the heat. Quickly remove the nuts from the oil and drain them on paper towels with a slotted spoon.

3. Sprinkle the yellow asafetida powder into the hot oil. Stir momentarily, drop in the rice, and stir-fry it in the oil for 2 or 3 minutes or until the rice grains become a little whitish in colour. When the stock is boiling, and the grains of rice are sufficiently toasted, pour the boiling stock into the rice. Add the cloves, ginger, bay leaves, thyme stalks, orange zest, salt and pepper. Raise the heat to high and quickly bring the rice to a full boil. Immediately reduce the heat to very low, cover with a tight-fitting lid, and gently simmer, without stirring, for 20–25 minutes or until the liquid is fully absorbed and the rice is tender and fluffy.

4. Remove the saucepan from the heat, allowing the delicate rice grains to firm up for 5 minutes. Lift the lid and carefully extract the cloves, thyme stalks, ginger and bay leaves. If all has gone well and you haven't stirred the rice while it was cooking, these should be sitting on the very surface of the rice. Finally, carefully fold in the currants, nuts and continental parsley and serve the rice hot.

Turkish Pilaf with Currants and Pine Nuts
served with
Malai Kofta (page 127)

HEARTY RICE AND MUNG BEAN HOTPOT (KHICHARI)

What would a vegetarian's life be without *khichari*? I eat it practically every day. *Khichari*, a flavoursome juicy stew of mung beans, rice and vegetables, is an ideal working-person's breakfast food — both nutritious and sustaining. It can be served any time a one-pot meal is required. It's delicious accompanied with a little yogurt, some wholemeal toast or *poories*, a few wedges of lemon or lime and a little melted ghee on top. *Khichari* is irresistible, and it's a very inexpensive way for vegetarians to derive all their protein needs. My spiritual master, Srila Prabhupada, rightly described *khichari* as "a poor man's feast".

Once you've made *khichari* a couple of times, you'll see how easy it is to use practically any type of rice, any variety of split or whole dried legume and virtually any vegetable combination and seasoning. The varieties are truly limitless. This recipe yields a tasty, semi-moist *khichari*. If this is your first experience of this dish, then welcome to the wonderful world of *khichari*.

PREPARATION AND COOKING TIME:
about 50 minutes
YIELD: enough for 4–6 persons

⅓ cup (85ml) split mung beans, about 65g
6 cups (1.5 litres) water
1 large green chili, seeded and finely chopped
one 2.5cm (1-inch) cube ginger, cut into julienne strips
2–5 bay leaves (depending on their freshness)
one 7.5cm (3-inch) cinnamon stick
¼ teaspoon (3ml) turmeric
2 whole star anise or 1½ teaspoons (7ml) fennel seeds
1 cup (250ml) Thai rice or a long-grain rice of your choice
1½–2 teaspoons (7–10ml) salt
2 cups (500ml) chopped vegetables, cut into 1.25cm (½-inch) cubes (try potatoes, carrots, green beans, sweet potatoes, pumpkin, radish or vegetables of your choice)
1 small bunch spinach, washed and chopped
2 tablespoons (40ml) ghee
2 teaspoons (10ml) cumin seeds
10-12 curry leaves
½ teaspoon (2ml) fenugreek seeds
½ teaspoon (2ml) yellow asafetida powder
1 cup (250ml) peeled, diced tomatoes
¾ cup (185ml) chopped fresh coriander leaves
extra ghee or butter

1. Wash the split mung beans in several changes of cold water. Place the beans in a heavy-based 5-litre/quart saucepan (preferably non-stick) with the water, turmeric, ginger, bay leaves, cinnamon, chili and star anise. (If substituting fennel seeds for the star anise, add them later as described.) Bring to the boil over high heat, then reduce to a gentle boil, partially covered. Careful — the water has a tendency to foam up and boil over. Boil, stirring occasionally, for about 20 minutes, or until the mung beans are soft and starting to break up.

2. Pour in the rice, add the salt and vegetables, and stir well. Increase the heat, bring to the boil, then reduce to a simmer, covering it with a tight-fitting lid. Cook the *khichari* for another 10 minutes, then stir in the spinach leaves. Replace the lid and keep cooking for another 5 minutes or so.

3. Now add the seasonings as follows: Heat the ghee in a small saucepan over medium-high heat. Sprinkle in the cumin seeds (if using fennel seeds, add them now). When the seeds darken a few shades, add the curry leaves. As soon as they crackle and darken in colour, add the fenugreek and cook until the fenugreek seeds darken slightly. Sprinkle in the yellow asafetida powder, lift the pan from the heat, and swirl the pan slightly. Lift the lid from the *khichari* and then pour in the contents of the saucepan of fried seasonings into the *khichari*. Stir to mix well, then replace the lid and simmer the *khichari* for another 10–15 minutes, or until the *khichari* is thick, the rice grains are soft and swollen and the vegetables are tender. If you desire a more moist *khichari*, add hot or boiling water now. Finally, stir in the tomatoes and chopped coriander leaves. Serve piping hot garnishing each portion with a trickle of warm ghee or butter.

SOUPS

Simple Carrot and Ginger Soup

Greek-style White Bean and Vegetable Soup (Fasoulada)

Mulligatawny Soup

Buttermilk Sambar

Hearty Dal with Vegetables (Dalma)

Black Bean Soup

Light and Tasty Italian Tomato Soup (Zuppa di Pomodoro)

Creamy, Fresh Green-Pea Soup

Roasted Capsicum, Peanut and Tomato Soup

Jamaican Pepperpot Soup

Broccoli Cheddar Soup

Wholesome Brown Lentil and Vegetable Soup

Chilled Avocado and Green Peppercorn Soup

Sweet Potato Soup with Corn and Chilies

Beetroot Soup (Borscht)

Maharastrian-style Sweet and Sour Chana Dal (Katachi Amti)

SIMPLE CARROT AND GINGER SOUP

The carrot is a popular vegetable the world over. It is a powerful cleansing food, and a rich source of vitamin A. It is well known for its numerous natural benefits and curative properties. Carrot soup, as well as being delicious, is an effective natural remedy for diarrhoea. It supplies fluid to combat dehydration, replenishes sodium, potassium, phosphorous, calcium, sulphur and magnesium, and is a good source of pectin.

The best carrot soup I ever tasted was made from carrots picked straight from the garden — sweet and delicious. This fresh tasting soup is flavoured with a hint of ginger. The added potatoes thicken and enrich the soup; you may choose to replace them with more carrots, or leave them out completely.

PREPARATION AND COOKING TIME:
about 30 minutes
YIELD: enough for 4 persons

2 tablespoons (40ml) butter
½ teaspoon (2ml) yellow asafetida powder
2 teaspoons (10ml) grated fresh ginger
700g topped, scraped and sliced carrots, about 4½ cups (1125ml)
1 cup (250ml) potatoes, diced
1½ teaspoons (7ml) salt
½ teaspoon (2ml) black pepper
at least 4 cups (1 litre) light vegetable stock or water
chopped continental parsley leaves for garnish

1. Melt the butter in a 3-litre saucepan over moderate heat. Sprinkle in the yellow asafetida powder and ginger, stirring briefly. Add the sliced carrots, potatoes, salt and pepper and sauté for 10 minutes, stirring occasionally. Add the stock or water, and bring to the boil, then reduce the heat and simmer the vegetables, covered, for 15 minutes, or until the vegetables are very tender.

2. Remove the pan from the heat, transfer the contents to a blender or food processor and process to a smooth purée.

3. Rinse the saucepan, return the soup to the pan, and gently reheat over moderate heat. For a thinner soup, add extra stock at this stage. Serve the soup hot with a sprinkle of freshly chopped continental parsley leaves.

GREEK-STYLE WHITE BEAN AND VEGETABLE SOUP (FASOULADA)

There's nothing like a steaming pot of hot soup to warm you up on a cold winter's day, and this one "does the trick". Probably every Greek housewife has a version of *fasoulada*, a full-bodied, thick rustic soup of white beans and vegetables. Any white beans are preferred, such as cannellini, black-eyed beans, lima, navy or haricot.

You can serve *fasoulada* as an entrée, or you can build a substantial meal around it by adding bread, olives and cheese.

BEAN SOAKING TIME: 1 hour or overnight
PREPARATION AND COOKING TIME:
about 1 hour
YIELD: enough for 6 persons

2 cups (500ml) haricot beans, about 375g,
or white beans of your choice

8 cups (2 litres) water

1 teaspoon (5ml) yellow asafetida powder

1½ cups (375ml) chopped, peeled tomatoes

¾ cup (185ml) diced carrot

1 cup (250ml) chopped celery, including leaves

2 tablespoons (40ml) tomato paste

¼ cup (60ml) chopped parsley

2–3 tablespoons (40–60ml) virgin olive oil

¼ teaspoon (1ml) freshly-ground black pepper

½ teaspoon (2ml) sugar

1½ teaspoons (7ml) salt

chopped parsley for garnish

1. Wash and drain the beans. Place them in a 5-litre/quart saucepan along with the 8 cups (2 litres) water, and bring to the boil over full heat. Allow the beans to boil for two minutes, then remove the saucepan from the heat, cover tightly and set aside for 1 hour, or until the beans double in size. Alternatively, soak the beans overnight, drain them, rinse and drain again.

2. Add all the other ingredients to the saucepan of soaked beans, except the salt and garnish. Return the pan to full heat, bring to the boil, then reduce the heat to a simmer, and cook, tightly covered, for about 1 hour, or until the beans are soft.

3. Stir in the salt and sprinkle each bowl of hot steaming soup with some of the reserved parsley. Succulent!

MULLIGATAWNY SOUP

To some, the name *"mulligatawny soup"* conjures up visions of dull, greasy, Indian restaurant concoctions, seasoned with supermarket curry powder. This is unfortunate and it is due to the soup's chequered legacy from the days of the British Raj. Actually, despite its bad reputation, this soup, of which there are hundreds of versions, is one of South India's outstanding contributions to the culinary world. This version is adapted from a recipe by Yamuna devi featured in her excellent book *Yamuna's Table*.

PREPARATION AND COOKING TIME:
about 45 minutes
YIELD: enough for 6 persons

one 7.5 cm (3-inch) cinnamon stick, broken in pieces
6 whole cloves
4 green cardamom pods
1 teaspoon (5ml) black peppercorns, preferably Malabar
6 cups (1.5 litres) light vegetable stock
1 tablespoon (20ml) grated fresh ginger
2 tablespoons (40ml) chopped cashews or almonds
1 cup (250ml) chopped potato
½ cup (125ml) chopped carrot
½ cup (125ml) chopped zucchini
½ cup (125ml) chopped cauliflower
½ cup (125ml) chopped pumpkin
½ teaspoon (2ml) turmeric powder
1 tablespoon (20ml) ghee
1 teaspoon (5ml) brown mustard seeds
1 teaspoon (5ml) cumin seeds
½ teaspoon (2ml) yellow asafetida powder
1½ teaspoons (7ml) salt
¼ teaspoon (1ml) freshly-ground black pepper
2 tablespoons (40ml) chopped fresh coriander leaves

1. Tie the cloves, cardamom pods and pepper corns in a piece of muslin. Place the vegetable stock in a 3-litre/quart saucepan

Buttermilk Sambar

over moderate heat, and add the spice bag, ginger, the nuts, vegetables and turmeric powder. Bring to the boil, reduce the heat to a simmer, cover the pan and cook for about 30 minutes, or until the vegetables are tender.

2. Allow the soup to cool a little, remove the spice bag, and pour the stock and vegetables into a food processor or blender. Process to a purée. Pass the mixture through a fine meshed sieve, pressing to extract as much of the liquid as possible. Rinse the saucepan.

3. Return the saucepan of soup to gentle heat. Prepare the final seasonings as follows: warm the ghee in a small pan over moderate heat. Add the mustard seeds. When they start to crackle, add the cumin seeds, then remove the pan from the heat. Sprinkle in the yellow asafetida powder, stir briefly and carefully pour the spice mixture into the soup. Stir to mix, and allow the spices to soak for a few minutes.

4. Add the salt, freshly-ground black pepper and serve hot in pre-warmed soup bowls, and garnish with the fresh, chopped coriander leaves.

BUTTERMILK SAMBAR

Sambar soups are a well-known favourite from the southern states of India. They vary immensely, although they are all traditionally served chili-hot. This one is based upon cooling buttermilk and laced with vegetables. It is essential that you don't overcook the fenugreek in both the spice paste and the seasoning, or else the *sambar* will have a bitter taste. Serve buttermilk *sambar* with hot plain rice, or for a full meal with *Hot and Spicy South Indian Tomato Rice, Savoury Lentil Doughnuts, South Indian Coconut Chutney* and *South Indian Carrot Salad.*

PREPARATION AND COOKING TIME:
about 35 minutes
YIELD: enough for 4–6 persons

2 tablespoons (40ml) oil
2 tablespoons (40ml) split toor dal
1½ teaspoons (7ml) coriander seeds
2 teaspoons (10ml) split urad dal lentils
6 large dried red chilies
2 teaspoons (10ml) fenugreek seeds

¾ teaspoon (3ml) yellow asafetida powder
½ cup (125ml) grated fresh coconut
2 teaspoons (10ml) shredded fresh ginger
3 cups (750ml) buttermilk
½ teaspoon (2ml) turmeric
1 teaspoon (5ml) salt

The final seasoning:

1 teaspoon (5ml) mustard seeds
1½ teaspoons (7ml) cumin seeds
1 large hot red chili sliced into thin rings
12 curry leaves
¾ teaspoon (3ml) fenugreek seeds
⅓ cup (85ml) fresh green peas
½ cup (125ml) eggplant cubes, diced 1.25cm (½ inch)
½ cup (125ml) potato cubes, diced 1.25cm (½ inch)

1. Prepare the spices as follows: Heat the oil in a wok or *karai* over moderate heat. When the oil is fairly hot, drop in the *toor dal*, coriander seeds, *urad dal* and chilies. Stir-fry the spices and lentils for 2 or 3 minutes or until the *urad dal* is golden brown and the *toor dal* is slightly browned around the edges. Drop in the fenugreek and yellow asafetida powder, and immediately remove the wok from the heat. Stir the fenugreek into the hot oil for a few moments and allow the spice mixture to cool. Spoon out the spices and lentils with a slotted spoon, being careful to leave the oil behind, and place them in a spice mill or coffee grinder. Grind to a fine powder.

2. Place the coconut, ginger and a few spoons of cold water in a food processor or blender and process to a smooth paste. Add the buttermilk, turmeric, salt and roasted ground spices, and process until well mixed.

3. Heat the oil that remains in the wok or *karai* over moderate heat. When hot, add the mustard seeds and fry them until they crackle, then add the cumin seeds, red chili and curry leaves, and fry for 30 seconds, or until the cumin darkens one or two shades. Drop in the fenugreek seeds, and when they go slightly darker, pour in ½ cup (125ml) cold water. Add the peas, eggplants and potato, stir and cover with a tight lid. Bring to the boil, then reduce the heat slightly and cook the vegetables for 10 minutes, or until they are tender.

4. Pour in the buttermilk mixture. Heat gently, but do not allow it to boil, otherwise it will curdle. When it is very hot, remove from the heat and serve immediately.

HEARTY DAL WITH VEGETABLES (DALMA)

Dal is the generic name for all members of the dried pea and bean family, and also the name of the dishes made from them. *Dal* is also the ultimate Indian comfort food. It's hearty, but not heavy, and is the protein-rich staple for millions. All dried beans are rich in iron, vitamin B and substantial amounts of incomplete proteins that yield their total nutritional value when combined with other proteins. So if you serve *dal* dishes with other protein-rich foods such as grains, nuts, yogurt or milk, you'll round out the full potential of nourishment dormant in the *dal*.

Dalma is a thick, robust, "stick-to-your-ribs" dish, rich in flavour but light on the digestion. It thickens substantially on sitting, but is delicious reheated; the flavours seem to improve on sitting. Serve *Hearty Vegetable Dal* with breads such as *Punjabi Baked Flatbread*, or *Trinidad-style Flatbread* and a salad dish such as *Creamy Banana and Yogurt Salad*, for a substantial and delightful meal.

DAL SOAKING TIME: 6 hours or overnight
PREPARATION AND COOKING TIME:
1–1½ hours
YIELD: enough for 4–6 persons

2 cups (500ml) yellow split peas
4–6 cups (1–1½ litres) water
1 teaspoon (5ml) turmeric
2 teaspoons (10ml) coriander powder
2 cups (500ml) selected vegetables from the following: cauliflower, carrots, sweet potatoes, pumpkins, zucchini, squash, potatoes and eggplants, cut 1.25cm (½-inch) cubes
3 or 4 large tomatoes, chopped
3 tablespoons (60ml) ghee or oil
2 teaspoons (10ml) fresh green chilies, chopped
1 teaspoon (5ml) yellow asafetida powder
½ teaspoon (2ml) cayenne pepper
1 teaspoon (5ml) cinnamon powder
½ teaspoon (2ml) nutmeg powder
1½ teaspoons (7ml) ginger powder
3 teaspoons (15ml) cumin powder
2 teaspoons (10ml) paprika powder
2 teaspoons (10ml) salt
2 teaspoons (10ml) sugar
3 teaspoons (15ml) lemon juice
packed ¼ cup (60ml) chopped fresh coriander leaves

1. Wash the split peas thoroughly in a sieve under cold running water until the water runs clear. Soak the split peas in a large bowl with 10–12 cups of water for at least 6 hours, or overnight.

2. Place 4 cups (1 litre) water in a large heavy-based saucepan and bring it to the boil over high heat. Drain the split peas and add them along with the turmeric and coriander powder to the boiling water. Reduce the heat to a simmer and cook without a lid and stirring occasionally for about 1–1½ hours, or until the *dal* is completely broken down and smooth. You will need to add water as the cooking proceeds, but keep the *dal* as thick as possible.

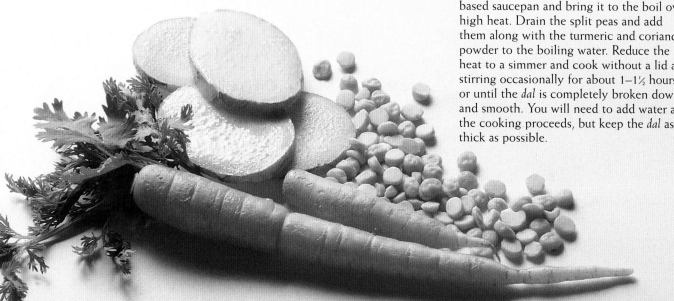

3. Meanwhile, while the *dal* is simmering, cook your selected vegetables — either grill, bake, or deep-fry them until tender. These three methods of cooking will intensify the flavour of the vegetables, caramelise their sugar content and render them delicious. When the *dal* is a soft thick purée, add all the cooked vegetables and the tomatoes and stir to combine well.

4. Warm the ghee or oil in a heavy 1-litre/quart saucepan or frying pan. When hot, add the chopped fresh chilies and sauté them for 1 or 2 minutes or until translucent and fragrant. Sprinkle in the yellow asafetida powder. Remove the ghee from the heat. Allow it to cool down until just very warm. Sprinkle all the remaining powdered spices into the warm oil and stir to mix. Add the spices and oil to the simmering soup and mix well to combine.

5. Fold the salt, sugar, lemon juice and fresh coriander leaves into the *dal*. Simmer for another 1 or 2 minutes, and serve hot.

BLACK BEAN SOUP

This is my vegetarian version of the hearty black bean soup so popular in the Caribbean. Black beans, also known as turtle beans, are a variety of kidney bean, *Phaseolus vulgaris*. They are a good source of vegetable protein and are exceptionally rich in dietary fibre. These shiny, black, kidney-shaped beans are native to Mexico where they were first cultivated. They're not always easy to find outside Latin America, the Caribbean and the USA. Asian grocers seem to be a reliable source, but be sure you don't come away with fermented cooked salted black beans, which are actually soy beans.

BEAN SOAKING TIME: 4 hours or overnight
PREPARATION AND COOKING TIME:
1¼–1½ hours
YIELD: enough for 4–6 persons

1½ cups (375ml) dried black beans
3 tablespoons (60ml) olive oil
2 small fresh red jalapeno chilies, seeded and finely chopped (leave the seeds in if you like the heat)
½ teaspoon (2ml) yellow asafetida powder
1 cup (250ml) finely sliced celery stalks and leaves
1 teaspoon (5ml) ground coriander seeds
1 teaspoon (5ml) ground cumin seeds
one large carrot, sliced
7½ cups (1825ml) vegetable stock
2 tablespoons (40ml) fresh lime or lemon juice
2 teaspoons (10ml) salt
¼ teaspoon (1ml) freshly-ground black pepper
½ cup (125ml) sour cream
coriander leaves for garnish

1. Pick over, sort and rinse the beans in a sieve under cold water. Soak them in plenty of cold water for 4 hours or overnight. Drain the beans.

2. Heat the olive oil in a 5-litre/quart saucepan over moderate heat. When the oil is fairly hot, drop in the chilies and sauté them for 2–3 minutes or until they become a little translucent. Drop in the yellow asafetida powder, celery, coriander and cumin powders and sauté for 3–5 minutes, or until the celery is translucent.

3. Add the drained beans, carrots and vegetable stock. Increase the heat, bring to the boil then reduce to moderately low. Partially cover the saucepan, and simmer for 1–1¼ hours or until the beans are very soft.

4. Remove the saucepan from the heat. In one or two batches, carefully blend the soup to a purée in a food processor or blender. Return the purée to the saucepan and add the lime or lemon juice, salt and pepper. Reheat the soup to a simmer and serve hot, garnishing each bowl with a dollop of sour cream and a sprinkle of fresh coriander leaves.

LIGHT AND TASTY ITALIAN TOMATO SOUP (ZUPPA DI POMODORO)

Fully ripe tomatoes fresh from the vine make the most flavoursome tomato dishes. When selecting tomatoes, choose unblemished fruits without bruising or splits. If you can't get fully ripened tomatoes, unripe ones can be ripened in a cupboard or on the bench away from direct sunlight at the optimum temperature of 20°C/68°F.

Remember that tomatoes don't fare well in the refrigerator — it's too cold for them. If the weather is hot and your ripe tomatoes must be stored, keep them in the crisper section of the fridge for as short a time as possible. Refrigerated tomatoes quickly lose their flavour and become sour. The best temperature for long-term tomato storage is 11°–12°C or 51°–53°F which is warmer than the refrigerator and cooler than most kitchens.

Note that due to their acidity, tomatoes will react with aluminium and non-stainless steel and produce a bitter taste. So be sure to choose a non-reactive stainless steel or enamel saucepan.

This soup is a rustic delight, flavoured with the Italian favourites: fragrant olive oil, fresh basil, and a sprinkling of mature parmesan cheese.

PREPARATION AND COOKING TIME: about 1 hour
YIELD: enough for 6 persons

1200g fresh ripe Italian plum tomatoes
1–2 tablespoons (20–40ml) extra virgin olive oil
½ teaspoon (2ml) yellow asafetida powder
packed ½ cup (125ml) fresh basil leaves, coarsely chopped
2 cups (500ml) water
1 ½ teaspoons (7ml) salt
¼–½ teaspoon (1–2ml) freshly-ground black pepper
2 teaspoons (10ml) sugar, optional
freshly grated parmesan cheese

1. Bring a large saucepan of water to the boil over full heat. Drop in the tomatoes, and remove the saucepan from the heat. When the tomato skins blister, carefully remove the tomatoes from the water and peel them. Remove the cores and finely chop the tomatoes.

2. Heat the olive oil in a 3-litre/quart saucepan over moderate heat. When warm, sprinkle in the yellow asafetida powder and sauté briefly. Add the tomatoes, basil, water, salt and pepper and stir to combine. Bring to the boil, then reduce the heat to low. Cook, well covered, stirring occasionally for about 45 minutes or until the tomatoes are very soft and tender. Stir in the optional sweetener, and serve hot in warm soup bowls with a sprinkle of freshly grated parmesan cheese.

CREAMY, FRESH GREEN-PEA SOUP

Whether you choose the shelling variety or the edible-podded variety, the best peas are the small, young sweet ones fresh from the vine. Because the sugars in the vegetables start to convert to starch from the moment they are picked, peas begin to lose their flavour literally moments after harvesting. So it goes without saying that the fresher the peas, the better the soup.

PREPARATION AND COOKING TIME:
about 20 minutes
YIELD: enough for 4 persons

¼ cup (60ml) butter
½ teaspoon (2ml) yellow asafetida powder
the inner leaves and heart of a lettuce, shredded, about 1 cup (250ml)
4 cups (1 litre) fresh green peas
4 cups (1 litre) light vegetable stock or water
1½ teaspoons (7ml) salt
1½ teaspoons (7ml) sugar
¼ teaspoon (1ml) freshly-ground black pepper
1 tablespoon (20ml) chopped fresh mint leaves
4 tablespoons (80ml) pouring consistency fresh cream

1. Melt the butter in a 3-litre/quart saucepan over moderate heat. Sprinkle in the yellow asafetida powder, sauté briefly, then add the lettuce and peas. Stir briefly, then cover the pan and braise the vegetables for 3–5 minutes, to intensify their flavours.

2. Lift the lid, add the stock or water, the salt, sugar, pepper and mint. Raise the heat, bring the soup to the boil, reduce the heat and simmer, covered, for 10–15 minutes, or until the peas are very tender.

3. Remove the saucepan from the heat and carefully pour the contents into a blender or food processor. Process to a smooth purée. Transfer the purée to a heavy metal sieve and, holding it over the saucepan, strain the soup through, scraping the underside until only dry residue remains in the sieve. Discard the residue. Gently reheat the soup, returning it to the boil. Serve the fresh green-pea soup hot, garnishing each bowl with a swirl of fresh cream.

ROASTED CAPSICUM, PEANUT AND TOMATO SOUP

This is a rich Latin American soup, with the smoky flavour of dried *chipotle* chilies available at Mexican grocery suppliers. If *chipotle* chilies are unavailable, use Spanish smoked hot paprika powder along with fresh, red *jalapeno* chilies.

PREPARATION AND COOKING TIME:
about 1–1¼ hours
YIELD: enough for 6–8 persons

3 medium red capsicums (peppers), cored, de-ribbed and quartered, about 400g after trimming
2 tablespoons (40ml) olive oil
½ teaspoon (2ml) yellow asafetida powder
2 dry chipotle chilies, seeds removed and cut into small pieces, or 1 fresh red jalapeno chili, seeded and sliced along with 1 teaspoon (5ml) Spanish smoked hot paprika powder
700g ripe tomatoes, blanched, peeled and coarsely chopped, about 2½ cups (625ml)

¼ cup (60ml) chopped fresh coriander leaves
and fine stalks

4 cups (1 litre) rich vegetable stock

2 teaspoons (10ml) salt

¼ teaspoon (1ml) freshly-ground black pepper

¼ cup (60ml) smooth peanut butter,
or more for a richer peanut flavour

2 tablespoons (40ml) chopped fresh coriander leaves for garnish

1. Pre-heat your griller. Place the capsicums, with their skins upwards under the griller and roast for 10–15 minutes or until their skins are blackened and blistered. Alternatively, if you don't have a griller, hold them over a flame with kitchen tongs. Remove the capsicums and place them in a plastic bag to steam for 15 minutes. Remove and rinse the capsicums under cold water, rubbing and peeling off the blackened skin. Chop the capsicums roughly and set them aside.

2. Warm the olive oil in a 3-litre/quart saucepan over moderate heat. Sprinkle in the yellow asafetida powder and sauté momentarily. Add the dry chili pieces or the fresh red chili slices. Stir briefly, then add the tomatoes, capsicums, coriander leaves and the smoked paprika, if using it. Raise the heat and, stirring occasionally, cook the tomatoes, peppers and coriander for 10 minutes or until the tomatoes break down.

3. Add the vegetable stock, salt and pepper, bring the soup to the boil and reduce the heat slightly. Cover with a lid and simmer for 25 minutes.

4. Remove the soup from the heat and stir in the peanut butter, mixing thoroughly. Pour the soup into a food processor or blender and process until very smooth. Return the soup to the rinsed-out saucepan and reheat over gentle heat. The soup should be creamy in consistency. If too thick, add a little more vegetable stock or water; or if you prefer you may like to add a little extra peanut butter now. Serve hot, with a garnish of fresh coriander leaves.

JAMAICAN PEPPERPOT SOUP

This recipe was inspired by and loosely based on a recipe by Dorinda Haffner in her popular book *"Dorinda's Taste of the Caribbean"*. My simple vegetarian version contains a selection of earthy root vegetables — taro, yam and sweet potatoes — which, as Dorinda explains, are known as "ground provisions" in the Caribbean. Pepperpot soup is a hearty winter fare. If taro, yam or sweet potatoes are not all available, you may like to substitute with potato, pumpkin, or cassava root. Try deep-frying or pan-frying the tofu before adding it to the soup.

PREPARATION AND COOKING TIME:
about 40 minutes
YIELD: enough for 6–8 persons

1 tablespoon (20ml) oil
2–3 large red or green chilies, seeded and chopped
½ teaspoon (2ml) yellow asafetida powder
1⅓ cups (335ml) taro root, about 250g, cubed 1.5cm (¾ inch)
1⅓ cups (335ml) yam, about 250g, cubed 1.5cm (¾ inch)
1⅓ cups (335ml) sweet potato, about 250g, cubed 1.5cm (½-inch)
4 cups (1 litre) rich vegetable stock
2 cups (500ml) thick coconut milk
250g firm tofu, cut 1.5cm (¾ inch) cubes
½ cup (125ml) chopped celery leaves
2 tablespoons (40ml) butter
1½–2 teaspoons (7–10ml) salt
½ teaspoon (2ml) freshly-ground black pepper
¼ bunch spinach leaves rolled into a tight log and sliced thin

1. Place the oil in a 5-litre/quart saucepan over moderate heat. When hot, drop in the chilies, sauté for 1 or 2 minutes, then sprinkle in the yellow asafetida powder and stir momentarily. Add the taro, yam and sweet potato and stir-fry for 1 or 2 minutes.

2. Pour in the vegetable stock and bring to the boil. Add the coconut milk, the tofu pieces, celery leaves, butter, salt and black pepper. Simmer the soup, covered, for 20 minutes, or until the vegetables are tender. In the last 5 minutes add the sliced spinach leaves. Serve hot.

Broccoli Cheddar Soup

BROCCOLI CHEDDAR SOUP

The Romans were fond of broccoli. Apicius, the ancient Roman food writer was known for his skill in cooking it. Although there were once many types, the green sprouting Calabrese is the best-known variety today.

Fresh and crisp broccoli marries well with tasty cheddar cheese in this stunningly simple, thick and tasty soup. I first tasted it on the winter lunchtime menu at Govinda's restaurant in Denver, Colorado, and it became my favourite.

PREPARATION AND COOKING TIME:
about 25 minutes
YIELD: enough for 4 persons

3 cups (750ml) water
250g broccoli, cut into small florets, about 2½ packed cups (625ml)
4 tablespoons (80ml) butter
½ cup (125ml) flour
½ teaspoon (2ml) yellow asafetida powder
2 cups (500ml) warm milk
1¼ cups (310ml) grated cheddar cheese, about 125g
½ teaspoon (2ml) freshly-ground black pepper
1 teaspoon (5ml) salt
1 tablespoon (20ml) finely chopped fresh parsley

Jamaican Pepperpot Soup

1. Place the water and broccoli in a 2-litre/quart saucepan and bring it to the boil over moderate heat. Reduce to a simmer and cook until the broccoli is just tender. Remove from the heat.

2. Meanwhile, in another 3-litre/quart saucepan, melt the butter over low to medium heat. Sprinkle in the yellow asafetida powder and sauté momentarily. Add the flour, and cook it, stirring continually until it darkens slightly. Carefully pour in the warm milk and stir with a wire whisk until it thickens. Fold in the cheese, black pepper and salt.

3. Pour the broccoli and water into the cheese sauce. Combine well, being careful not to break up the broccoli florets. Sprinkle in the chopped parsley and serve immediately.

WHOLESOME BROWN LENTIL AND VEGETABLE SOUP

Lentils are sometimes called "the poor man's meat". Of all the dried pulses, with the exception of the soy bean, lentils contain the most protein — 100g of lentils contain 25g of protein, more weight-per-weight than beef.

Remember that, like all legumes, once lentils are in an acid medium, they will not get any softer, no matter how long they are cooked. So make sure they are tender before adding the lemon juice to this soup.

This distinctly Middle Eastern flavoured soup is a good one if you're in a hurry. Brown lentils, sometimes called green lentils, don't need soaking before being cooked.

PREPARATION AND COOKING TIME: about 45–50 minutes
YIELD: enough for 4–6 persons

1 cup (250ml) brown lentils
6 cups (1.5 litres) water
3 tablespoons (60ml) olive oil
½ teaspoon (2ml) yellow asafetida powder
1 cup (250ml) potatoes, diced into 1.25cm (½-inch) cubes
½ teaspoon (2ml) freshly-ground black pepper
1 cup (250ml) chopped celery, including leaves
1 cup (250ml) chopped silverbeet (Swiss chard) leaves, or spinach
1 tablespoon (20ml) ground coriander powder
½ teaspoon (2ml) cumin powder
2 tablespoons (40ml) lemon juice
¼ cup (60ml) chopped parsley leaves
¼ cup (60ml) chopped coriander leaves
1½ teaspoons (7ml) salt

1. Rinse the lentils under cold running water, then place them with the water in a 3-litre/quart saucepan over moderate heat. Bring to the boil, then reduce the heat to a simmer. Cook for 15–20 minutes or until the lentils start to break up.

2. Warm the oil in another small saucepan over moderate heat. When warm, sprinkle in the yellow asafetida powder. Drop in the potatoes and black pepper, increase the heat and sauté the potatoes for 2 or 3 minutes. Add the celery and fry for 1 more minute. Pour the vegetables and flavoured oil into the simmering soup.

3. Cook the soup for another 15 minutes, or until the potatoes begin to soften. Then add the silverbeet (Swiss chard) leaves, the ground coriander, cumin and lemon juice. Allow the soup to cook for another 10 minutes, or until the vegetables are all sufficiently tender and the lentils are completely smooth. Finally add the parsley, coriander leaves and salt. Serve the soup hot.

CHILLED AVOCADO AND GREEN PEPPERCORN SOUP

Green peppercorns are picked unripe, and are usually preserved in brine. They have an invigorating, lively taste and combine well with the delicate flavour of avocados.

This velvety-smooth chilled soup is an ideal addition to a summer menu. It is uncooked and practically effortless to prepare. Select ripe but blemish-free avocados that feel heavy for their size.

PREPARATION TIME: 10 minutes
REFRIGERATION TIME: at least 1 hour
YIELD: enough for 4–6 persons

3 medium-sized ripe avocados, about 600g
1 teaspoon (5ml) salt
1 tablespoon (20ml) fresh lime or lemon juice
½ teaspoon (2ml) yellow asafetida powder
1 tablespoon (20ml) fresh coriander leaves
4 cups (1 litre) rich vegetable stock, or more for a thinner soup
1 tablespoon (20ml) green peppercorns preserved in brine, drained and rinsed
½ cup (125ml) crème fraîche
extra ¼ cup (60ml) crème fraîche for garnish
extra 1 tablespoon (20ml) coriander leaves for garnish
a few green peppercorns for garnish

1. Cut the avocados in half, remove the stones, and scoop out the flesh into a food processor. Add the salt, lime juice, yellow asafetida powder, coriander leaves, half the stock, 2 teaspoons (10ml) of the peppercorns, and the cream. Process to a smooth purée. Add the remaining stock and process again. Add a little extra stock now if you desire a thinner consistency.

2. Pour the soup into a large bowl. Fold in the other 2 teaspoons (10ml) green peppercorns. Cover and refrigerate for at least 1 hour.

3. Serve the soup in individual bowls with a swirl of the reserved *crème fraîche*, a few peppercorns and the garnish of fresh coriander leaves.

SWEET POTATO SOUP WITH CORN AND CHILIES

The sweet potato, like the ordinary potato, was cultivated in pre-historic Peru. It is now grown around the world and comes in hundreds of varieties, the most common being yellow and white. As a general rule, the paler the colour, the drier the flesh. The darker tubers become more moist and sweet when cooked.

Whichever variety of sweet potato you prefer, they combine beautifully with another South American favourite — fresh corn. For contrasting texture, I have left the corn kernels whole in this heart-warming and tasty soup. If you prefer, you can blend the corn to a purée with the sweet potatoes.

PREPARATION AND COOKING TIME:
about 40 minutes
YIELD: enough for 4–6 persons

¼ cup (60ml) butter, about 50g
1 teaspoon (5ml) yellow asafetida powder
4¾ cups (1185ml) sweet potato, about 650g, diced
4 cups (1 litre) rich vegetable stock
1¼ cups (310ml) cooked corn kernels, about 200g
1 green jalapeno chili, seeded and finely diced
1½ teaspoons (7ml) salt (less if using a salty stock)
½ teaspoon (2ml) freshly-ground black pepper
whole coriander leaves for garnish

1. Melt the butter in a 3-litre/quart saucepan over moderate heat. Sprinkle in the yellow asafetida powder and drop in the sweet potatoes. Sauté the potatoes for 2 or 3 minutes, then add the vegetable stock. Bring to the boil and cook for 15–20 minutes, or until the sweet potatoes are tender but not broken down. Remove the saucepan from the heat.

2. Strain the sweet potatoes, being careful to reserve all the liquid. Return the cooking liquid to the rinsed-out saucepan. Place the sweet potatoes in a food processor and reduce them to a purée. Add a little cooking liquid if needed.

3. Add the sweet potato purée to the cooking liquid and return to moderate heat. Add the cooked corn, chili, salt and pepper. Simmer the soup for another 10 minutes, then serve hot with crusty bread and a garnish of fresh coriander leaves.

BEETROOT SOUP (BORSCHT)

Beetroots are of great therapeutic value. They have properties to clean the kidneys and gall bladder. Being rich in alkaline elements, beetroots are also useful in aiding the natural processes of elimination. The juice is extremely useful in the treatment of anaemia, and also in the healing of gastric ulcers, piles and circulatory disorders.

What I like the most about beetroots, though, is that my mother used to cook them in the most delicious way, combined simply with potatoes and sour cream. I can still remember the taste of this simple, comforting chunky soup, eaten hot as the cold English rain lashed the window panes. This recipe is almost like my mother used to make — she added eggs to her version of this classic European dish. Mine is much less rich without the eggs, so you needn't feel guilty about the sour cream.

PREPARATION TIME: about 10 minutes
COOKING TIME: about 1 hour
YIELD: enough for 6 persons

6 medium beetroots, scrubbed and halved, about 1kg after trimming
2 bay leaves
6 cups (1.5 litres) water
1½ teaspoons (7ml) salt
5 old, medium-sized potatoes, peeled and cut into 2.5cm (1-inch) cubes, about 600g
2 tablespoons (40ml) fresh lemon juice
½ teaspoon (2ml) black pepper
1 tablespoon (20ml) sugar
1 cup (250ml) sour cream
fresh dill sprigs for garnish

1. Place the halved beetroots and the bay leaves in a 5-litre/quart saucepan over full heat, and cover with the water. Add one teaspoon (5ml) salt, bring to the boil, then reduce the heat and simmer the beetroots for one hour or until they are tender.

2. Meanwhile, boil the potatoes in a separate saucepan in lightly salted water until tender. Remove the potatoes and strain off the liquid. Set the potatoes aside, covered.

3. Remove the beetroots from the water, strain the liquid and reserve it. Rinse the saucepan and return the cooking water to it. Peel the skins off the beetroots under cold running water. Cut the beetroots into 1.5cm (¾-inch) cubes. Return the beetroot to the beetroot water. Add the lemon juice, the remaining salt, pepper and sugar, and place over moderate heat.

4. When the beetroots and their broth are hot, and you are ready to serve, divide the cooked potatoes between warmed serving bowls. Ladle the beetroot chunks and liquid — as much or as little as you desire — over the potatoes. Dollop with a generous spoon or two of sour cream. Garnish with the dill sprigs and serve immediately.

1 cup (250ml) hot water
⅓ cup (85ml) peanuts, about 50g, roasted and powdered in a spice mill or coffee grinder
1 tablespoon (20ml) jaggery or brown sugar
1 teaspoon (5ml) salt
2 tablespoons (40ml) ghee
1 teaspoon (5ml) chickpea flour
½ teaspoon (2ml) yellow asafetida powder
1 teaspoon (5ml) garam masala
1½ teaspoons (7ml) chili powder
1 handful fresh coriander leaves, chopped

1. Rinse the *chana dal* under cold running water until it runs clear. Place the *dal* in a large bowl of cold water and allow it to soak for 6 hours, or overnight.

2. Soak the tamarind in 1 cup (250ml) hot water for 15 minutes. When the tamarind is soft, squeeze it through a sieve to extract the tamarind purée. Set the purée aside.

3. Drain, rinse and drain the *dal* again. Place it with the 5 cups (1250ml) water, along with the turmeric, in a 2-litre/quart saucepan over moderate heat. Bring to the boil and simmer, covered for at least one hour, or until the *dal* is soft and broken down. For a very smooth soup, you may wish to blend the soup at this stage, and you may wish to add more water.

4. Add the ground peanut powder, the tamarind purée, the sweetener and the salt to the simmering *dal*. Stir to combine well. Note that after you add the sour tamarind purée, the *dal* will not break down any further.

5. Fry the final seasonings as follows: Place the ghee in a small pan over moderate heat. When the ghee is fairly hot, add the chickpea flour, and stirring, fry it until it darkens a few shades. Add the yellow asafetida powder, sauté momentarily, then add the *garam masala* and chili powder. Swirl the pan to mix, then immediately pour the contents into the simmering *dal*. Stir to mix well, sprinkle with coriander leaves and serve hot.

MAHARASTRIAN-STYLE SWEET AND SOUR CHANA DAL (KATACHI AMTI)

Chana dal, a variety of small chickpea, is one of India's most important pulses. The whole dried seeds are split and separated, are buff to bright yellow in colour, and about 0.5cm (¼-inch) in diameter. *Chana dal* is classically used in thick-textured *dal* purées and soups. Note that imported *dals* arrive minimally processed, so be sure to pick through, wash and rinse the legumes very carefully before proceeding with the recipe.

DAL SOAKING TIME: 6 hours or overnight
PREPARATION TIME: 15 minutes
COOKING TIME: 1¼–1½ hours
YIELD: enough for 4–6 persons

1 cup (250ml) chana dal
5 cups (1250ml) water
½ teaspoon (2ml) turmeric
1 walnut-sized lump tamarind, about 50g

BREADS

Punjabi Baked Flatbread (Naan)

Super-flaky Wholemeal Griddle-fried Breads (Parathas)

Dense and Delicious German Sourdough Bread (Pumpernickel)

Herbed Bread Rolls

Steamed Semolina Bread (Dhokla)

Trinidad-style Flatbread (Roti)

Light and Moist Rye Bread

Stuffed Italian Flatbread (Focaccia)

Old English Saffron Bread

Buckwheat Chapatis

Leavened Turkish Flatbread (Pide)

Puffed Fried Sesame Breads (Til Poories)

Spicy Cajun Cornbread

PUNJABI BAKED FLATBREAD (NAAN)

This popular leavened bread, especially enjoyed in Punjab in north-west India and Pakistan, is cooked in a traditional coal or wood-fired clay oven called a *tandoor*. Many versions of this flat bread are found throughout central Asia, from Iran in the East to the Soviet countries in the North. The breads, enriched with milk, yogurt and butter, are slapped onto the inner walls of the hot oven where they cook quickly, partially puffing, and taking on a smoky flavour. The occasional charred spot from where the flames lick them adds a delightful crisp textured crust. This recipe calls for a household griller, which does a pretty good job. If you have a *tandoor* oven, all the better. *Naan* are traditionally sprinkled with *kalonji* seeds that are also known as *nigella* seeds and occasionally misnamed as onion seeds. *Kalonji* seeds are available at Indian and specialty grocers.

DOUGH RESTING TIME: about 4½ hours
PREPARATION TIME: about 30 minutes
COOKING TIME: about 6 minutes per bread
YIELD: 6 naan

2 teaspoons (10ml) dried yeast
1 teaspoon (5ml) sugar
2 tablespoons (40ml) warm water
¼ cup (60ml) warm milk
¼ cup (60ml) yogurt
4 tablespoons (80ml) melted butter or ghee
3 cups (750ml) plain flour
1 teaspoon (5ml) salt
½ teaspoon (2ml) baking powder
1 teaspoon (5ml) kalonji seeds
about ½ cup (125ml) extra warm water
2 teaspoons (10ml) extra kalonji seeds

1. Combine the yeast, sugar and warm water in a small bowl and set aside for 5–10 minutes, or until the mixture becomes frothy.

2. Mix the frothy yeast mixture with the warm milk, yogurt and melted butter or ghee. Combine the flour, salt, baking powder and 1 teaspoon (5ml) *kalonji* seeds in a large bowl, and add the blended wet ingredients. Mix well, adding a little of the extra warm water at a time until the mixture leaves the side of the bowl and becomes a non-sticky, kneadable dough. Knead for 6–8 minutes or until smooth and elastic. Transfer the dough to an oiled bowl and set it aside in a warm place for about 4 hours or until it is well risen.

3. Punch the dough down and knead it briefly, adding a little flour if it is sticky. Divide the dough into 6 pieces and form each piece into a smooth ball. Place the balls on an oiled plate and cover them with plastic wrap. Allow the balls to rest for 10–15 minutes.

4. Pre-heat the griller to the highest setting. Place a shelf 12.5cm (5 inches) under the heat source, and pre-heat your baking sheet. Roll and stretch a ball of dough into a teardrop shape, about 25cm (10 inches) long and 12.5cm (5 inches) wide at its base. Repeat for one more ball of dough and spray the bread with water. Sprinkle on half the extra *kalonji* seeds.

5. Place the breads under the griller and cook them for about 3 minutes on each side, or until they rise and turn golden brown. Avoid placing the breads too close to the griller, otherwise the breads may not fully cook inside before browning. If you wish, allow the breads to become slightly toasted, with a few charcoal flecks.

6. Remove the breads from the oven, cover them with a clean teatowel and repeat the procedure for the remaining breads. Serve the *naan* hot or warm.

SUPER-FLAKY WHOLEMEAL GRIDDLE-FRIED BREADS (PARATHAS)

One of the most famous Indian breads, *parathas*, are fully cooked on a griddle and basted with ghee to make them crisp and rich. Plain *parathas* such as those featured here are rolled in a special way: The sequence of rolling out the pastry, spreading ghee on the surface, then re-folding and re-rolling results in the formation of a multitude of layers. When the *parathas* are heated, the air and water vapour expanding between the layers forms a flaky puff-like pastry in the same way that Western-style puff pastry is produced. Note that to cook your *parathas* you will need one or two cast iron griddles or non-stick frying pans, a rolling pin, a pastry brush and a smooth rolling area. Serve *parathas* hot or at room temperature with chutneys such as *Spicy Guava Jam*, a dry vegetable dish such as *Sautéed Potatoes with Cashews* or a moist vegetable dish such as *Green Papaya and Potato Tarkari*.

PREPARATION TIME: about 15 minutes
DOUGH RESTING TIME: ½–3 hours
COOKING TIME: 35–45 minutes
YIELD: 10 parathas

2½ cups (625ml) sieved chapati flour (atta)
1½ teaspoons (7ml) salt or a little less if using salted butter in the pastry
5 tablespoons (100ml) melted butter or ghee
up to ⅔ cup (165ml) warm water
extra chapati flour for dusting
about ½ cup (125ml) extra melted ghee for cooking

1. Mix the flour and salt in a large bowl. Drizzle in the melted butter or ghee and rub it in with your fingertips until the mixture has the consistency of coarse meal. Add about three-quarters of the warm water, gathering the mixture into a rough mass. Add more water, if required, to form a medium-soft dough. Knead the dough for 10 minutes, or until silky smooth and pliable. Leave the dough to rest for 30 minutes to 3 hours, covered with an inverted bowl.

2. Re-knead the dough briefly. Form it into a smooth log and cut it into 10 equal-sized pieces. Form a portion of the dough into a smooth round patty. On a lightly floured surface, roll the patty of dough into a 19cm (7½-inch) wide, evenly round disc of pastry. Pour 1½ teaspoons (7ml) melted ghee into the centre of the disk, and spread it lightly with your fingers. With a knife, make a cut from the centre of the circle to the outer edge. Roll the pastry disc, starting at the cut edge, into a tight cone. Lift the cone, sit it on its base and press the point down with the palm of your hand to reduce it to a roughly circular patty of dough again. Repeat this procedure for the remaining pieces of pastry.

3. Lightly re-flour your rolling surface. Carefully roll out a piece of dough into a 16.5cm (6-inch) disk, being careful to avoid pressing too hard. Pre-heat one or two pans or griddles over moderate heat for 2 or 3 minutes. Spread a little ghee on the griddle and gently slip on a disc of pastry. Cook the bread for 1½ minutes and then drizzle another teaspoon of ghee around the edges and on top of the *paratha*, and cook for another minute, or until the *paratha* is marbled with reddish-gold spots. Turn over the *paratha* and drizzle another teaspoon of ghee on the surface. To encourage the *paratha* to cook evenly, rub the bread in a circular motion with the bottom of a spoon. Cook for 1 or 2 minutes more or until the bread is crisp and shows reddish-brown spots all over. Remove the *paratha*, and keep warm in a clean tea towel. Repeat for the remaining breads. Serve the *parathas* hot.

DENSE AND DELICIOUS GERMAN SOURDOUGH BREAD (PUMPERNICKEL)

This is a richly flavoured, traditional German sourdough bread, naturally leavened without yeast. Dark and tasty, it is less sweet than commercial *pumpernickel* and more closely resembles the German black bread, *schwartzbrot*. It's slow cooking time ensures that it will keep very well.

PREPARATION TIME: a few minutes
FERMENTING TIME: 16–20 hours
COOKING TIME: 5–6 hours
YIELD: 1 loaf

3 cups (750ml) coarse rye flour
1¾ cups (435ml) coarse wheat flour
1¼ cups (310ml) coarse barley flour
2 teaspoons (10ml) salt
½ teaspoon (2ml) powdered fennel seeds
½ teaspoon (2ml) powdered anise seeds
½ teaspoon (2ml) powdered caraway seeds
½ teaspoon (2ml) powdered coriander seeds
2 teaspoons (10ml) treacle
600ml water, heated to about 65°C/150°F

1. Combine all the dry ingredients in a large bowl. Dissolve the treacle in the warm water and pour the water into the dry mix to form a moist dough. Knead briefly. Press the dough into a 3-litre/quart capacity rectangular bread-baking tin and flatten the top.

2. Cover the bread tin with oiled plastic wrap and leave in a warm place (30°C/85°F) for 16–20 hours. If the temperature is right, the dough will naturally ferment and rise in the tin. (The sour fermented aroma is quite natural.) Remove the plastic wrap and replace with a tight covering of foil.

3. Pre-heat the oven to 107°C/225°F. Fill a large baking pan with boiling water and place at the bottom of the oven. Sit a rack over the pan and place the bread tin on top of the rack. Bake the bread for 5–6 hours or until it feels firm and looks dark.

4. For the final stage of baking, remove the foil and the baking pan of water from the oven, and increase the oven temperature to 175°C/350°F. Bake the bread for another 30–60 minutes or until the top of the bread is crusty.

5. Remove the loaf, cool on a wire rack and leave 24 hours before cutting into very thin slices when required. Store in foil or plastic wrap.

HERBED BREAD ROLLS

In this recipe, small bun-sized pieces of herbed and yeasted dough are arranged in a quiche pan or shallow cake tin fairly close together, then baked. They come to the table joined together in a singular circular cluster, and diners can break off a roll as desired.

PREPARATION TIME: about 30 minutes
DOUGH RESTING TIME: First rise: 1 hour
Second rise: 30 minutes

BAKING TIME:
30–35 minutes
YIELD: 18 rolls

1 teaspoon (5ml) dried yeast
about 1¼ cups (310ml) warm water
1 teaspoon (5ml) sugar
3 cups (750ml) plain unbleached bread flour
1 teaspoon (5ml) salt
3 teaspoons (15ml) oil
1 teaspoon (5ml) fresh thyme leaves, minced
1 teaspoon (5ml) fresh oregano leaves, minced
2 teaspoons (10ml) fresh basil leaves, chopped
½ teaspoon (2ml) yellow asafetida powder
poppy seeds, sesame seeds, fine oatmeal or dried herbs for topping

1. Combine the yeast, a few teaspoons of warm water, and the sugar in a small bowl. Set aside for 10 minutes, or until the mixture is frothy.

2. Whisk together the flour and salt. Add the oil, herbs and yellow asafetida powder to the frothy yeast mixture. Make a well in the centre of the flour and pour in the yeast mixture. Add three-quarters of the warm water, and mix. Add enough of the remaining water, if required, to make a soft but non-sticky dough. Knead the dough for 5–8 minutes. Place the dough in an oiled bowl, cover with plastic wrap and leave in a warm place for one hour, or until doubled in bulk.

3. Punch down the dough and divide into 18 even-sized pieces. Shape them by rolling them around under cupped hands on a floured board or marble slab, then arrange them fairly close together in a lightly oiled, 25cm (10-inch) quiche pan or round, shallow baking dish. Keep in mind that the rolls will approximately double in size. Allow the rolls to rise again for about 30 minutes. Spray with water and sprinkle with poppy seeds, sesame, fine oatmeal or dried herbs.

4. Pre-heat the oven to 220°C/430°F and bake the rolls for 30–35 minutes or until golden brown and hollow-sounding when tapped on the base. Serve as described.

STEAMED SEMOLINA BREAD (DHOKLA)

This savoury golden bread is a specialty of the State of Gujarat in western India. There's practically as many recipes for *dhokla* as there are Gujarati housewives — and that's a lot! Some recipes for *dhokla* call for chickpea flour; there's another version that uses semolina. Here's a recipe that's practically instant, using semolina with a little chickpea flour and rice flour added which requires no batter resting time and a short cooking time. Because *dhokla* is steamed instead of baked, the top of the bread is soft and shiny rather than brown and crisp. *Dhokla* is usually served warm or at room temperature, with meals, or as a snack, with chutneys. It is usually cut into 3.75cm (1½-inch) pieces and served with a colourful garnish of snowy white fresh coconut, fresh coriander and a fried seasoning of mustard and sesame. It's delicious — once you've tasted *dhokla*, you'll make it again and again.

PREPARATION TIME: a few minutes
COOKING TIME: 20 minutes
YIELD: about 30 pieces

1 cup (250ml) semolina
2 teaspoons (10ml) rice flour
1 tablespoon (20ml) chickpea flour
1 teaspoon (5ml) salt
¼ teaspoon (1ml) turmeric
1 teaspoon (5ml) fresh ginger, minced
1 or 2 small fresh chilies, finely minced
10 fresh curry leaves, very finely shredded
2 tablespoons (40ml) chopped fresh coriander leaves
1½ tablespoons (30ml) oil
½ cup (125ml) yogurt
up to ½ cup (125ml) cold water
1 teaspoon (5ml) Eno powder (fruit salts, available from chemist)

The topping:

1 tablespoon (20ml) oil
½ teaspoon (2ml) mustard seeds
½ teaspoon (2ml) sesame seeds
2 tablespoons (40ml) fresh coriander leaves
⅓ cup (85ml) grated fresh coconut

1. Whisk together the semolina, rice flour, chickpea flour, salt and turmeric in a medium-sized mixing bowl. Drop in the minced ginger, chilies, the curry leaves and the coriander leaves. Pour in the oil, the yogurt and half the water, and whisk again. While whisking, add more of the water to bring the mixture to an almost pourable batter consistency. Depending on the variety of semolina and the thickness of the yogurt, you may require more or less water.

2. Place a few inches of water in a deep 5-litre/quart saucepan. Select a shallow 22.5cm (9-inch) cake tin that will comfortably sit inside the saucepan. Set it on top of an upside down bowl or container inside the saucepan, enabling the tin to sit above the water level and below the top of the saucepan, leaving room for a tight-fitting lid. This will ensure that the bread steams trouble-free. Place the saucepan over full heat and bring the water to a boil.

3. Spray or rub a thin film of oil in the tin. Set the tin in the steaming saucepan. When the water is fully boiling, the steaming tin is in place and the tight-fitting lid to the saucepan is on hand, quickly whisk in the Eno powder into the batter. This will aerate the mixture, an essential step in the steaming process. Quickly pour and scrape the batter into the oiled tin, level it briefly with a spatula and immediately put on the lid. Steam the *dhokla* over full heat for 15–20 minutes or until the *dhokla* is fully set and does not stick to a knife point when inserted.

4. When the bread is fully cooked, lift it from the saucepan while still in its tin, and set it aside for 10 minutes to cool and firm up. Cut the bread into 3.75cm (1½-inch) squares or diamond shapes.

5. For the final seasoning, heat the oil in a small saucepan. When hot, sprinkle in the mustard and sesame seeds. When the mustard seeds pop, crackle and turn greyish, and the sesame seeds are a few shades darker and fragrant, pour and spread the seasoning over the *dhokla*. Sprinkle with the freshly grated coconut and fresh coriander leaves. Serve warm or at room temperature.

TRINIDAD-STYLE FLATBREAD (ROTI)

As Dorinda Haffner points out in her book *Dorinda's Taste of the Caribbean*, "a good 40 per cent of the Trinidadian population is of Indian ancestry, and Indian cuisine has added greatly to the richness and variety of the local diet". Thin, slightly chewy *roti* breads hot off the griddle make delicious wrappers for dry vegetable dishes. Cold *rotis* are great filled with salad.

The best utensil for griddle-baking your *roti* is a *tava*, an Indian-style iron griddle with a slightly concave shape. *Tavas* are available at Indian grocery stores. If unavailable, use a non-stick frying pan.

PREPARATION TIME: 25–30 minutes
DOUGH RESTING TIME: about 1 hour
COOKING TIME: about 25 minutes
YIELD: twelve 23cm (9-inch) breads

about 11 tablespoons (220ml) warm water
2 teaspoons (10ml) dried yeast
1½ teaspoons (7ml) sugar
3 cups (750ml) plain bread flour
3 teaspoons (15ml) baking powder
½ teaspoon (2ml) salt
1½ tablespoons (30ml) oil
a little oil for brushing the pan

1. Combine 2 tablespoons (40ml) warm water, the yeast, and the sugar in a small bowl. Leave in a warm place for 10 minutes, or until frothy.

2. Sift together the flour, baking powder, and salt in a large bowl. Make a well in the centre of the flour and pour in the oil, the frothy yeast mixture, and about 6 tablespoons (120ml) warm water. Gather the mixture into a lump, and form it into a firm, non-sticky kneadable dough. If too dry, add a few more tablespoons of water. Knead the dough for about 5 minutes, then place it in an oiled bowl covered with oiled plastic wrap. Leave aside in a warm place for 1 hour, or until doubled in size.

3. Briefly re-knead the dough. Roll it out into an evenly shaped tube, and cut it into 12 pieces. Roll each piece into a very thin disc measuring about 22.5cm (9-inches) wide.

4. Pre-heat your *tava* or non-stick pan over fairly high heat. When the pan is hot, brush or spray the surface with a little oil and immediately lower one bread onto the surface. In a few moments bubbles will appear on the bread's surface. Firmly press around the edges of the bread with a folded tea towel. Cook for about 1½–2 minutes, then turn the bread over and cook it on the other side for 1–1½ minutes. Some parts of the bread, although probably not all, will puff up. Regulate the heat so that the brown spots, which will naturally appear on the surface of the breads, do not become burnt spots. Regularly brush or spray the surface with the oil, and continue to cook your *roti* until they are all done. Serve hot or cold.

LIGHT AND MOIST RYE BREAD

Studded with caraway seeds, this distinctively flavoured rye bread is mellowed with the addition of wheat flour. And although rye bread can often be dense and heavy, this one is very light in texture due to the addition of gluten flour. If you're sensitive to gluten, replace the gluten flour with more wholemeal flour.

You may prefer to use fresh or compressed yeast. If that's the case, you'll need more yeast than the recipe suggests. Dried yeast is at least twice as potent, weight for weight, as compressed yeast. Keep in mind that if you use more yeast than necessary, the bread will go stale and dry very quickly. The less yeast used, the more moist the loaf. You may also want to "prove" your bread for longer. The general rule of thumb is this: The longer the fermentation time, the better the flavour and texture, and a vastly improved crust. Rye bread is best served a day or two after baking and is traditionally cut into very thin slices.

PREPARATION AND COOKING TIME:
20–25 minutes
DOUGH RESTING TIME: 3 hours
BAKING TIME: about 1 hour
YIELD: 2 medium loaves

3½ cups (875ml) rye flour
2½ cups (625ml) wholemeal flour
1½ cups (375ml) gluten flour

3 teaspoons (15ml) fine sea salt
2 teaspoons (10ml) dried yeast
3 teaspoons (15ml) caraway seeds, or more if desired
3½ cups (875ml) warm water
1 tablespoon (20ml) treacle
1–2 teaspoons (5–10ml) caraway seeds for sprinkling on top

1. Mix the flours and the 3 teaspoons (15ml) caraway seeds and salt together in a large bowl.

2. Combine the yeast with a little of the warm water in a small bowl, and leave aside in a warm place for 10 minutes, or until frothy.

3. Dissolve the treacle in the remaining warm water.

4. Pour the frothy yeast mixture and the treacle and water mixture into the bowl of flour. Mix thoroughly to a soft dough. It will probably be a little sticky, but that's the nature of rye flour. Knead the dough for 5 minutes, then transfer it to a clean bowl. Cover the bowl with oiled plastic wrap, and leave the bread to rise in a warm place for about 2 hours, or until doubled in size, or longer if you wish.

5. Lightly oil two, 2-litre oblong loaf tins. Punch down the dough and form it into a shape roughly the length of the tins. Place the dough in the tins, moisten the surface of the dough with a little water, and sprinkle and press on the remaining caraway seeds. Brush a little oil on top of the breads (this helps them stay moist). Cover the bread tins with oiled plastic wrap and leave them in a warm, undisturbed place for at least 1 hour, or until the breads rise high in their tins.

6. Pre-heat the oven to 210°C/410°F. Remove the plastic wrap and bake the breads for about 1 hour or until golden brown and hollow sounding when tapped on the base. When cooked, turn the loaves out of their tins onto a wire rack to cool.

STUFFED ITALIAN FLATBREAD (FOCACCIA)

Focaccia has become a national dish of Italy, and many regional versions can be found, all quite different. My version is probably a cross between the local country cuisine of the Puglia region, where breads are enriched with the ingredients of the pastoral people such as tomatoes, herbs and oil, and southern versions adding cheese. This recipe makes a large thick *focaccia* (it can only just be called a "flatbread") filled with a variety of tasty, herby, melty mouth-watering ingredients. Serve *focaccia* hot from the oven for a taste treat.

PREPARATION TIME: about 30 minutes
TOTAL DOUGH RISING TIME: 45 minutes
BAKING TIME: about 40 minutes
YIELD: 1 thick 25cm (10-inch) bread

The dough:

3 teaspoons (15ml) dried yeast
1 cup (250ml) warm water
½ teaspoon (2ml) sugar
3 cups (750ml) unbleached plain bread flour
1 teaspoon (5ml) yellow asafetida powder
½ teaspoon (2ml) salt

4 tablespoons (80ml) olive oil

The filling:

2 cups (500ml) grated cheddar cheese
2 cups (500ml) grated mozzarella cheese
½ cup (125ml) freshly grated parmesan cheese
½–¾ cup (125–185ml) halved or chopped olives (kalamata are highly recommended)
packed ½ cup (125ml) coarsely chopped oil-packed sundried tomatoes
packed ½ cup (125ml) chopped fresh basil leaves
1–2 tablespoons (20–40ml) oil from sundried tomatoes
½ teaspoon (2ml) freshly-ground black pepper

The topping:

a little olive oil for brushing on the bread
dried basil for sprinkling
coarse sea salt (optional)

1. Stir the dried yeast into ¼ cup (60ml) of the warm water. Sprinkle in the sugar and leave in a warm place for about 10 minutes, or until frothy.

2. Sift the flour, yellow asafetida powder and salt into a large bowl. Pour in the frothy yeast mixture, the olive oil and the remaining water. Mix well and knead on a floured surface for about 8–10 minutes, or until the dough is velvety and soft. Place the dough in a lightly oiled bowl and cover the bowl with oiled plastic wrap. Leave the dough in a warm, draught-free place for about 45 minutes, or until doubled in size.

3. Punch the dough down and remove it from the bowl. Place it on a lightly floured surface and knead it briefly. Divide the dough into two equal portions. Roll out one portion to a 25cm (10-inch) round disk and place it on a well-oiled baking sheet. Sprinkle on half the cheeses, leaving a 1.25cm (½-inch) border of dough. Evenly cover the cheese with the olives, sundried tomatoes and basil leaves. Drizzle over the oil from the sundried tomatoes, and sprinkle on the black pepper. Cover with the remaining cheese. Moisten the outer border of exposed dough with water.

4. Pre-heat the oven to 220°C/430°F. Roll out the other portion of dough to exactly the same size and carefully lift it on top of the filled base. Tightly seal the top to the bottom, making sure no filling is exposed. Brush the surface of the *focaccia* with olive oil, sprinkle with basil and the optional sea salt. Place the *focaccia* in the centre of the pre-heated oven, and bake for 30 minutes, or until the top is golden brown. Remove and carefully place the bread on a rack to cool, or cut into wedges and serve immediately.

Note: For variety, or just plain indulgence, try adding one or more of the following ingredients to the *focaccia* filling: 1–2 cups thinly-sliced grilled or pan-fried zucchini; 1–2 cups steamed or pan-fried tender asparagus; 1–2 cups capsicum strips; 1–2 cups grilled or pan-fried eggplant slices; 1–2 cups marinated artichoke hearts.

Old English Saffron Bread

Tinted marigold yellow with saffron threads, this English bread was a favourite for tea in the seventeenth and eighteenth centuries in Cornwall and the south-west of England. In the Victorian period, cooks called it "cake" rather than bread, but it was cooked as bread or buns. It is highly delicious with a prominent heady flavour from the saffron infusion. Note that this bread dries out quite quickly, so eat it fresh, although it can be toasted.

The recipe calls for plaiting of the loaf rather than using a bread tin. Because of the loaf's intricate shape and the fact that it is baked "free-standing", be sure to use a strong bread flour. As far as plaiting is concerned, if you have ever plaited hair, you'll get it first time. If not, try practising with three tightly rolled-up tea towels on the kitchen table. If you can't get it, just make a solid loaf. It will still taste delicious.

PREPARATION TIME: 50–60 minutes
TOTAL DOUGH RESTING TIME:
about 2¾ hours, or longer
BAKING TIME: about 30 minutes
YIELD: 1 large loaf

2 teaspoons (10ml) saffron threads
⅓ cup (85ml) water
½ cup (125ml) butter
4–4½ cups (1000–1125ml) unbleached plain bread flour
1 teaspoon (5ml) salt
1½ teaspoons (7ml) dried yeast
1 tablespoon (20ml) sugar
1 cup (250ml) warm milk
¼ cup (60ml) buttermilk
1 teaspoon (5ml) nutmeg
1 teaspoon (5ml) ground caraway seeds
½ teaspoon (2ml) cinnamon powder
½ teaspoon (2ml) mace powder
8 cloves, powdered
1⅓ cups (335ml) currants

For the glaze:

3 tablespoons (60ml) sugar
2 tablespoons (40ml) water
¼ teaspoon (1ml) lemon juice

dough into a ball, and place it to rise in a buttered bowl, covered in plastic wrap, in a slightly warm place for 1½ hours, or until doubled in size.

4. Punch down the dough. Roll it on a lightly floured surface into a 25cm (10-inch) circle. Sprinkle evenly with the currants. Fold the edges in towards the centre to form a ball, working the currants into the dough. Let the dough rest, covered, for 8–10 minutes.

5. Divide the dough into thirds. Shape each third into a 35cm (14-inch) rope. Place the ropes side by side on a lightly buttered large baking sheet. Beginning at one end, braid the dough, tightly interweaving the pieces without stretching them. Pinch the ends of the strands together and tuck them under. Leave the loaf to rise again, covered with waxed paper, for one hour or until doubled in size.

6. Pre-heat the oven to 210°C/410°F. Heat the sugar and water together in a small saucepan over moderate heat for the glaze. Boil for 1 minute, remove from the heat and add the lemon juice.

7. Bake the bread in the centre of the oven for 10 minutes. Then reduce the heat to 195°C/385°F and bake for another 20 minutes, or until the bottom sounds hollow when tapped. Remove the bread from the baking sheet and place on a wire rack. While the bread is hot, brush it very generously all over with the sugar glaze. Cool and serve.

1. Carefully grind the saffron threads to a powder in a spice mill or coffee grinder. Place the saffron and water in a small saucepan and heat to barely simmering. Reduce the heat to very low and simmer gently for 15 minutes, or until the water is a rich red colour. Remove the saucepan from the heat. Place the butter in the saucepan and allow it to melt into the saffron infusion. Put the saucepan aside.

2. Sift the flour and salt into a large bowl. In another large bowl, mix together the warm milk, yeast and sugar. Stir to dissolve the yeast and set it aside in a warm place for 10 minutes or until frothy.

3. Stir the saffron infusion and butter mixture into the frothy yeast mixture. Add the buttermilk, nutmeg, the ground caraway, cinnamon powder, mace powder and ground cloves. Whisk in 2 cups (500ml) of the flour and combine until very smooth. Gradually stir in enough of the remaining flour to make a medium-stiff dough. Knead the dough on a lightly floured surface for about 10 minutes, or until smooth and elastic. Shape the

BUCKWHEAT CHAPATIS

Buckwheat is not technically a grain, but it lends itself to breads and pancakes as it behaves like a grain. In India and elsewhere, on the grain-free Vaisnava fasting day of *Ekadasi*, buckwheat, as well as other pseudo-grains, like chestnut flour and tapioca flour, are used in a variety of versatile ways. If you like the taste of buckwheat, you'll love these tender versions of India's most popular flatbread, the *chapati*. Buckwheat contains no gluten, so those of you who can't eat wheat will find this recipe appealing. As far as equipment is concerned, you'll need at least one non-stick frypan, (two or three are better), a rolling pin, a smooth surface for rolling, and some kitchen tongs.

PREPARATION TIME: 15 minutes
COOKING TIME: 25–35 minutes
YIELD: 10 large chapatis

2 cups (500ml) buckwheat flour, about 250g
½ teaspoon (2ml) salt
300g peeled potatoes, about 3 medium-sized potatoes, cut into large pieces
3 tablespoons (60ml) water
a good quantity of extra buckwheat flour for dusting and rolling
melted butter or ghee (optional, for spreading over the chapatis after they've been cooked)

1. Combine the buckwheat flour and salt in a large bowl.
2. Boil the potatoes in sufficient water until they are very soft. Remove, drain and mash them. Measure the quantity of mashed potatoes. You will need 1 cup (250ml).

Place the measured quantity of mashed potatoes in a large metal sieve over a large kitchen bowl. Push and rub the potato through the sieve and collect it in the bowl.

3. Pre-heat the large non-stick frying pan, or pans over moderate heat. Combine the warm mashed potato with the buckwheat flour. Add the water a little at a time to form a soft, but not sticky dough. Turn the dough onto a clean, smooth working surface, sprinkled with buckwheat flour. Turn and knead the dough for one or two minutes.

4. Pinch off 10 even-sized lumps of dough and form them into smooth balls, pressing and kneading them gently into thick patties. Dredge a patty of dough in flour and place it on the flour-strewn surface. Carefully roll it with a dry, flour-sprinkled rolling pin to a fairly thin, even, smooth disc about 15cm (6 inches) in diameter. If it sticks to the pin, re-roll it and apply more flour. A little care needs to be taken here since the dough contains no gluten and is very delicate.

5. Very carefully pick up the disc of dough and quickly transfer it to the frying pan. Slip it onto the hot pan, taking care to avoid wrinkling it. Cook it for about 1 minute on the first side. The top of the bread should start to show small bubbles, or it may even fully puff up in the pan — even better! Turn it over, being careful not to tear it, and cook it on the reverse side. When a few dark spots appear on the underside, lift the *chapati* with kitchen tongs to about 5cm (2 inches) over a full flame, if you are using gas. If using an electric stove, you'll need to sit a cake cooling rack above, but not touching, the element. The *chapati* should swell into a puffy balloon. Cook it until it shows a few more darker spots, then place it in a bowl or basket covered with a clean cloth, and continue cooking the rest of the *chapatis*. When they are cooked and stacked, you may like to butter them. Serve buckwheat *chapatis* hot, or keep them warm, well covered, in a pre-heated warm oven for up to half an hour.

Leavened Turkish Flatbread (Pide)

LEAVENED TURKISH FLATBREAD (PIDE)

Turkish people probably eat as much bread in one day as an Australian eats in a week! *Pide* (pronounced *pee-day*) is a traditional flatbread eaten in Turkey and Northern Iraq. In Istanbul, it is popular during the month of Ramadan, where it is purchased hot from the bakery to take home for Iftar, breaking the fast. It is not unusual to see giant loaves, 90cm (36 inches) long and 30cm (12 inches) wide coming out of the traditional village ovens. I have adapted the recipe for breads that will fit in a "normal" Western kitchen oven. You will need two large baking sheets on which to bake the bread.

DOUGH RESTING TIME: about 2½ hours
PREPARATION TIME: 40–50 minutes
COOKING TIME: 10–15 minutes
YIELD: makes 4 oval breads, about 20cm (10 inches) long

4½ cups (1125ml) plain unbleached bread flour
1 teaspoon (5ml) sugar
2 teaspoons (10ml) dried yeast
1½ teaspoons (7ml) salt
3 tablespoons (60ml) olive oil
1¼ cups (310ml) warm water, plus an extra ⅓ cup (85ml)
1 tablespoon (20ml) sesame seeds
extra 2 tablespoons (40ml) olive oil

1. Combine the yeast and sugar with 2 tablespoons (40ml) warm water in a small bowl. Set aside in a warm place for 10 minutes or until frothy. Combine the flour and salt in a large bowl.

2. Pour 1¼ cups (310ml) of the water into the flour mixture along with the 3 tablespoons (60ml) oil and the frothy yeast mixture. Mix the dough, adding enough of the remaining water to form a soft, pliable, but non-sticky dough. Turn the dough out onto a lightly-floured board and knead it for 8–10 minutes, or until it is very smooth and elastic. Place it in a lightly oiled bowl, cover the bowl with oiled plastic wrap and leave it in a warm place for one hour, or until doubled in size.

3. Punch down the dough, then cover it again and let it rise for another hour. Pre-heat your oven to the highest setting. Punch the dough down once more, and knead it again briefly. Divide the dough into four equal-sized lumps. Form each lump into a smooth ball, and roll each ball into a 20cm (8-inch) disc, about 0.5cm (¼-inch) thick. Place one bread on a lightly oiled baking sheet and stretch it into an oval shape, about 25cm (10 inches) long. Place another bread next to it and repeat the shaping. Shape the two other breads in the same manner and place them on the second baking sheet. Spray the breads lightly with water. Sprinkle on some sesame

seeds, and with wet fingertips, make deep depressions all over the surface of the breads, without breaking through to the base.

4. Leave the breads to sit for 20 minutes, then place them into the lower quarter of the pre-heated oven. If two baking sheets can't fit on one shelf, cook in two batches. After 5 minutes of cooking, open the oven door and brush the breads with the optional olive oil. Quickly return the breads to the oven and bake for another 5 or 10 minutes, or until they are lightly golden brown. Repeat for the rest of the bread. *Pide* are most delicious served hot.

PUFFED FRIED SESAME BREADS (TIL POORIES)

Sesame, known as *til*, is probably the oldest of all cultivated seed crops, and has been regarded as a food of high value throughout Asia since ancient times. Charak, the great medical authority of ancient India, has said that "of all the oils, sesame oil is the best. It has the finest flavour, and a high boiling point". From the health point of view, a high boiling point is deemed a great advantage, indicating that less molecular restructuring takes place in sesame oil than any other seed oil.

The seeds are almost tasteless when raw, but gentle roasting brings out a very agreeable, nutty flavour. It is this nutty flavour that makes *til poories* so distinctive. Gossamer-thin sesame flavoured *poories* are always a treat when served hot and crisp, but are equally tasty cold.

Try to obtain the unhulled variety of sesame (rich in protein and calcium) from health food stores. The best flour to use is *chapati* flour, also known as *atta*, which is available from Indian and specialty stores.

PREPARATION TIME: 15 minutes
DOUGH RESTING TIME: 30 minutes to 3 hours
COOKING TIME: 30 minutes
YIELD: 16 medium-sized poories

Puffed Fried Sesame Breads (Til Poories) served with Savoury Chickpeas in Tomato Glaze (page 140)

⅓ cup (85ml) sesame seeds
2 cups (500ml) sifted chapati flour, atta
½ teaspoon (2ml) salt
2 tablespoons (40ml) melted ghee or oil
⅔ cup (165ml) warm water
ghee or oil for deep-frying

1. Place the sesame seeds in a heavy pan over moderately low heat. Stirring frequently, dry roast them until they turn a few shades darker. Transfer the seeds to a plate, and allow them to cool. Grind them to a fine powder in an electric spice mill or with a mortar and pestle.

2. Combine the flour, sesame and salt in a large sieve over a large mixing bowl. Sieve the ingredients into the bowl. Mix in the salt then drizzle in the ghee or oil. Rub the ghee into the flour until the mixture resembles coarse meal. Add half the water and work it into a mass. Slowly pour in more of the water, incorporating it with your other hand to form a medium-soft, non-sticky dough. Turn the dough onto a clean working surface and knead it for 5–8 minutes or until it is silky smooth. Cover and leave for 30 minutes to 3 hours.

3. Knead the dough for another minute. Divide the dough in half. Form each half into a long smooth rope of dough, about 20cm (8 inches) long. Cut it into 8 portions. Repeat for the other half of the dough.

4. Pre-heat the ghee or oil in a wok or deep pan over low heat. Meanwhile, with a rolling pin, roll all the balls of dough into smooth, wrinkle-free discs of pastry, about 12.5 cm (5 inches) wide. To avoid the *poories* sticking, you may require a tiny amount of

flour on the rolling surface, but try to avoid it as the flour will burn in the cooking oil.

5. Increase the ghee temperature to about 185°C/365°F. There should be a slightly smoky haze above the surface. Lift up a rolled *poori* and gently slip it into the hot oil, making sure it doesn't fold over. It will briefly sink and then rise to the surface. Hold it under the surface as it rises with a slotted spoon. It should puff up like a balloon. Immediately turn it over and cook it on the other side for a few seconds, or until it goes a golden brown. Turn the *poori* over to the original side, fry until golden, then lift the *poori* out carefully with a slotted spoon and place it in a colander lined with paper towels. Repeat for all the *poories*, being careful not to stack them on top of each other so as to avoid breakage. Serve the *poories* hot, warm or cold.

SPICY CAJUN CORNBREAD

The Creoles and Cajuns of southern Louisiana have their own distinctive and spicy cuisine. This tasty cornbread, spiked with herbs and spices, is tasty and easy to prepare. Serve *Spicy Cajun Cornbread* as an accompaniment to a moist vegetable dish, or with a salad and soup for a light meal.

PREPARATION AND COOKING TIME:
about 30 minutes
YIELD: 1 small loaf

1 cup (250ml) polenta
½ cup (125ml) plain flour
1 tablespoon (20ml) baking powder
1 teaspoon (5ml) salt
1 teaspoon (5ml) Spanish-style hot smoked paprika powder or ½ teaspoon (2ml) cayenne and ½ teaspoon (2ml) sweet paprika
½ teaspoon (2ml) yellow asafetida powder
¼ teaspoon (1ml) dried oregano
¼ teaspoon (1ml) dried thyme leaves
¼ teaspoon (1ml) freshly-ground black pepper
¼ teaspoon (1ml) white pepper
2 tablespoons (40ml) minced fresh green chilies
1 cup (250ml) buttermilk
3 tablespoons (60ml) oil
¾ cup (185ml) shredded tasty cheese

1. Pre-heat the oven to 220°C/430°F. Combine the polenta, flour, baking powder, salt, paprika, yellow asafetida powder, oregano, thyme, the two peppers and chilies in a large bowl. Stir to mix well. In another small bowl, whisk together the buttermilk and oil.

2. Combine the dry and moist ingredients to form a thick batter. Add the cheese and mix well.

3. Spoon the mixture into an oiled 17.5cm (7-inch) long loaf pan, or a 22.5cm (9-inch) pie dish. Place in the pre-heated oven and bake for 20 minutes, or until golden on top. Slice and serve warm.

VEGETABLE DISHES

Sautéed Potatoes with Cashews

Spicy Javanese Eggplant (Balado Terong)

Mixed Vegetable Curry with Coconut Milk

Hot Roasted Jacket-baked Potatoes with Arugula Pesto

Cauliflower Korma

Roasted Antipasti Vegetable Platter with Lemony Herb Pesto

Bengali Spinach (Sak)

Stuffed Baked Eggplants (Melanzane Ripieni al Forno)

Spicy Bengali Potatoes

Greek-style Eggplant Casserole (Moussaka)

Stir-fried Asian Vegetables

Green Papaya and Potato Tarkari

Quick and Tasty Stir-fried Lettuce

Chickpea and Cauliflower Curry

Fried Plantain Rounds in Tomato Sauce

Fried Bitter Melon Chips (Karela Bhaji)

Tender Pan-fried Asparagus

Simple Gujarati Pumpkin

Braised Fennel

Spinach with Pine Nuts and Raisins

Stuffed Baby Pumpkins

Brussels Sprouts, Potatoes and Peas with Sour Cream

Quick and Simple Snake Beans

SAUTÉED POTATOES WITH CASHEWS

When selecting potatoes, keep in mind that soil is a natural preservative — washed potatoes don't keep as well as unwashed ones. Choose potatoes that are firm to the touch and without blemishes. Avoid at all costs potatoes with green patches or sprouts — these indicate the presence of toxic alkaloids.

Marble-sized waxy new potatoes are ideal for this elegant dish. Their delicate skins will almost float off during scrubbing. If you use larger new potatoes, cook them whole and slip off the skins when cool.

Crisp toasted cashews added at the end make a good foil for the soft, creamy texture of the potatoes.

PREPARATION AND COOKING TIME:
about 20 minutes
YIELD: enough for 4–6 persons

800g new potatoes
3 tablespoons (60ml) ghee or good quality olive oil
1½ teaspoons (7ml) mustard seeds
2 teaspoons (10ml) split urad dal
20 fresh curry leaves
1 tablespoon (20ml) minced, fresh ginger
2 medium-sized green chilies, seeded and finely chopped
4 tablespoons (80ml) coarsely-shredded fresh coconut
1½ teaspoons (7ml) salt
2 teaspoons (10ml) lemon juice
⅓ cup (85ml) toasted cashew halves

1. Wash the potatoes and place them whole and unpeeled in a 5-litre/quart saucepan of cold water. Bring the water to the boil and cook the potatoes until they are just tender. Drain, cool and peel the potatoes, and cut them into 1.5cm (¾-inch) cubes.

2. Pour the ghee into a wok or large pan, and place over moderate heat until a slight haze forms over the pan. Drop in the mustard seeds. When they start to crackle, lower the heat a little and add the *urad dal*. Stir it gently until it turns a rich golden colour. Add the curry leaves, ginger and chili and sauté for 1 minute or until their fragrance is quite noticeable. Sprinkle in the shredded coconut, stir briefly, then add the potatoes and salt. Gently sauté for 1 or 2 minutes, or until the potatoes are fully coated with the spices and coconut. Finally add the lemon juice and cashews. Serve hot.

SPICY JAVANESE EGGPLANT (BALADO TERONG)

Balado Terong is a spicy eggplant dish from Padang, the capital of West Sumatra Province in Western Java. The enterprising Minangkabau people of West Sumatra have taken their rich, spicy cuisine called "Masakan Padang" and made it famous by setting up restaurants all over Indonesia and, indeed, all over the world. This cuisine is characterised by plenty of rich coconut milk and chilies. Serve *Balado Terong* with plain rice.

PREPARATION AND COOKING TIME:
about 30 minutes
YIELD: enough for 4 persons

750g small thin eggplants, about 5 or 6, cut into 1.5cm (¾-inch) rings
oil for deep frying
3 large tomatoes, cut in quarters
3 or 4 large red chilies
2 tablespoons (40ml) oil
two 1.5cm (¾-inch) cubes galangal root, or ½ teaspoon (2ml) powdered laos
half a blade fresh lemon grass
2 salam leaves or curry leaves
2 tablespoons (40ml) palm sugar
1 teaspoon (5ml) salt

1. Place the tomatoes and whole chilies in a blender or food processor. Blend until smooth, remove the purée and set it aside.

2. Pour the oil for deep-frying into a wok or pan over high heat. When the oil is hot, drop in the eggplant pieces in 2 or 3 batches, and deep-fry them until they are tender enough to pierce with a knife point. Set the eggplants aside to drain.

3. Heat another pan or wok over moderate heat. Add the 2 tablespoons (40ml) oil. When hot, drop in the *galangal* and lemon grass. Sauté for one minute, or until fragrant. Add the curry leaves or *salam* leaves, fry momentarily, then add the tomato purée. If using powdered *laos* instead of *galangal*, add it now. Cook the tomatoes for 5 or 10 minutes, or until thick and saucy.

4. Add the sugar and salt, stir to dissolve, and gently fold in the eggplant pieces. Serve hot.

MIXED VEGETABLE CURRY WITH COCONUT MILK

This is a colourful, smooth and tasty combination of lightly seasoned vegetables smothered in a coconut-flavoured gravy. Vary the combination of vegetables according to taste and availability — try squash, Brussels sprouts or peas, sweet potatoes, broccoli, to name but a few. This recipe is very adaptable. You can increase its heat by adding more chilies and you can adjust the juiciness of the dish by adding more or less water or coconut milk. Serve it fairly dry with breads, or more moist with rice.

PREPARATION AND COOKING: 30–40 minutes
YIELD: enough for 6 persons

3 tablespoons (60ml) ghee
1 tablespoon (20ml) minced fresh ginger
2–3 hot green chilies, seeded and chopped
one 2.5cm (1-inch) cinnamon stick
10 fresh curry leaves
½ teaspoon (2ml) yellow asafetida powder
1½ cups (325ml) stringless green beans, cut into 3.75cm (1½-inch) lengths, about 200g
1½ cups (325ml) potatoes, cut into 1.5cm (¾-inch) cubes, about 250g
1½ cups (325ml) pumpkin, cut into 1.5cm (¾-inch) cubes, about 250g
1½ cups (325ml) zucchini, cut into 1.5cm (¾-inch) cubes, about 200g
1½ cups (325ml) cauliflower, cut into florets, about 200g
1½ cups (325ml) carrots, cut into 1.25cm (½-inch) chunks, about 250g
1 teaspoon (5ml) turmeric
1 teaspoon (5ml) coriander powder
1½–2 teaspoons (7–10ml) salt
1 teaspoon (5ml) sugar
1 cup (250ml) coconut milk
½ cup (125ml) water
¼ cup (60ml) chopped fresh coriander leaves

1. Place the ghee in a heavy 5-litre/quart saucepan over moderate heat. When hot, drop in the ginger and chilies and sauté for 1–2 minutes. Add the cinnamon stick and curry leaves, and sauté for another minute. Sprinkle in the yellow asafetida powder. Stir briefly, then add all the vegetables, the turmeric, coriander powder, salt and sugar. Stir the vegetables in the flavoured ghee until well coated.

2. Pour in the coconut milk and water. Reduce the heat and simmer slowly, well covered, for 30–40 minutes, or until the vegetables are tender. The quantities suggested yield a fairly dry curry, cooked slowly for 30–40 minutes. If a more moist curry is desired, increase the quantity of coconut milk to 1½ cups (375ml) and the water to 1 cup (250ml), and cook over a higher heat for less time. Fold in the chopped fresh coriander leaves and serve hot.

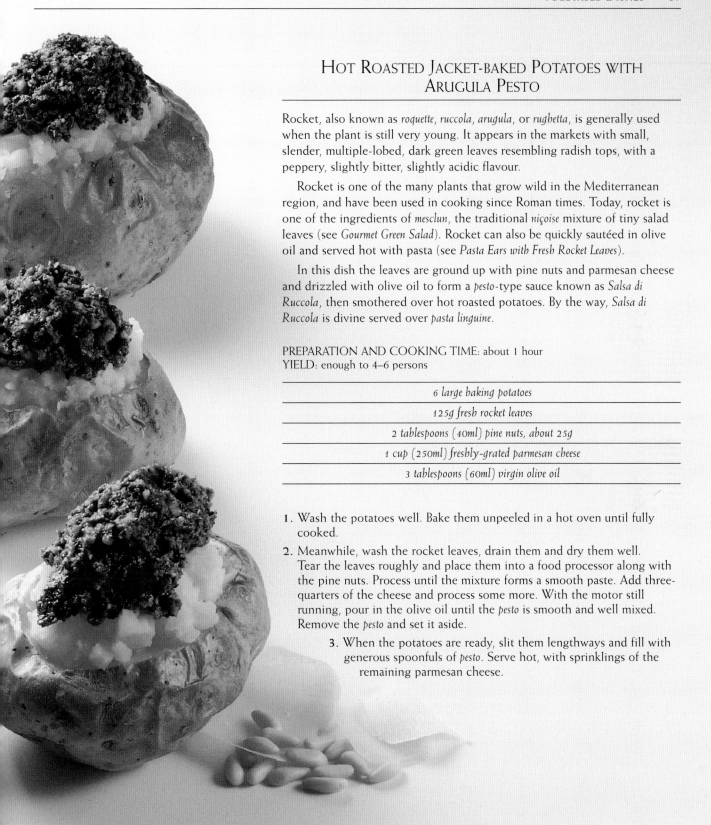

HOT ROASTED JACKET-BAKED POTATOES WITH ARUGULA PESTO

Rocket, also known as *roquette*, *ruccola*, *arugula*, or *rughetta*, is generally used when the plant is still very young. It appears in the markets with small, slender, multiple-lobed, dark green leaves resembling radish tops, with a peppery, slightly bitter, slightly acidic flavour.

Rocket is one of the many plants that grow wild in the Mediterranean region, and have been used in cooking since Roman times. Today, rocket is one of the ingredients of *mesclun*, the traditional *niçoise* mixture of tiny salad leaves (see *Gourmet Green Salad*). Rocket can also be quickly sautéed in olive oil and served hot with pasta (see *Pasta Ears with Fresh Rocket Leaves*).

In this dish the leaves are ground up with pine nuts and parmesan cheese and drizzled with olive oil to form a *pesto*-type sauce known as *Salsa di Ruccola*, then smothered over hot roasted potatoes. By the way, *Salsa di Ruccola* is divine served over *pasta linguine*.

PREPARATION AND COOKING TIME: about 1 hour
YIELD: enough to 4–6 persons

6 large baking potatoes
125g fresh rocket leaves
2 tablespoons (40ml) pine nuts, about 25g
1 cup (250ml) freshly-grated parmesan cheese
3 tablespoons (60ml) virgin olive oil

1. Wash the potatoes well. Bake them unpeeled in a hot oven until fully cooked.
2. Meanwhile, wash the rocket leaves, drain them and dry them well. Tear the leaves roughly and place them into a food processor along with the pine nuts. Process until the mixture forms a smooth paste. Add three-quarters of the cheese and process some more. With the motor still running, pour in the olive oil until the *pesto* is smooth and well mixed. Remove the *pesto* and set it aside.
3. When the potatoes are ready, slit them lengthways and fill with generous spoonfuls of *pesto*. Serve hot, with sprinklings of the remaining parmesan cheese.

CAULIFLOWER KORMA

I've not named this recipe after myself! Rather, the name *korma*, sometimes spelled *quorma*, indicates a fragrant braised dish often containing yogurt and sweet spices, and thickened with either ground white poppy seeds or a paste of ground almonds. This Mogul-influenced style of cooking invariably centres around non-vegetarian ingredients. My version features cauliflower, the "queen" of vegetables. Serve *Cauliflower Korma* hot with flatbreads or rice.

PREPARATION AND COOKING TIME:
50–60 minutes
YIELD: enough for 4–6 persons

1 cup (250ml) blanched almonds
1 tablespoon (20ml) anise seeds
one 10cm (4-inch) cinnamon stick
6 cloves
4 cardamom pods
5 small green chilies, seeded
one 1.5cm (¼-inch) cube peeled fresh ginger
1 cup (250ml) yogurt
2 teaspoons (10ml) salt
2 teaspoons (10ml) sugar
4 tablespoons (80ml) ghee or oil
1 large firm cauliflower, about 1kg, cut into 16 large pieces

1. Dry-roast the almonds on a tray in a moderate oven for 10–15 minutes or until golden brown. Remove and allow them to cool. Grind the almonds to a fine powder in a spice mill or coffee grinder. Set the powder aside.

2. Set a heavy frying pan over low to moderate heat. When the pan is hot, sprinkle in the aniseed, cinnamon, cloves and cardamom, and dry roast the spices for 3–5 minutes or until they darken a few shades and give off a strong aroma. Grind the spices to a fine powder in a spice mill or coffee grinder. Set aside.

3. Place the green chilies and ginger in a food processor fitted with a metal blade. Process until finely chopped. Add the yogurt, the salt, sugar, the powdered almonds and 1 cup (250ml) cold water. Process to a smooth, saucy paste. Add the ground, roasted spices. Process a little more and then remove the paste and set it aside.

4. Heat the ghee in a heavy 5-litre/quart, preferably non-stick, saucepan over moderate heat. Drop in the cauliflower pieces and stir-fry them for 5 minutes or until they soak up the ghee and become golden on their extremities.

5. Pour in the paste and stir to mix. Increase the heat, bring the sauce to the boil, then reduce the heat to very low. You may need to add more water as the sauce thickens. Cook for 25–30 minutes, partly covered, stirring often or until the sauce thickens to the desired consistency and the cauliflower is tender but not falling apart. Serve hot.

ROASTED ANTIPASTI VEGETABLE PLATTER WITH LEMONY HERB PESTO

The process of heat-roasting vegetables caramelises their natural sugars and intensifies their flavour. You can roast them in the oven or over live charcoals, which imparts a unique smoky flavour. Whichever way you choose, keep in mind that although the vegetables you select need not be exotic, they must be fresh. As soon as vegetables are harvested, they begin to loose their natural sugars. The following recipe is for oven-roasted vegetables. I have given a suggested list of vegetables to choose from. Note that the cooking time varies, and you can cook vegetables that have similar cooking times together.

ROASTING TIME: varies according to the vegetables selected
PESTO PREPARATION TIME: a few minutes
YIELD: enough roasted vegetables for 4–6 persons, and a little over 1 cup (250ml) pesto

The vegetables (select 6 or more):

2 medium red, green or yellow capsicums (peppers), or a combination, trimmed and cut into 4 lengthwise
½ small butternut pumpkin (cut lengthwise) seeded and quartered lengthwise
3 long thin eggplants trimmed and halved lengthwise
10 or 12 asparagus spears, preferably 1.25cm (½-inch) thick, trimmed
12 baby carrots, scraped
3 medium zucchinis or summer squash, trimmed and halved lengthwise
4 small sweet potatoes, or potatoes, sliced thin
3 large firm roma tomatoes, halved lengthwise
½ small fennel bulb, trimmed and sliced into 1.25cm (½-inch) slices
½ cup (125ml) artichoke hearts in oil, drained
6 small white radishes
2 ears fresh sweet corn, cut in thirds
olive oil for brushing
salt for sprinkling

The lemony herb pesto:

3 tablespoons (60ml) pine nuts
packed ⅓ cup (85ml) chopped basil leaves
packed ¼ cup (60ml) chopped continental parsley leaves
packed ¼ cup (60ml) chopped coriander leaves
1 teaspoon (5ml) fresh thyme leaves
⅓ cup (85ml) olive oil
2–3 tablespoons (40–60ml) lemon juice
½ teaspoon (2ml) salt
¼ teaspoon (1ml) freshly-ground black pepper
½ teaspoon (2ml) yellow asafetida powder
3 tablespoons (60ml) freshly-grated parmesan cheese

To prepare the vegetables:

Pre-heat the oven to 260°C/500°F. Select a large baking sheet and vegetables of your choice. Note that roasting times are approximate. Cook in the upper one-third of your oven, turning the vegetables when required.
Capsicums: roast for 10 minutes or until the skins are black. Place in a plastic bag to steam for 10 minutes, then peel.
Butternut pumpkin: brush with olive oil and sprinkle with salt. Roast for 8 minutes each side.
Eggplants: brush with olive oil and sprinkle with salt. Roast for 8–10 minutes.
Asparagus: brush with olive oil and sprinkle with salt. Roast in a single layer for 8–12 minutes.
Baby carrots: brush with olive oil and sprinkle with salt. Roast for 8–10 minutes.
Zucchini: brush with olive oil and sprinkle with salt. Roast for 8–10 minutes.
Sweet potato or potato: brush with olive oil and sprinkle with salt. Roast for 10–12 minutes.
Roma tomatoes: brush with olive oil and sprinkle with salt. Roast for 5 minutes.
Fennel: brush with olive oil and sprinkle with salt. Roast for 12–15 minutes.
Artichoke hearts: sprinkle with salt. Roast for 10 minutes
White radishes: brush with olive oil and sprinkle with salt. Roast for 8 minutes.
Fresh corn: brush with olive oil and sprinkle with salt. Roast for 8–10 minutes.

To prepare the pesto:

Place the pine nuts, basil, parsley, coriander and thyme in a food processor fitted with a metal blade. Process until a smooth purée. With the blades turning, pour the olive oil in a thin steady stream. Add the lemon juice, salt, pepper, yellow asafetida powder and parmesan cheese, and process until well blended.

To assemble the platter:

Arrange your selection of roasted vegetables on a large serving platter. Dab with teaspoons of herb *pesto*, and serve with extra *pesto* in a small bowl.

BENGALI SPINACH (SAK)

Green leafy vegetables constitute the basis of a group of well-loved dishes in India known as *sak*. There are over 50 varieties of popular cooked greens in India, and, depending on regional cuisines, they can be flavoured with a variety of seasonings toasted in either ghee, mustard oil, sesame oil or peanut oil.

This lightly seasoned dish is based on a Bengali recipe that I first tasted in the holy city of Sridham Mayapur. The spinach is only lightly cooked, and the seasoning is subtle and unobtrusive to allow the full flavour of the greens to emerge.

Feel free to experiment by adding other greens — as long as no less than half of the greens are spinach — such as turnip, beet or radish greens, kale, collard, mustard greens, sorrel, or silverbeet (Swiss chard).

Avoid cooking the greens in aluminium or cast-iron, since they tend to discolour and absorb flavours from the pan. Stainless steel, enamel or iron, or a non-stick surface is ideal.

PREPARATION AND COOKING TIME:
about 15 minutes
YIELD: enough for 6 small side-dish size servings

2kg spinach, about 2 large bunches, washed and chopped
1 tablespoon (20ml) ghee
1 teaspoon (5ml) cumin seeds
¼ teaspoon (1ml) fenugreek seeds
1 teaspoon (5ml) chopped and seeded green chilies
2 teaspoons (10ml) freshly minced ginger
2 teaspoons (10ml) sugar
½ teaspoon (2ml) salt
¼ teaspoon (1ml) nutmeg powder
2 teaspoons (10ml) butter
1½ teaspoons (7ml) lemon juice

1. Place the spinach in a 5-litre/quart saucepan over moderate heat. Sprinkle on a few drops of water. Place a lid on the pan and cook the spinach for about 5 minutes, or until it softens. Remove the spinach from the pan and drain off all the liquid. You may wish to reserve it for soup stocks.

2. Rinse the saucepan and dry it. Pour the ghee into the saucepan and place it over moderate heat. When hot, add the cumin seeds and fry them until they turn a shade or two darker. Sprinkle in the fenugreek seeds and fry them very briefly until they darken slightly. Add the chili and ginger, and stir them for half a minute, then add the drained spinach. Stir briefly, then add the sugar, salt, nutmeg, butter and lemon juice.

3. Cook the spinach for 1 or 2 minutes more, then remove from the heat and serve immediately.

STUFFED BAKED EGGPLANTS (MELANZANE RIPIENI AL FORNO)

Many cuisines of the world offer a version of stuffed eggplants. On my last trip to Milan I was most impressed when I tasted them filled with a thick and richly flavoured combination of tomatoes, fresh basil, breadcrumbs and tasty parmesan cheese. Here's the recipe.

PREPARATION AND COOKING TIME:
35–45 minutes
BAKING TIME: about 20 minutes
YIELD: 8 stuffed eggplant halves

4 medium-sized eggplants, about 750g
¼ cup (60ml) olive oil
½ teaspoon (2ml) yellow asafetida powder
2 cups (500ml) fresh tomato purée
½ cup (125ml) tomato paste
¼ cup (60ml) packed fresh basil leaves, about ¼ large bunch basil, chopped
2 teaspoons (10ml) salt
1 tablespoon (20ml) sugar
½ teaspoon (2ml) freshly-ground black pepper
¾ cup (185ml) parmesan cheese
1½–2 cups (375–500ml) breadcrumbs
2 tablespoons (40ml) reserved parmesan cheese

1. Wash the eggplants, and trim the stalk end, being careful to slice off the very minimum of flesh. Cut the eggplants in half, lengthwise. Place them in a large saucepan of lightly salted boiling water, and boil them for 5–7 minutes or until they are just tender enough for their flesh to be spooned out. Remove and drain the eggplant halves.

2. With a spoon, scoop out the flesh from the eggplants, being careful to allow a little flesh around the narrow neck of the eggplant to remain intact. This will ensure that the eggplant shell doesn't collapse and loose its shape. Set the shells of the eggplant aside. Coarsely chop the eggplant flesh. Squeeze out as much liquid as you can from the chopped eggplant.

3. Place the olive oil in a large frying pan over high heat. When hot, sprinkle in the yellow asafetida powder, then drop in the chopped eggplant flesh. Fry, stirring often, for 6–8 minutes, or until the eggplant is very tender.

4. Pour in the tomato purée, and stir in the tomato paste, basil, salt, sugar and black pepper. Reduce the heat slightly and, stirring often, cook the mixture for another 5 or 6 minutes or until fairly thick and reduced. Remove the pan from the heat and stir in the cheese and 1½ cups (625ml) of the breadcrumbs. The mixture should now be very thick. Add a little extra breadcrumbs if required.

5. Pre-heat the oven to 200°C/390°F. Spoon the mixture into the eggplant shells, packing and piling it up until all the filling is used. Sprinkle the reserved cheese on top, place the eggplants on an oiled baking sheet or in a casserole dish and bake in the pre-heated oven for 20 minutes, or until the tops are golden brown. Serve hot or warm.

SPICY BENGALI POTATOES

This is a delicious, dry-textured potato dish with multi-levels of subtle flavours. Avoid over boiling the potatoes.

PREPARATION AND COOKING TIME:
about 20 minutes
YIELD: enough for 4 persons

500g washed small new potatoes
2 teaspoons (10ml) chopped, fresh ginger
3 fresh green chilies, seeded and chopped
½ cup (125ml) yogurt
2 teaspoons (10ml) coriander powder
2 teaspoons (10ml) salt
½ teaspoon (2ml) turmeric powder
¼ teaspoon (1ml) ground black pepper
1½ teaspoons (7ml) sugar
2 tablespoons (40ml) ghee
1 teaspoon (5ml) cumin seeds
10 fresh curry leaves
⅛ teaspoon (0.5ml) cinnamon powder
⅛ teaspoon (0.5ml) clove powder
⅛ teaspoon (0.5ml) cardamom powder
3 tablespoons (60ml) chopped fresh coriander leaves.

1. Place the whole potatoes in a large saucepan of water. Bring to the boil over full heat and cook the potatoes until they are just tender. Drain the potatoes, cool them a little, and peel them. Cut them into 2.5cm (1-inch) chunks, and set them aside in a bowl.

2. Drop the chilies and ginger into a food processor and blend until smooth. Add the yogurt, ground coriander, salt, black pepper, turmeric and sugar, and process again. Pour and scrape this mixture into the bowl of cooked potatoes, and carefully mix well to combine. Set the mixture aside to marinate for 10 minutes.

3. Heat the ghee in a large pan or wok over moderate heat. Sprinkle in the cumin seeds. When they darken a few shades, add the curry leaves, stir briefly, then add the potato mixture. Stir the potatoes carefully through the spices, and pan-fry for 5 minutes, or until they are dry and crusty.

4. Sprinkle in the cinnamon, cloves and cardamom powders. Mix well, sprinkle with chopped fresh coriander leaves and serve hot.

GREEK-STYLE EGGPLANT CASSEROLE (MOUSSAKA)

This is a delicious vegetarian counterpart of the famous Greek eggplant-based casserole. In my version, the eggplants are first grilled, then layered in a casserole dish with lentils, topped with tasty cheese sauce, and baked. If you wish, the eggplant slices can be deep-fried instead of grilling, yielding a richer dish. To save time, grill the eggplants while the lentils are cooking.

PREPARATION, GRILLING AND COOKING TIME: about 40 minutes
BAKING TIME: about 1 hour
YIELD: enough for 6–8 persons

1½ kg eggplants, sliced 0.5cm (¼-inch)
olive oil

For the lentils:

2 cups (500ml) uncooked brown lentils, about 400g
2 tablespoons (40ml) olive oil
1 teaspoon (5ml) yellow asafetida powder
1 cup (250ml) chopped peeled tomatoes
2 tablespoons (40ml) tomato paste
2 teaspoons (10ml) brown sugar
2 teaspoons (10ml) salt
¼ teaspoon (1ml) black pepper
2 tablespoons (40ml) chopped parsley

For the cheese sauce:

¼ cup (60ml) butter
⅓ cup (85ml) flour
2 cups (500ml) milk
⅛ teaspoon (0.5ml) nutmeg powder
¼ cup (60ml) grated parmesan cheese, plus 2 tablespoons (40ml) for garnish
½ teaspoon (2ml) salt
¼ teaspoon (1ml) black pepper

To prepare the eggplants:

1. Pre-heat your griller to high. Oil the base of a baking sheet that will fit under the griller. Add a layer of eggplant and brush the surface of the eggplants with oil. Place them under the hot griller, and cook for 5–10

minutes, or until they are lightly golden. Turn the eggplants, brush again with oil, and cook them until lightly golden and soft enough to pierce with a knife point. Remove the cooked eggplants and stack them on a plate. Repeat the grilling until all the batches of eggplants are cooked. Alternatively, deep-fry or pan-fry your eggplants.

To prepare the lentils:

1. Place the uncooked lentils in a 5-litre/quart saucepan over full heat along with 3 or 4 litres of boiling unsalted water. Bring to the boil, then reduce the heat slightly and cook the lentils until they are soft enough to squeeze between your thumb and forefinger. Remove and drain the lentils, reserving the liquid for soup stock, if you wish.

2. Rinse the saucepan, then add the oil and return the saucepan to moderate heat. When the oil is hot, sprinkle in the yellow asafetida powder and sauté it momentarily. Add the tomatoes, increase the heat and cook for about 5 minutes, or until the tomatoes soften and separate from the oil. Stir in the cooked, drained lentils, add the tomato paste, brown sugar, salt, black pepper and parsley. Reduce the heat and, stirring when necessary, cook the mixture for about 10 minutes, or until it is fairly dry.

To prepare the cheese sauce:

1. Melt the butter in a 2-litre/quart saucepan over low heat, stir in the flour and cook over gentle heat for 2 minutes, or until the flour changes colour slightly.

2. Add the milk, increase the heat and bring to the boil while stirring constantly. Let the mixture bubble for about 1 minute, then remove the sauce from the heat, and whisk in the nutmeg, cheese, salt and black pepper. Cover the top of the sauce with buttered paper if not using straight away to avoid formation of a thick skin.

To assemble the dish:

1. Butter a 32.5cm × 22.5cm × 5cm (13-inch × 9-inch × 2-inch) oven dish. Place a layer of one-third of the eggplant in the base. Top with half the lentils, then add a second layer of eggplants. Spoon on the second layer of lentils and top with the remaining one-third of eggplants. Spread the cheese sauce on top, and sprinkle with the remaining parmesan cheese.

2. Bake the casserole in a moderate oven, 180°C/355°F, for one hour or until the sauce is slightly golden brown. Allow the *moussaka* to stand for 10 minutes before cutting into squares and serving.

STIR-FRIED ASIAN VEGETABLES

Although you're probably familiar with most of the vegetables listed below for this delicious, crisp, vegetable combination, you may not know about yam beans. Available at most Chinese (or especially Vietnamese) greengrocers, yam beans are crisp, disc-shaped, light brown tubers with pronounced segments, sometimes known as *jicama* (pronounced *hee-kama*). Yam beans have a slightly sweet flavour and a crunchy flesh. Peeled and sliced, they can be eaten raw as well as stir-fried, where they soak up the flavours they're cooked with. They can be used in place of bamboo shoots.

Winged beans, also available at Asian grocers, have a delicious asparagus-like flavour. If unavailable, substitute with blanched asparagus, snake beans, or stringless green beans. You may like to add raw or fried firm tofu to this combination. Serve with hot, plain rice.

PREPARATION AND COOKING TIME:
about 20–30 minutes
YIELD: enough for 4–6 persons

200g snow peas
200g winged beans, sliced
¼ cup (60ml) oil
200g baby green eggplants, quartered lengthwise

1½ tablespoons (30ml) fine julienned strips fresh ginger
2 small red chilies, seeded and finely sliced
¾ teaspoon (3ml) yellow asafetida powder
6 baby bok choy, outer leaves removed, cut into half lengthwise
4 or 5 tender stems of choy sum, cut into 10cm (4-inch) lengths
2 tablespoons (40ml) soy sauce
300g yam beans, sliced into straws, 1.25cm × 1.25cm × 7.5cm (½-inch × ½-inch × 3-inches)
2 teaspoons (10ml) palm sugar, crushed
leaves from 1 small bunch coriander, chopped

1. Boil a small saucepan of water and blanch the snow peas for a few minutes until light green and tender-crisp. Remove and drain them. Repeat for the winged beans.

2. Set the oil in a large wok over high heat. When the oil is very hot, slip in the eggplant quarters. When they are just tender to knife point, remove and drain them.

3. Drop the ginger and chilies into the remaining hot oil, stir-fry for a few moments, sprinkle in the yellow asafetida powder, then add the *bok choy, choy sum,* snow peas and winged beans. Stir-fry until the vegetables are wilted. Pour in the soy sauce, and continue to stir-fry the vegetables. If you like your vegetables a little more tender, place a lid on the wok and steam the vegetables the rest of the way. Half way through the cooking, stir in the yam bean straws. When the vegetables are sufficiently crisp-tender, fold in the palm sugar, fried eggplant pieces and coriander leaves. Serve immediately.

1 teaspoon (5ml) cumin seeds
½ teaspoon (2ml) yellow asafetida powder
4 bay leaves
2 teaspoons (10ml) coriander powder
2 cups (500ml) semi-cooked green peas or uncooked frozen peas
1 teaspoon (5ml) cayenne pepper
1 teaspoon (5ml) sugar
1 teaspoon (5ml) garam masala

1. Soak the papaya cubes in water for 15 minutes. Rinse and drain them.

2. Place the cardamom and cinnamon in an electric coffee grinder, blender or mortar, and process to a fine powder.

3. Pour the ghee into a 3-litre/quart saucepan and warm it over moderate heat. When fairly hot, sprinkle in ½ teaspoon (2ml) turmeric powder and 1 teaspoon (5ml) salt. Stir to mix, then add the potato cubes. Shallow-fry the potatoes, stirring often, until they are golden, crusty, crispy, and yield easily to a knife point. Remove them with a slotted spoon and place them in a small bowl.

4. Sprinkle the cumin seeds into the remaining hot ghee. When they darken a few shades, sprinkle in the yellow asafetida powder, then the papaya pieces. Stir-fry the papaya for 5 minutes. Sprinkle in the cinnamon and cardamom powders, add the bay leaves, the coriander powder, the green peas, the remaining 1 teaspoon (5ml) salt, the remaining 1 teaspoon (5ml) of turmeric, the cayenne, sugar and 2 cups (500ml) water. Reduce the heat a little, place a lid on the saucepan, and cook for 15 minutes, or until the papaya is tender. You may need to add a little more water — the vegetable dish should be quite moist.

5. Finally add the *garam masala* and the pototoes, mix well and serve hot with rice. For a full meal selection, cook the tarkari a little drier and wrap in *Trinidad-style Flatbreads*, and serve with *Tender Eggplant Pickles*, *Plain Basmati Rice*, and *Spinach with Pine Nuts and Raisins*.

GREEN PAPAYA AND POTATO TARKARI

Modern scientific investigation into the properties of the papaya have confirmed many of the ancient beliefs in its virtues. The most important of these virtues is the discovery of the protein-digesting enzyme in the milky juice or latex. The enzyme is reputed to be so powerful that it can digest 200 times its own weight in protein.

Green papaya is eaten as a vegetable in India and South-East Asia. It has a mild, neutral taste which soaks up the flavours of whatever it is cooked with. Select firm papayas with dark skin and white flesh. This Bengali dish is a fine example of the versatility of green papaya.

PREPARATION AND COOKING TIME:
about 40 minutes
YIELD: enough for 4–6 persons

4 cups (1 litre) green papaya, 1 small papaya, about 500g, peeled and diced into 1.25cm (½-inch) cubes
4 cardamom pods
one 7.5cm (3-inch) cinnamon stick
3 tablespoons (60ml) ghee
1½ teaspoons (7ml) turmeric
2 teaspoons (10ml) salt
1 cup (250ml) potato cubes, cut 1.25cm (½-inch)

QUICK AND TASTY STIR-FRIED LETTUCE

Although generally known as a salad vegetable, lettuce can be cooked, and is delicious when braised quickly over high heat with a few other ingredients. Serve as a hot side dish as part of an Asian-style meal. Note that the success of this dish depends on a wok. A large wok, at least 35cm (14-inches) wide, really has no substitute. Also, a wok burner, or some other source of high heat, is essential. It should also be noted that to get the best result with this dish, as in all Chinese-style dishes, you should be prepared to serve it as soon as it is cooked.

PREPARATION AND COOKING TIME:
a few minutes
YIELD: enough for 4 persons

2 medium, firm iceberg lettuces, washed, drained and dried
1½ teaspoons (7ml) cornflour
1½ tablespoons (30ml) cold water
3 tablespoons (60ml) water, or light vegetable stock
1½ teaspoons (7ml) sugar
¼ teaspoon (1ml) salt
3 teaspoons (15ml) light soy sauce
1½ tablespoons (30ml) peanut oil
½ teaspoon (2ml) minced fresh ginger
¼ teaspoon (1ml) yellow asafetida powder

1. Remove any withered or discoloured outer leaves from the lettuces. Cut the lettuces in half lengthways and then cut each half in four.
2. Blend the cornflour and 1½ tablespoons (30ml) cold water in a small bowl.
3. Combine the water or stock, sugar, salt and soy sauce in another small bowl. Make sure all your ingredients are close to the stove.
4. Place the dry wok over high heat. When the wok is very hot, add the oil, swirl it around carefully and immediately add the ginger, yellow asafetida powder and lettuce simultaneously. Stir-fry, tossing the leaves gently for 30 seconds. Add the water, sugar, salt and soy sauce combination.

5. Move the lettuce to the side of the wok and pour in the cornflour mixture. Stir to thicken, folding the lettuce thoroughly in the sauce. Serve the dish immediately.

CHICKPEA AND CAULIFLOWER CURRY

Chickpeas are a cousin to the smaller *chana dal.* They are pale buff to light brown, and look like wrinkled peas. They are used in many Latin American cuisines — Spanish-speaking countries refer to them as *garbanzo,* and in Italy they are called *ceci.* They are no less loved in India, where they are a popular choice served in a variety of yogurt or tomato-based savoury sauces. They team up well with many vegetables, such as with tender cauliflower in this classic, succulent and flavoursome Bengali dish. As with all legume dishes, it is appropriate to serve this curry with a plain rice, or with a bread, such as *Punjabi Baked Flatbread, Puffed Fried Sesame Breads,* or *Super-flaky Wholemeal Griddle-fried Breads.*

CHICKPEA SOAKING TIME: 8 hours or overnight
CHICKPEA COOKING TIME: about 1 hour
PREPARATION AND REMAINING COOKING TIME: about 15–20 minutes
YIELD: enough for 4 persons

¾ cup (185ml) dried chickpeas
3–4 tablespoons (60–80ml) ghee
1 teaspoon (5ml) turmeric
1½ teaspoons (7ml) salt
2½ cups (625ml) cauliflower, about 250g, cut into very small florets

The paste masala:

one 7.5cm (3-inch) cinnamon stick
the seeds from 8 cardamom pods
1 teaspoon (5ml) cumin powder
1½ teaspoons (7ml) coriander powder
½ teaspoon (2ml) asafetida powder
3 teaspoons (15ml) very finely minced fresh ginger
1½ tablespoons (30ml) water

Other ingredients:

1 teaspoon (5ml) cumin seeds
1 large green chili, chopped, or more for a hotter dish
2 bay leaves
2 teaspoons (10ml) jaggery or brown sugar

1. Soak the chickpeas in 4 cups (1 litre) water for at least 8 hours or overnight at room temperature.

2. Drain the chickpeas and transfer them to a 3-litre/quart saucepan with 6 cups (1.5 litres) water. Bring to the boil over high heat, reduce to a simmer and cook, covered, until the chickpeas are butter soft. Drain, reserving the cooking liquid.

3. Grind the cinnamon and whole cardamom to a fine powder in an electric coffee mill or spice grinder. Transfer the powder to a small bowl. Add all the other ingredients for the paste *masala* and mix to form a wet paste.

4. Warm the ghee in a 3-litre/quart saucepan over moderate heat. When the ghee is fairly hot, sprinkle in the turmeric and salt, then drop in the cauliflower pieces. Shallow fry the cauliflower, turning often, being careful not to break them, for 5–10 minutes, or until the pieces are just tender. Remove the cauliflower pieces with a slotted spoon and place them in a small bowl.

5. Drop the cumin, chili and bay leaves into the ghee that remains in the saucepan, and fry until the cumin darkens a few shades. Add the spice paste and fry it for 1 or 2 minutes, or until the ghee oozes out. Add the cooked chickpeas, cauliflower pieces, a few tablespoons of the reserved chickpea cooking liquid, and the jaggery or brown sugar. Continue to cook over moderate heat, covered, for 5–10 more minutes, adding more chickpea liquid if required to keep the dish fairly moist. Serve hot with rice.

FRIED PLANTAIN ROUNDS IN TOMATO SAUCE

Plantains are one of the less-sweet members of the genus *Musa*. Big, firm and starchy, they are widely used as a staple food in many places. Unlike the banana which they resemble, they need to be cooked before they can be eaten. Care needs to be taken before peeling plantains — they can make your hands go black and sticky. Try rubbing your hands with a little oil or a little lime juice beforehand.

I first tasted this delicious dish in 1991 at a feast commemorating Krishna's birthday at the Hare Krishna temple complex in Los Angeles. I was immediately hooked on its stunning taste and luscious texture. I asked the cook, Krishna Kumari devi, for the recipe, and here it is.

PREPARATION AND COOKING TIME:
about 45 minutes
YIELD: enough for 4–6 persons

ghee for deep-frying
1 kg slightly under-ripe plantains, *about 3 large plantains,*
peeled and bias-cut into 1.25cm (½-inch) rounds
2 tablespoons (40ml) ghee
2 teaspoons (10ml) good quality sea salt *(try Celtic salt)*
1½ teaspoons (7ml) cumin seeds
1 teaspoon (5ml) crushed dried chilies
½ teaspoon (2ml) yellow asafetida powder
3 cups (750ml) fresh tomato purée
2 teaspoons (10ml) coriander powder
2 teaspoons (10ml) sweet paprika
2–3 tablespoons (40–60ml) of fresh coriander for garnish (optional)

1. Heat ghee to a depth of 5cm (2 inches) in a wok or deep-frying vessel over moderately high heat. When hot, about 190°C/375°F, fry a handful of plantain rounds for 2 or 3 minutes or until they become medium dark-brown in colour. Remove and place them in a colander. Sprinkle with some of the Celtic salt. Repeat until all the plantain rounds are fried, drained and salted.

2. Pre-heat the oven to 180°C/355°F. Place the 2 tablespoons (40ml) ghee in a 5-litre/quart saucepan over moderate heat. When the ghee is fairly hot, sprinkle in the cumin seeds and sauté them until they darken a few shades. Add the dried chilies, sprinkle in the yellow asafetida powder, and immediately pour in the tomato purée. Add the coriander powder, paprika powder, and bring to a boil, stirring. Reduce the heat and simmer the sauce for 5–10 minutes.

3. Carefully place the fried plantain rounds into the tomato sauce and stir to mix. Return the sauce to a simmer for one minute. Turn off the oven, place the saucepan, tightly covered in the oven, and leave for about 30 minutes. This will allow the plantains to soak up the hot sauce and become plump and juicy. You may need to carefully warm the saucepan over a low heat before serving, garnished with the optional chopped, fresh coriander leaves.

FRIED BITTER MELON CHIPS (KARELA BHAJI)

In the ancient Indian medical science, *Ayurveda*, bitter melons are well-known for their ability to cleanse the blood, aid digestion and encourage a failing appetite. Fried chips of bitter melon are well-loved in India, and are generally eaten in small appetiser quantities at the outset of a full lunch or dinner. To reduce their bitterness, the melons are rubbed in salt before cooking. You'll find bitter melons in Asian and Indian food stores. Always look for small melons that are dark green in colour and heavy for their size.

PREPARATION AND SALTING TIME: 30 minutes
COOKING TIME: 10 minutes
YIELD: enough for 4–6 persons

4 small or 2 medium-sized bitter melons, about 250g
salt
¼ teaspoon (1ml) turmeric
¼ teaspoon (1ml) cayenne pepper
2 tablespoons (40ml) rice flour or 1 tablespoon (20ml) rice flour and 1 tablespoon (20ml) chickpea flour

1. Trim the ends off the bitter melons. Slice them in half lengthways, remove the seeds and then slice them lengthways into long strips, 0.5cm (¼-inch) wide. Cut the strips into lengths about 3.75cm (1½ inches). Alternatively, cut each half crosswise to yield semi-circular strips of melon.
2. Place the bitter melon pieces in a bowl, sprinkle liberally with salt and place a weight on them. Set them aside for at least half an hour.
3. Rinse the melon pieces under running water and drain them. Pat them with paper towels until they are almost dry.
4. Pour 5cm (2 inches) oil or ghee into a deep-frying vessel. Place the pan over moderate heat and bring to a temperature of 190°C/375°F.
5. Sprinkle the turmeric, cayenne and flour over the melon pieces and toss gently to coat. When the oil is hot, drop in a small handful of flour-coated melon chips. Fry them for about 2½ minutes, or until crisp and golden. Remove and drain them on paper towels. Fry the remaining bitter melon chips in batches. Serve hot, warm or room temperature. For extra crispness, I like to double-fry the melon chips: allow the cooked chips to cool, then fry again briefly in hot oil.

TENDER PAN-FRIED ASPARAGUS

Modern botany recognises about 150 species of the genus *Asparagus*, but only one — *Asparagus officinalis* — the cultivated vegetable — is of culinary interest. Within that species, the most common are the green and white asparagus. Purple asparagus is also becoming quite fashionable, although it is simply a variety of green asparagus, and reverts to green if it's cooked for more than half a minute or so.

All these three kinds of asparagus are cooked in the same way: snap each spear at its natural breaking point and discard the end (it's good in vegetable stocks). For green or purple asparagus, peel the lower half of the remaining stem with a vegetable peeler or small sharp knife. The skin on white asparagus tends to be a little tougher, so peel it almost to the tip.

To steam asparagus, either stand it in a special asparagus cooker, or lay it flat in a wide pan of boiling water and cook for about 2 minutes — less for thin spears. Carefully lift out the asparagus, refresh it under gently running cold water, and drain on a folded kitchen towel.

Here's something a little different to do with slender, young green asparagus. Serve *Tender Pan-fried Asparagus* as *antipasto*, entrée or a side dish accompanying a main meal.

PREPARATION AND COOKING TIME:
about 20 minutes
YIELD: enough for 4–6 persons

300g slender, fresh asparagus
2–3 tablespoons (40–60ml) plain flour
sprinkle sea salt
sprinkle freshly-ground black pepper
2–3 teaspoons (10–15ml) lemon juice
2–3 tablespoons (40–60ml) olive oil, or enough to thinly cover the base of a 22.5cm (9-inch) frying pan

1. Trim the hard ends from the asparagus, and remove any tough skin from around the base of the stalks with a vegetable peeler.

2. Bring a saucepan of lightly salted water to the boil over full heat. Drop in the trimmed asparagus. When the water returns to the boil, cook the asparagus for 1 or 2 minutes, or until their stems are just tender. Remove the asparagus, drain on paper towels and allow to cool.

3. Toss the asparagus in the plain flour to lightly coat it. Heat the olive oil in a 22.5cm (9-inch) heavy frying pan over moderate heat. When fairly hot, add enough stalks of floured asparagus to fit loosely in one layer. Fry the asparagus, turning once, for 2 minutes, or until the asparagus is lightly crisped. Remove the asparagus and keep it warm while draining on paper towels. Fry the remaining asparagus. Serve hot sprinkled with the salt, a grating of freshly-cracked black pepper and a splash of lemon juice.

SIMPLE GUJARATI PUMPKIN

This dish proves just how delicious pumpkin can be if teamed up with the correct flavour partners. My proofreader rang me especially to tell me that she had cooked it for her son who normally hates pumpkin. He loved it. Don't take my word for it though — try it for yourself.

Succulent *Gujarati Pumpkin* is excellent served with hot *chapatis*.

PREPARATION AND COOKING TIME:
about 1 hour
YIELD: enough for 6 persons

2 tablespoons (40ml) oil or ghee
1 teaspoon (5ml) fenugreek seeds
½ teaspoon (2ml) yellow asafetida powder
1kg pumpkin, cut into 1.5cm (¾-inch) cubes
1 cup (250ml) water

1½ teaspoons (7ml) salt

½ teaspoon (2ml) turmeric

½ teaspoon (2ml) red chili powder

1 teaspoon (5ml) coriander powder

1½ teaspoons (7ml) jaggery or brown sugar

1 tablespoon (20ml) lemon juice

handful fresh coriander leaves, chopped

1. Heat a wok or deep sauté pan over moderate heat. Add the oil or ghee, and when slightly hot, add the fenugreek seeds. Fry them until they turn

one or two shades darker. Be careful not to darken them too much, or they will turn bitter. Add the yellow asafetida powder, sauté momentarily, add the pumpkin, water, salt, turmeric, chili, and coriander powder. Stir, then cover, raise the heat, bring the mixture to the boil, then reduce to a simmer and cook for about 15–20 minutes, or until the pumpkin is tender, preferably with a little liquid left in the pan.

2. Add the sweetener and lemon juice, heat through, then remove the pan from the heat, sprinkle with fresh coriander leaves and serve hot.

BRAISED FENNEL

The bulbous Florence fennel root, known as *finocchio*, has a delicious, sweet aniseed flavour. Fennel's gently pervasive aroma and delicious flavour are not its only benefits: it is also a soothing digestive. My favourite fennel recipes, including this one, come from Italy; some recipes suggest serving fennel sliced raw or blanched in salads, or steamed, baked or braised, with parmesan cheese. This recipe from Tuscany preserves the full flavour of the fennel by slow braising with vegetable stock. It is finished off in the oven with parmesan cheese. Select fennel bulbs about the size of tennis balls — larger bulbs may be a little stringy and strong flavoured.

PREPARATION AND COOKING TIME:
about 1 hour
BAKING TIME: 15–20 minutes
YIELD: enough for 4–6 persons

2 large fennel bulbs, about 900g
50g butter
about ⅓ cup (200ml) vegetable stock
2 tablespoons (40ml) lemon juice
1 teaspoon (5ml) salt
sprinkle freshly-ground black pepper
sprinkle freshly-grated nutmeg
1 tablespoon (20ml) olive oil (optional)
4 tablespoons (80ml) grated parmesan cheese

1. Wash the fennel bulbs and cut off any bruised leaves and hard stems. Quarter each bulb lengthwise, removing the hard core.
2. Heat the butter in a heavy-based casserole, add the fennel and cook over medium heat for 10 minutes. Stir in about ⅔ cup (165ml) vegetable stock and lemon juice. Cover, and simmer gently over low heat for about 45 minutes, or until the fennel is tender. Add a little more stock if it sticks, but not too much. I like it when the pan is almost dry and the fennel is tender and ready to finish off in the oven.
3. Pre-heat the oven to 220°C/430°F. Remove the fennel from the pan with a slotted spoon and transfer it to a shallow ovenproof dish. Sprinkle on the salt, black pepper and nutmeg, trickle over the oil if desired, and cover with the grated parmesan cheese. Bake for 15–20 minutes or until golden on top. Serve hot.

SPINACH WITH PINE NUTS AND RAISINS

Spinach needs thorough washing before cooking. Careful observation of the following suggested procedure will save you from "gritty spinach syndrome".

Cut off the roots and base of the stems and discard them. Place the leaves in a sink or large bowl filled with cool water. Allow the spinach to soak for no more than 5 minutes — any longer will result in soggy wilted leaves. Remove the leaves to a colander and rinse them under cold running water. Drain them, then clean out the sink and repeat the above procedure. Welcome to the grit-free zone.

The sweetness of raisins is a natural foil to the slightly astringent taste of the spinach in this Mediterranean-inspired side dish. Crunchy pine nuts round out the taste and textural experience.

STUFFED BABY PUMPKINS

Practically any vegetable lends itself to stuffing — ornamental baby pumpkins are no exception. In this case, they are filled with plump *arborio* rice, folded with crunchy vegetable chunks and basil-laced ricotta cheese. Stuffed baby pumpkins are great served as an entrée before a Mediterranean flavoured meal or as part of a picnic lunch.

PREPARATION AND COOKING TIME:
1–1¼ hours
YIELD: 8 stuffed baby pumpkins

½ cup (125ml) Italian superfino rice such as arborio
1 cup (250ml) water
1¼ teaspoons (6ml) salt
8 small ornamental pumpkins, about 7.5 cm (3 inches) wide
½ cup (125ml) ricotta cheese
2 tablespoons (40ml) olive oil
2 tablespoons (40ml) lemon juice
3 tablespoons (60ml) chopped basil leaves
½ teaspoon (2ml) freshly-ground black pepper
½ teaspoon (2ml) yellow asafetida powder
¼ cup (60ml) finely chopped red capsicum
¼ cup (60ml) finely chopped green capsicum

To prepare the rice:

1. Place the rice, water and ½ teaspoon (2ml) salt in a 1-litre/quart saucepan over high heat. Bring to the boil, reduce the heat to low and simmer for 18–20 minutes, or until the grains are tender. Remove the saucepan from the heat, spoon the rice out into a sieve and rinse it under cold running water to cool. Drain well, and reserve the rice.

To prepare the pumpkins:

1. Pre-heat the oven to 220°C/430°F. Slice the pumpkin across about 0.5cm (¼-inch) below their lowest surface point to form lids. Scoop out the seeds and discard them.

2. Return the lids to the pumpkins, place the pumpkins on a baking sheet and bake for 15–30 minutes, or until tender. Some varieties of pumpkins take longer to cook than others. Remove the pumpkin from the oven.

PREPARATION AND COOKING TIME:
about 15 minutes
YIELD: enough for 4–6 persons as a side dish

1kg fresh spinach
1 tablespoon (20ml) olive oil
⅓ cup (85ml) pine nuts
½ cup (125ml) seeded raisins
¾ teaspoon (3ml) salt
freshly-ground black pepper

1. Wash the spinach as described above. Pat the leaves dry or shake them well. Place the spinach in a covered 5-litre/quart saucepan and cook over low heat for 5 minutes or until the spinach leaves are softened. Drain well.

2. Heat the oil in a pan or wok over moderate heat. When the oil is fairly hot, drop in the pine nuts and stir them for 1 or 2 minutes, or until lightly golden. Add the raisins and stir until they are plump and puffed. Add the spinach and salt, and toss quickly over high heat. Sprinkle with the ground black pepper and serve immediately.

3. Scoop out as much cooked flesh from inside the body and lid of the baked pumpkins as practical, leaving enough to allow the pumpkins to stand freely without collapsing. Chop the pumpkin flesh.

To prepare the filling and assemble the pumpkins:

1. Combine the ricotta cheese, 1 tablespoon (20ml) of the olive oil, the lemon juice, basil, the remaining salt, pepper, cooked rice, and chopped pumpkin flesh in a large bowl.

2. Heat the remaining olive oil in a small frying pan over moderate heat. When hot, sprinkle in the yellow asafetida powder and chopped red and green capsicum pieces. Sauté the capsicum for 2 or 3 minutes, or until softened. Transfer the capsicums and flavoured oil to the bowl of filling, and fold to combine all the ingredients. Carefully spoon the filling into the pumpkins, packing them full. Replace the lids and serve.

BRUSSELS SPROUTS, POTATOES AND PEAS WITH SOUR CREAM

Brussels sprouts may not be everyone's favourite vegetable, but they're delicious combined with golden cubes of deep-fried potatoes, green peas and folded with mildly seasoned sour cream. Serve this tasty and versatile dish as part of a special banquet or feast menu, with a soup and bread for a warming winter's meal, or with rice.

PREPARATION AND COOKING TIME:
30–40 minutes
YIELD: enough for 4–6 persons

2 large baking potatoes, peeled and cut into 1.25cm (½-inch) cubes, 500g, weighed after peeling
ghee or oil for deep-frying
1 cup (250ml) green peas
2 tablespoons (40ml) ghee or oil
10–15 fresh curry leaves
½ teaspoon (2ml) yellow asafetida powder
750g small, firm Brussels sprouts, ends cut off and cut in half lengthwise
¼ teaspoon (1ml) coarsely-ground black pepper
½ teaspoon (2ml) ginger powder
½ teaspoon (2ml) turmeric
¼ teaspoon (1ml) cayenne pepper
1–1½ teaspoons (5–7ml) salt
1 cup (250ml) sour cream, at room temperature
1 tablespoon (20ml) chopped fresh coriander leaves or parsley

1. Rinse the potato cubes in cold water. Drain and pat them dry. Place enough ghee in a deep pan or wok that will well cover the quantity of potatoes. Heat the ghee to 190°C/375°F. Deep-fry the potato cubes for 8–10 minutes, or until they are lightly golden brown. You may need to fry them in two batches. Remove the potatoes and drain them on paper towels.

2. Place the peas in a small saucepan and cover them with water. Bring to the boil, and cook the peas for 5–8 minutes, or until tender. Drain and set aside, reserving the water.

3. Heat the 2 tablespoons (40ml) ghee or oil in a 3-litre/quart saucepan over moderate heat. When fairly hot, drop in the curry leaves and sauté them for a few moments. Sprinkle in the yellow asafetida powder, stir momentarily and then drop in the Brussels sprouts halves. Sauté them in the fragrant

oil for 3 or 4 minutes. Sprinkle in the black pepper, ginger powder, turmeric, cayenne pepper and salt, stir to mix and add ½ cup (125ml) water. Stir briefly, place a lid on the saucepan and cook over moderate heat for 10 minutes or until the Brussels sprouts are just tender when stabbed with a knife point. Add the peas, potatoes, and herbs and then fold in the sour cream. Add a little of the reserved pea water if the dish is a little dry. Serve immediately.

QUICK AND SIMPLE SNAKE BEANS

Snake beans are popular in both Indian and South-East Asian cuisine, and are becoming a popular addition to our cooking repertoire. As their name suggests, these round-bodied beans are 30–40cm long. They're hard to miss! You'll find them in Indian and Asian vegetable markets and even well-stocked supermarkets. Serve simple snake beans as a hot side dish, straight from the pan.

PREPARATION AND COOKING TIME:
about 10 minutes
YIELD: enough for 4 persons

2 tablespoons (40ml) unsalted butter
300g snake beans, tips and ends removed, and cut into equal 10cm (4-inches) lengths
¾ teaspoon (3ml) salt
⅛ teaspoon (0.5ml) freshly-ground black pepper

1. Melt the butter over moderately low heat in a heavy frying pan that has a lid. Add the beans to the melted butter, splash them with a few drops of water, sprinkle with salt and pepper, and cover them tightly with the lid. Raise the heat slightly, and cook the beans for about 6 or 7 minutes, shaking the pan occasionally to avoid the beans sticking or burning. You may need to sprinkle in a little extra water once or twice.

2. When the beans are tender, remove the lid, evaporate any remaining water, and serve immediately.

SALADS

Tomato, Basil and Fresh Mozzarella Salad (Insalata Caprese)

Warm Vegetable Salad with Greek-style Oil and Lemon Dressing

Creamy Banana and Yogurt Salad (Kela Raita)

Mexican Broad Bean Salad (Ensalada de Habas)

Couscous Salad

Thai-style Green Papaya Salad

Mediterranean Rice Salad (Insalata di Riso)

Kumara Salad

Bavarian Potato Salad

Sicilian-style Roasted Sweet Peppers in Olive Oil (Insalata di Peperoni Arrostiti)

Daikon Radish Salad

South Indian Carrot Salad

Japanese-style Spinach with Sesame Dipping Sauce

Spanish-style Curly Endive Salad (Xato)

Fresh Chilies in Seasoned Yogurt (Chili Raita)

Quinoa Tabbouleh Salad

Warm Potato Salad with Vietnamese Greens

Gourmet Green Salad with Herbed French Dressing

TOMATO, BASIL AND FRESH MOZZARELLA SALAD (INSALATA CAPRESE)

I tasted this ultra-delicious combination of fresh buffalo-milk mozzarella cheese, slices of ripe tomatoes and fresh basil leaves for the first time while in Rome. The pure white mozzarella had been literally made fresh that morning and came floating in whey in little plastic bags. For the best results, select the freshest mozzarella and basil leaves, aromatic virgin olive oil and vine ripe tomatoes.

PREPARATION TIME: a few minutes
YIELD: enough for 4 persons

250g buffalo-milk mozzarella or bocconcini, sliced into 0.5 cm (¼-inch) rounds
a few fresh basil leaves, shredded, for garnish
3 or 4 medium-sized ripe roma tomatoes, sliced into 0.5 cm (¼-inch) rounds
sea salt
coarsely-ground black pepper
2–3 tablespoons (40–60ml) extra virgin olive oil
12–15 whole large fresh basil leaves

Decoratively arrange the slices of cheese, whole basil leaves and tomato slices in overlapping rings on a serving platter. Just before serving, sprinkle over the salt, the black pepper, drizzle with the extra virgin olive oil and garnish with the shredded basil leaves.

WARM VEGETABLE SALAD WITH GREEK-STYLE OIL AND LEMON DRESSING

Greek oregano, *rigani*, is a stronger, sharper version of the familiar Italian herb. The word *oregano* derives from the Greek, meaning "joy of the mountains", and was well-known to the ancient Greeks. Today it covers the hills and mountain slopes of Greece, perfuming the air with its flavour. You can find bunches of dried *rigani* in Greek stores; it is worth seeking out to give an authentic flavour to the traditional *latholemono* dressing that goes with this very palatable warm vegetable salad — a delicious meal in itself when accompanied by crusty bread.

PREPARATION AND COOKING TIME:
about 15 minutes
YIELD: enough for 4–6 persons

1½ cups (375ml) yellow button squash cut into wedges or sections, about 200g
1½ cups (375ml) green beans cut into 5cm (2-inch) lengths, about 200g
1½ cups (375ml) cauliflower cut into medium-sized florets, about 200g
1½ cups (375ml) broccoli cut into medium-sized florets, about 200g
1½ cups (375ml) zucchini cut into wedges, about 200g
leaves from half bunch silverbeet (Swiss chard), slightly blanched in boiling water and drained, about 200g

1. Cook the vegetables in lightly salted water until completely cooked but still firm. Drain them thoroughly. Briefly blanch the silverbeet (Swiss chard) leaves in the water and drain.

2. Arrange the vegetables on a bed of the slightly blanched silverbeet (Swiss chard) leaves on the platter you wish to serve them.

3. Mix the dressing ingredients well (recipe follows), and pour the dressing on top of the warm vegetables. Serve immediately.

Greek-style Oil and Lemon Dressing (Latholemono):

½ cup (125ml) olive oil
¼ cup (60ml) lemon juice
1 tablespoon (20ml) rigani, or 2 tablespoons (40ml) fresh oregano leaves, chopped
¼ teaspoon (1ml) yellow asafetida powder
½ teaspoon (2ml) salt
½ teaspoon (2ml) freshly-ground black pepper

Combine all the ingredients in a screw-top jar, seal and shake well or combine in a bowl and whisk.

CREAMY BANANA AND YOGURT SALAD (KELA RAITA)

Raita is a name given to a wide range of raw or semi-cooked fruit and vegetable salads served on the Indian subcontinent. These simple, easy-to-prepare salads provide a light, cooling contrast to an elaborate meal. *Raita* generally features one or two main ingredients that float in lightly seasoned, creamy fresh yogurt. This *raita* has an intriguing flavour, combining sweet, sour and hot tastes, with a pungent kick of *rai* (mustard seeds) — hence the name *raita*. I have suggested that you can temper the tartness of the yogurt by substituting some of it with *crème fraîche* or sour cream. Serve *kela raita* in small, half-cup bowls.

PREPARATION AND COOKING TIME:
10 minutes
CHILLING TIME: 2–3 hours
YIELD: enough for 4–6 persons

2 cups (500ml) plain yogurt (or 1¼ cups [310ml] sour cream or crème fraîche and ¾ cup [185ml] plain yogurt)
¾ teaspoon (3ml) salt
2 tablespoons (40ml) finely-chopped fresh mint leaves
1½ cups (375ml) peeled and thinly-sliced, firm ripe bananas, about 2 medium-sized bananas
2 tablespoons (40ml) mild olive oil or avocado oil
1 teaspoon (5ml) black mustard seeds
1 or 2 hot green chilies, seeded and cut into paper thin, julienne strips
½ teaspoon (2ml) garam masala

1. Whisk the yogurt, or yogurt and cream mixture, with the salt and mint in a 1-litre/quart bowl. Fold in the bananas, cover, and refrigerate for at least 2–3 hours.

2. Heat the oil in a small saucepan over moderate heat. When the oil is hot but not smoking, add the mustard seeds. When they pop and crackle, remove the pan from the heat, toss in the strips of green chili, swirl and tilt the pan and then pour the seasonings into the yogurt mixture. Stir well. Serve the *raita* in small bowls, sprinkled with a garnish of *garam masala*.

MEXICAN BROAD BEAN SALAD (ENSALADA DE HABAS)

Dried broad beans, also called *fava* beans, are known by the name *habas* in Spanish. They appear in many dishes throughout South and Central America. In this simple but hearty salad from central Mexico, *fava* beans are combined with chopped tomatoes, chilies and fresh *cilantro* (coriander) leaves and drenched in a tangy lime juice and olive oil dressing. The skin is traditionally left on the beans, making them quite chewy. If you prefer, you may like to pop the beans out of their "jackets" before proceeding on with the recipe. I have replaced the onions in this recipe with "you-know-what" — asafetida. For an authentic Mexican flavour, try to procure *jalapeño* chilies, and Mexican oregano. *Fava* beans are easily available from Mexican suppliers, or from Middle Eastern grocers, where they go by the name *ful* beans.

BEAN SOAKING TIME: 24 hours
BEAN COOKING TIME: 15 minutes
PREPARATION TIME: 15–20 minutes
YIELD: enough for 4–6 persons

1¼ cups (310ml) uncooked dried broad beans (fava beans) — any size or variety
4 tablespoons (80ml) fresh lime juice or lemon juice
3 tablespoons (60ml) virgin olive oil
½ teaspoon (2ml) dried oregano
1½ teaspoons (7ml) salt
¾ teaspoon (3ml) yellow asafetida powder
3 jalapeño chilies, seeded and cut into julienne strips
3 tablespoons (60ml) coarsely-chopped fresh coriander (cilantro) leaves
1 cup (250ml) finely-diced unpeeled tomatoes
3 tablespoons (60ml) chopped fresh coriander leaves for garnish

1. Soak the beans in a large container of cold water and leave in a cool place for 24 hours.

2. If you wish to remove the skins from the beans, do it now, before you cook them. The best way is to squeeze the bean hard, a little off-centre. It should pop out of its thick skin. If it resists, tear a little skin first. If you prefer a more authentic chewy texture, miss out this step.

3. Drain the beans, rinse them, and drain them again. Place the beans in a 3-litre/quart saucepan with plenty of cold water over high heat. Bring to the boil, then reduce the heat and simmer the beans for about 15–20 minutes, or until they are soft. Drain the beans thoroughly, transfer to a serving bowl, and allow them to cool slightly.

4. Combine the lime juice, olive oil, oregano, salt and yellow asafetida powder in a small bowl. Mix the chili strips, the chopped coriander leaves and the tomatoes with the beans. Pour on the dressing, mix well, and allow the salad to marinate for at least 45 minutes. Garnish with the extra chopped coriander and serve at room temperature.

COUSCOUS SALAD

Couscous, the famous grain product of North African fame, makes a great salad base. Teamed up with a selection of vegetables, tender chickpeas, crunchy peanuts and a mint-parsley, tahini-laced dressing, it is a substantial addition to a summer menu.

PREPARATION AND COOKING TIME:
about 15 minutes
YIELD: enough for 6 persons

The couscous:

1½ cups (375ml) water
1½ teaspoons (7ml) salt
1½ tablespoons (30ml) olive oil
1½ cups (375ml) couscous

The dressing:

4 tablespoons (80ml) lemon juice
2 tablespoons (40ml) olive oil
2 teaspoons (10ml) sugar
3 tablespoons (60ml) tahini
4 tablespoons (80ml) fresh mint leaves, chopped
1½ teaspoons (7ml) salt
1 teaspoon (5ml) freshly-ground black pepper
½ teaspoon (2ml) yellow asafetida powder
4 tablespoons (80ml) fresh parsley, chopped

The remaining ingredients:

⅓ cup (85ml) tomato, diced 0.5cm (¼-inch)
¼ cup (60ml) red capsicum, diced 0.5cm (¼-inch)
¼ cup (60ml) green capsicum, diced 0.5cm (¼-inch)
¼ cup (60ml) green beans, cut into 1.25cm (½-inch) lengths and steamed
½ cup (125ml) cooked chickpeas
½ cup (125ml) unpeeled, diced Lebanese-style cucumbers
½ cup (125ml) sultanas
¼ cup (60ml) chopped green olives
¼ cup (60ml) small, roasted peanut halves

To prepare the couscous:

1. Bring to the boil the water, salt and olive oil in a 1 or 2-litre/quart saucepan. Remove the saucepan from the heat, stir in the *couscous* grains and set the saucepan aside, covered, for 10 minutes. Fluff the grains with a fork, and transfer the cooked *couscous* to a serving bowl. Allow to cool thoroughly.

2. Combine all the dressing ingredients in a small bowl. Mix the rest of the ingredients with the cooled *couscous*. Add the dressing, mix well and serve.

THAI-STYLE GREEN PAPAYA SALAD

Green papaya (paw paw) is a popular ingredient in Thai cooking. This is my less aggressive version of a bold flavoured dish from north-east Thailand that's usually served with a main course and plain rice. This dressing is traditionally pounded coarsely on a large stone mortar yielding a salad with a hot, sour, salty flavour with a hint of sweetness. Green papaya can be obtained at any Asian specialty store when in season.

PREPARATION AND COOKING TIME:
about 15 minutes
YIELD: enough for 4 persons

½ cup (125ml) snake beans, about 60g, cut into 1.5cm (½-inch) lengths

½ cup (125ml) roasted peanuts

3 or 4 hot green chilies

1 tablespoon (20ml) palm sugar

2 tablespoons (40ml) fresh lime juice or lemon juice

1 medium-sized tomato, quartered

200g green papaya, peeled and shredded into long even fine shreds

1 teaspoon (5ml) yellow asafetida powder

1 teaspoon (5ml) sea salt, or more for an authentic salty taste

2 tablespoons (40ml) chopped fresh coriander leaves

1. Steam the beans over boiling water until tender. Set them aside to cool.

2. To prepare the dressing: Place the roasted peanuts, chili, palm sugar, lime juice and tomato in a food processor fitted with a metal blade. Coarsely chop the contents with a few quick on/off bursts, then scrape the dressing into a small bowl. Combine the cooled steamed beans, the papaya and the dressing in a bowl. Add the yellow asafetida powder, the salt and half the chopped coriander. Mix well and serve immediately, garnished with the remaining coriander leaves.

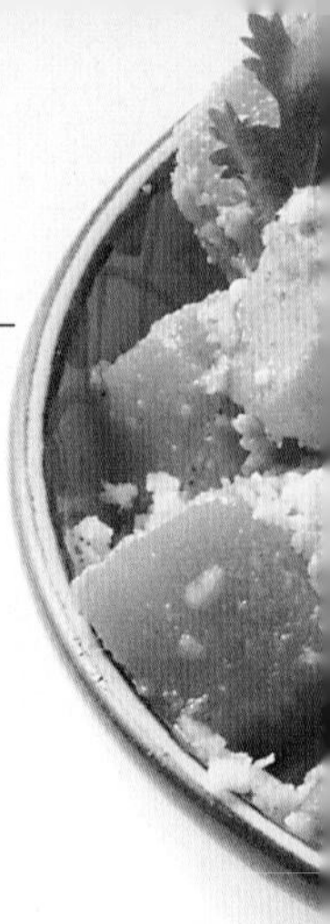

MEDITERRANEAN RICE SALAD (INSALATA DI RISO)

Plump and tender Italian *superfino* rice, such as *arborio*, lends itself perfectly to this fresh-tasting salad. Studded with a multi-coloured selection of raw, fresh vegetables and black olives, *Insalata di Riso* is a winner on hot, lazy days.

PREPARATION AND COOKING TIME:
25–35 minutes
YIELD: enough for 4–6 persons

The rice:

1 cup (250ml) uncooked Italian superfino rice, such as arborio
4½ cups (1125ml) water
1½ teaspoons (7ml) salt

The vegetables:

¾ cup (185ml) zucchini, diced into 0.5cm (¼-inch) cubes
¾ cup (185ml) grated carrot
¾ cup (185ml) pitted, chopped black olives, such as Gaeta or Kalamata
¾ cup (185ml) ripe, but firm, plum tomatoes, cored, seeded and diced into 0.5cm (¼-inch) cubes
¾ cup (185ml) yellow capsicum, diced into 0.5cm (¼-inch) cubes

The dressing:

¼ cup (60ml) extra virgin olive oil
1½ teaspoons (7ml) salt
¾ teaspoon (3ml) freshly-ground black pepper
1½ tablespoons (30ml) balsamic vinegar or lemon juice

1. Place the rice, water and salt in a 2 or 3-litre/quart saucepan and bring to the boil over medium-high heat. Stir once, reduce the heat to low and simmer well covered for 18 minutes or until the rice is tender but still firm. Drain the rice in a colander and refresh it under cold water. Drain well and set aside to fully cool.

2. Combine the vegetable ingredients with the cooled, drained rice in a large serving bowl. Mix the dressing ingredients together, and toss with the rice and vegetables. Serve at room temperature.

KUMARA SALAD

This is an unusual yet delectable "east-meets-west" combination of red-skinned, yellow-fleshed New Zealand sweet potatoes known as *kumaras*, coupled with South Indian seasonings. It would be equally delicious using red-, orange- or white-fleshed sweet potatoes, or even yams.

PREPARATION AND COOKING TIME: about 25 minutes
YIELD: enough for 6 persons

6 cups (1.5 litres) kumaras, about 1kg, cut into 1.5cm (½-inch) cubes
2 tablespoons (40ml) olive oil, plus 2 teaspoons (10ml)
½ teaspoon (2ml) yellow asafetida powder
¾ teaspoon (3ml) garam masala
½ teaspoon (2ml) cayenne pepper
1 tablespoon (20ml) seeded, finely-chopped green chili
2 tablespoons (40ml) fresh lime or lemon juice
½ teaspoon (2ml) salt
¼ cup (60ml) finely-shredded fresh coconut
2 tablespoons (40ml) roasted peanuts, powdered
1 tablespoon (20ml) sesame seeds, preferably unhulled, dry-roasted and powdered
2 tablespoons (40ml) fresh coriander leaves for garnish

1. Place the *kumaras* in ample boiling water in a 5-litre/quart saucepan and boil over full heat until the potatoes are tender but not overcooked. Remove and drain the potatoes, covering them to keep them warm.

2. Pour 2 teaspoons (10ml) olive oil in a wok or large pan over moderate heat. When hot add the yellow asafetida powder, stir briefly, then remove the pan from the heat. Allow the oil to cool a little, then add the *garam masala*, cayenne and chili. Mix well, then add the lime juice, salt and the rest of the olive oil. Fold in the *kumaras* and stir gently to coat them with the spices. Add the coconut, peanut powder and toasted sesame seed powder, and stir gently to combine.

3. Allow the salad to cool and the flavours to mingle, then serve with a garnish of fresh coriander leaves.

BAVARIAN POTATO SALAD

At a quick glance, the gentle fronds of dill can be easily mistaken for fennel; their seasons overlap. But dill is earlier, and its leaves are a darker green. The invigorating flavour of fresh dill leaves marries well with creamy potato salads, such as this one from Germany.

There are practically as many versions of this recipe as there are Bavarian kitchens. You may like to add dill-flavoured pickled cucumbers — a popular choice. Some recipes add diced sweet apple — I would add about ⅓ cup (85ml). And many German potato salad aficionados would insist on adding mustard (German, of course) — ½–1 teaspoon (2–5ml) would do the trick.

PREPARATION AND COOKING TIME:
about 20–30 minutes
YIELD: enough for 6 persons

The vegetables:

1kg new potatoes
¼ cup (60ml) green capsicum, diced 0.5cm (¼-inch)
¼ cup (60ml) red capsicum, diced 0.5cm (¼-inch)
½ cup (125ml) peeled cucumbers, diced 0.5cm (¼-inch)
⅓ cup (85ml) cubed tomatoes
4 small radishes, cut into thin wedges

The dressing:

1¼ cups (310ml) sour cream
4 tablespoons (80ml) lemon juice
2 tablespoons (40ml) melted butter
2 tablespoons (40ml) chopped fresh dill leaves
2 tablespoons (40ml) sugar
¼ teaspoon (1ml) freshly-ground black pepper
1½ teaspoons (7ml) sweet paprika
2 tablespoons (40ml) olive oil
1½ teaspoons (7ml) salt

1. Scrub the potatoes and boil them whole in a large saucepan of lightly salted water until tender. Drain them, peel them and chop them into 1.5cm (¾-inch) cubes.

2. Combine the dressing ingredients. Gently fold the warm potatoes into the dressing and leave for about 30 minutes for the flavours to mingle. Finally, fold in the peppers, cucumber, tomato and radish. Serve at room temperature, or chilled.

SICILIAN-STYLE ROASTED SWEET PEPPERS IN OLIVE OIL (INSALATA DI PEPERONI ARROSTITI)

Roasted peppers (capsicums), sprinkled with salt and covered with fragrant olive oil make an ideal *antipasto*. They are also a perfect accompaniment to a casual lunch. Roasting your own peppers is far more rewarding — and economical — than purchasing ready-made jars from the supermarket. Home-roasted peppers last at least a week if stored under oil and longer if kept in the refrigerator.

PREPARATION AND COOKING TIME:
20 minutes
YIELD: enough for 6 persons

6 large, fleshy, red peppers, or a combination of red, yellow and green peppers
salt
pepper
4 tablespoons (80ml) olive oil

1. Cut the peppers in half lengthways. Remove the membranes, stalk and seeds. Lay the peppers cut-side down on a baking sheet, and place them under a hot griller for 10 minutes, or until blackened and blistered. Remove and quickly put the peppers into a plastic bag. Close tightly and leave for 20 minutes. This steaming will help loosen the skins.

2. Remove the peppers from the bag, and peel off their skin. Holding the peppers under cold running water while doing this helps speed up the process. Serve *Insalata di Peperoni Arrostiti* cold, sprinkled with salt and pepper and drizzled with olive oil.

Note: If you don't have a griller, you can roast your peppers in a hot oven (200°C/390°F) for about 30 minutes. If you don't have either an oven or a griller, hold the peppers over a gas flame with a pair of kitchen tongs until the peppers are blackened and blistered, then proceed as above.

DAIKON RADISH SALAD

Radishes range in colour from white to red to black — the varieties are numerous. Daikon radish, known also as white winter radish, Japanese radish, or *mooli*, is well-loved throughout Asia. It is a healthy vegetable with a fresh, slightly peppery-mustard taste and a clean crisp texture, which makes it an ideal salad ingredient.

When selecting daikon, choose roots which are firm to the touch and slightly shiny. *Mooli* doesn't keep very well, so be sure to use it within a week. My *Daikon Radish Salad* is actually a cross between a salad and a pickle, and is based on an old Chinese recipe. It's easy to prepare and even though it contains only a few ingredients, it tastes remarkably exotic.

PREPARATION TIME: 25 minutes
MARINATING TIME: a few hours, or overnight
YIELD: enough for 4–6 persons

650g daikon radish (1 very large daikon radish, or a few small ones)
3 tablespoons (60ml) lemon juice, lime juice or white vinegar
1 teaspoon (5ml) dark Chinese sesame oil
1 teaspoon (5ml) salt
1½ tablespoons (30ml) sugar
2 teaspoons (10ml) finely-chopped, fresh coriander leaves

1. Peel the radish, and cut it into 5cm (2-inch) sections. Cut each section lengthwise into 0.5cm (¼-inch) slices. Pile a bundle of slices on top of each other and slice them into 0.5cm (¼-inch) strips lengthwise. When all the radish is chopped, transfer to a suitably sized bowl.
2. Combine the lemon juice, sesame oil, salt and sugar. Pour this dressing over the radish, and leave to marinate for a few hours or overnight. Before serving, add the coriander and mix well. Serve at room temperature or chilled.

SOUTH INDIAN CARROT SALAD

This is a delicious, fresh-tasting side salad from Karnataka State in south-west India that brings out the very best in the humble but versatile carrot. Cream-coloured split *urad dal* lentils add a nutty flavour when toasted, and are available from Indian grocery stores.

PREPARATION AND COOKING TIME:
10 minutes
YIELD: enough for 4 persons

500g carrots, about 4 large ones, peeled, shredded medium coarse
1 large hot green chili, seeded and sliced into julienne strips
leaves from 1 small bunch fresh coriander, coarsely-chopped
1 teaspoon (5ml) salt
3 teaspoons (15ml) oil
¾ teaspoon (3ml) black mustard seeds
1 teaspoon (5ml) cumin seeds
10 fresh curry leaves
1 teaspoon (5ml) split urad dal
½ teaspoon (2ml) yellow asafetida powder
2 tablespoons (40ml) lemon juice

1. Combine the shredded carrots, the chili, fresh coriander leaves and salt in a large bowl.
2. Place the oil in a small saucepan over moderate heat. When hot, sprinkle in the mustard seeds. When they start to crackle, drop in the cumin seeds, curry leaves and *urad dal* lentils. When the *urad dal* starts to darken to a golden brown, remove the pan from the heat, sprinkle in the yellow asafetida powder, swirl the pan momentarily, then pour the spices and oil into the carrot mixture. Pour in the lemon juice, combine well and serve.

JAPANESE-STYLE SPINACH WITH SESAME DIPPING SAUCE

This is a very easy dish to prepare, and can be made in advance, especially since the spinach is not added to the sauce before serving, and the sauce improves on sitting. Serve as an accompaniment to any Asian style meal, or any-time for "something a little different".

PREPARATION TIME: about 20 minutes
SAUCE RESTING TIME: about 30 minutes
YIELD: enough for 4–6 persons

The dipping sauce:

3 tablespoons (60ml) sesame seeds
2 tablespoons (40ml) soy sauce
1 tablespoon (20ml) lemon juice
1 teaspoon (5ml) black mustard seeds ground to a powder and soaked in 1 teaspoon (5ml) water for 10 minutes, or 1 teaspoon (5ml) commercial mustard powder
½ teaspoon (2ml) yellow asafetida powder
2 teaspoons (10ml) finely-grated fresh ginger
500g fresh spinach leaves, weighed after removing all stems

1. Place a non-stick frying pan over medium heat. Sprinkle on the sesame seeds, and, stirring occasionally, toast them until they turn fragrant and a darker shade of brown. Be careful not to burn them. Remove and grind the seeds to a powder in a coffee grinder or spice mill.

2. Combine the ground sesame, soy sauce, lemon juice, soaked or pre-prepared mustard, yellow asafetida powder and ginger in a small bowl. The sauce will actually be quite thick — more like a loose paste. Leave it aside for about 15 minutes for the flavours to mix and intensify.

3. Wash the spinach, drain it and place it in a 5-litre/quart saucepan over moderate heat with only the water that clings to the leaves. Cook without stirring for about 5 minutes or until the spinach is wilted, soft and tender, but not overdone.

4. Carefully drain the spinach, forcing out as much water as possible. Press and form the spinach into a 1.25cm (½-inch) thick log, then slice it into 7.5cm (3-inch) lengths. Arrange the spinach on a platter, and serve at room temperature with the dipping sauce.

SPANISH-STYLE CURLY ENDIVE SALAD (XATO)

White-green curly endive is a hardy winter salad vegetable with a sharp, slightly bitter flavour. This salad has its origins in Spain's Catalonia region, where it is known as *xato* (pronounced *shar-toh*). Endive, teamed up with a tangy dressing spiked with ground, toasted almonds and red chilies, makes for a sharp-tasting, attention-grabbing entrée, or accompaniment to a main meal.

PREPARATION AND COOKING TIME:
about 20 minutes
YIELD: enough for 6–8 persons

2 small heads of fresh, young, curly endive, about 400g in total
15 blanched and toasted whole almonds
2 large dried red chilies, seeded
¼ cup (60ml) olive oil
½ teaspoon (2ml) yellow asafetida powder
3 tablespoons (60ml) lemon juice
½ teaspoon (2ml) salt
½ teaspoon (2ml) sugar

1. Separate the curly leaves of the endive from its base. Rinse the leaves well in cold water — curly endive can be very gritty. Thoroughly shake the leaves and pat them with paper towels. It's important to remove all the moisture you can. Cut the leaves into 7.5cm (3-inch) sections. Arrange the leaves in a large serving bowl or platter.

2. Place the almonds and chilies together in a spice mill and grind them to a fine powder.

3. Warm 2 teaspoons (10ml) of olive oil in a small saucepan over low heat. Sprinkle in the yellow asafetida powder and swirl the pan momentarily. Pour this fragrant oil into a small bowl. Add the rest of the olive oil, the lemon juice, the nut and chili powder, the salt and sugar. Whisk the dressing well. Just before serving, toss the dressing into the endive leaves and serve.

FRESH CHILIES IN SEASONED YOGURT (CHILI RAITA)

Chili Raita makes a zesty accompaniment to a meal that doesn't contain much heat. The bite of the chilies is tempered by the cooling effect of the yogurt.

PREPARATION AND COOKING TIME:
20–25 minutes
YIELD: enough for 4 persons as a side dish

100g fresh green chilies, sliced lengthwise, seeds removed
1 tablespoon (20ml) oil
¼ teaspoon (1ml) mustard seeds
¼ teaspoon (1ml) yellow asafetida powder
¼ teaspoon (1ml) turmeric powder
1 tablespoon (20ml) water
1 cup (250ml) yogurt
2 tablespoons (40ml) freshly-grated coconut
½ teaspoon (2ml) sugar
1 teaspoon (5ml) salt
1–2 tablespoons (20–40ml) fresh coriander for garnish

1. Pour the oil in a small pan or wok over moderate heat. When the oil is hot, sprinkle in the mustard seeds, and fry until they crackle. Add the yellow asafetida powder, turmeric and chili halves, stir briefly, reduce the heat, and fry, stirring occasionally for 3–5 minutes, or until the chilies soften a little. Add the water, cover the pan, reduce the heat to low and cook for a further 5–10 minutes, or until the chilies are tender. Remove the lid and set the chilies aside to cool.

2. Add the yogurt, coconut, sugar and salt to the cooled chilies. Mix well, transfer to a serving bowl and serve garnished with fresh coriander leaves.

QUINOA TABBOULEH SALAD

Quinoa (pronounced *keen-wa*) is a pseudo-grain that has been cultivated in the South American Andes for 5,000 years. Given the name "the mother grain" by ancient farmers, it was much revered. Like buckwheat, it is called a grain, but actually it is the

fruit of the plant in the *Chenopodium* family. The most common pale yellow *quinoa* variety looks like a cross between millet and yellow mustard seeds.

As far as food value is concerned, one researcher has said that "while no single food can supply all of the essential life-sustaining nutrients, *quinoa* comes as close as any other in the vegetable or animal kingdom". *Quinoa* contains more protein than any other grain, has a good balance of amino acids and is light on the digestion. *Quinoa* can be cooked just like rice and is especially favoured by those Vedic vegetarians who fast from grains on the Ekadasi day. It makes a light alternative to *bulgur* (cracked wheat) in my version of the famous Middle Eastern lemon-mint-parsley laced *tabbouleh* salad.

Note that *quinoa* should always be briefly rinsed in cold water before using, to remove any bitterness. *Quinoa* is available from health food shops and grain stores.

PREPARATION AND COOKING TIME:
about 35 minutes
YIELD: enough for 6 persons

1¾ cups (435ml) quinoa, about 340g
3½ cups (875ml) water
2 teaspoons (10ml) salt
½ teaspoon (2ml) yellow asafetida powder

¼ cup (60ml) fresh lemon juice
¼ cup (60ml) olive oil
¼ teaspoon (1ml) coarsely-ground black pepper
1 cup (250ml) fresh parsley, finely chopped
2 tablespoons (40ml) fresh mint leaves, chopped
¾ cup (185ml) cucumbers, finely diced
½ cup (125ml) tomatoes, finely diced
lettuce leaves for serving

1. Rinse the *quinoa* in a large fine sieve under cold water until the water runs clear. Drain the *quinoa* well.

2. Place the water and 1 teaspoon (5ml) salt in a heavy 2-litre/quart saucepan and bring it to the boil over moderate heat. Add the *quinoa*, return to the boil, reduce the heat and simmer, covered, for 10–15 minutes or until the grains are translucent and fully cooked and the *quinoa*'s spiral-shaped germ ring has separated. Remove the pan from the heat and set it aside, covered, for 10 minutes to allow the *quinoa* to firm up.

3. Spoon out the *quinoa* and spread it on a flat dish to fully cool. Then combine it with the yellow asafetida powder, lemon juice, olive oil, the remaining salt, black pepper, parsley and mint in a large bowl. Add the cucumber and tomatoes and toss to combine all the ingredients. Chill and serve *Quinoa Tabbouleh* in lettuce leaves.

WARM POTATO SALAD WITH VIETNAMESE GREENS

The Vietnamese green herb featured in this simple but stunningly flavoured potato salad is known as Vietnamese mint. This pungent herb (*Persicaria odorata*, syn. *Polygonum odoratum*) is not a true mint but widely known by this common name. It is also known as Cambodian mint, hot mint, and *laksa* leaf. The leaves are narrow and pointed with distinctive dark markings in the centre. In Vietnamese cooking, the herb is not cooked, but rather used in salads, or eaten as a fresh accompaniment to the well-known Vietnamese spring rolls. I've found its pungent flavour to be a good foil to the smooth flavour and texture of potatoes and sour cream. Vietnamese mint is available in small bunches from Vietnamese suppliers where it is known as *rau ram*, or from Malaysian or Indonesian suppliers where it is known as *daun kesom* or *daun laksa*.

PREPARATION AND COOKING TIME:
15–20 minutes
YIELD: enough for 4 persons

4 large potatoes, about 600g
2 tablespoons (40ml) oil
½ teaspoon (2ml) yellow asafetida powder
½ cup (125ml) sour light cream
1 tablespoon (20ml) lemon juice
¾–1 teaspoon (3–5ml) salt
¼ teaspoon (1ml) freshly-ground black pepper
leaves from 1 small bunch Vietnamese mint, rau ram, coarsely chopped, about ¼ cup (60ml)

1. Boil the potatoes whole in a large saucepan of lightly salted water until they are tender. Remove and drain them, peel them and cut into 1.5cm (¾-inch) cubes.

2. Warm the oil in a small saucepan over low heat. Sprinkle in the yellow asafetida powder, sauté momentarily, and remove from the heat.

3. Whisk together the sour cream, lemon juice, salt and pepper in a large bowl. Pour in the oil and yellow asafetida powder mixture and combine well. Fold in the warm potatoes and the Vietnamese mint. Serve immediately, or chill and serve cold.

GOURMET GREEN SALAD WITH HERBED FRENCH DRESSING

These days it's easy to purchase a ready-mixed combination of baby salad greens from any well-stocked fruit and vegetable supplier. If you prefer to make your own combinations, here's a couple of selections with a tasty herbed oil and lemon dressing, inspired by the traditional *niçoise* mixture of tiny salad leaves known as *mesclun*.

Tender greens selection:
PREPARATION TIME: a few minutes
YIELD: enough for 4–6 persons

50g baby spinach
50g metzuma (mizuna)
50g rocket leaves (arugula)
50g green oak leaf lettuce, leaves separated

Combine all the greens. You may like to add watercress, or *mâche* (lamb's lettuce) as an alternative to, or in conjunction with, the above selection. Serve with the dressing that follows the next recipe.

Semi-bitter combination:
PREPARATION TIME: a few minutes
YIELD: enough for 4–6 persons

½ small radicchio lettuce
1 small bunch rocket leaves (arugula)
1 small butter lettuce

Separate the butter lettuce leaves from their base, and tear them into large pieces. Discard any large stems from the bunch of rocket.
Tear the radicchio leaves into large bite-sized pieces. Combine the salad leaves and serve with the dressing. Recipe follows.

Herbed French dressing:
PREPARATION TIME: a few minutes
YIELD: about ½ cup (125ml)

½ cup (125ml) extra virgin olive oil
2 tablespoons (40ml) fresh lemon juice
¼ teaspoon (1ml) salt
¼ teaspoon (1ml) freshly cracked black pepper
¼ teaspoon (1ml) Dijon mustard, or to taste
1 teaspoon (5ml) fresh oregano leaves, chopped
1 teaspoon (5ml) fresh basil leaves, chopped
1 teaspoon (5ml) fresh thyme leaves, chopped
2 teaspoons (10ml) honey

Whisk all the ingredients together until well-blended; or combine all the ingredients in a lidded jar and shake vigorously until emulsified.

Note: You may like to "jazz-up" the salads with any of the following additions: well-chopped toasted walnuts, pecans or hazelnuts; toasted pine nuts; halved and seeded black and green grapes; trimmed and blanched slender asparagus; tender, ripe, sliced fresh pears; marinated and sliced artichoke hearts; kalamata olives; sliced baby cucumbers; tender slices of avocado; blanched bias-cut slices of baby zucchini; wedges of tender, steamed or oven-roasted baby beetroots; steamed and julienned baby carrots; tiny blanched broccoli florets; slices of fresh fennel root; blanched snow peas; slices of roasted red peppers.

SAVOURIES

Indonesian Crispy Corn Fritters (Perkedel Jagung)

Cheesy Vegetable Tart

Coconut Milk and Rice Flour Crêpes Stuffed with Seasoned Potatoes
(Masala Dosa)

Herby Pan-fried Potato Cakes (Hash Browns)

Juicy Curd "Steaks"

Mayapur-style Stuffed Vegetable Pastries (Samosas)

Succulent Satay Sticks with Peanut Sauce

Pan-warmed Wheat Turnovers Stuffed with Goat's Cheese and Sundried Tomatoes
(Quesadillas)

Spinach and Curd Cheese Patties (Kofta)

Vegetarian Cornish Pasties

Fried Tofu with Sesame Sauce

Potato Nuggets

Savoury Lentil Doughnuts (Vadai)

Tender Potato Pockets (Knishes)

Party Pizzas

Savoury Fresh Cheese Balls in Creamy Tomato Sauce (Malai Kofta)

INDONESIAN CRISPY CORN FRITTERS (PERKEDEL JAGUNG)

Although rice is the staple diet of most of the people of Indonesia, corn is another important mainstay, especially in the drier eastern provinces, and also during the dry season in the whole of Indonesia. Corn is prepared in many ways, this being one of the most tasty. Serve crispy *Perkedel Jagung* alongside rice dishes, accompanied with *Hot Chili Relish*, or alone with just a squeeze of lemon.

PREPARATION AND COOKING TIME:
40–50 minutes
YIELD: about 25 fritters

2½ cups (625ml) raw corn kernels fresh from the cob, about 3 or 4 large cobs
3 large hot green chilies, seeded and chopped
½ cup (125ml) plain flour
½ cup (125ml) rice flour
¼ teaspoon (1ml) baking powder
2 teaspoons (10ml) salt
2 teaspoons (10ml) coriander powder
1 teaspoon (5ml) sugar
½ teaspoon (2ml) cayenne pepper or chili powder
1 teaspoon (5ml) yellow asafetida powder
oil for frying
6 candle nuts, or large macadamia nuts
up to ¾ cup (185ml) cold water
packed ½ cup (125ml) chopped celery leaves and stalk

1. Coarsely chop or crush the corn kernels to form a mixture of whole and semi-crushed pieces.

2. Combine the flour, rice flour, baking powder, salt, coriander powder, sugar, cayenne and yellow asafetida powder in a large bowl.

3. Pour a few tablespoons of oil into a small saucepan over moderate heat. Drop in the candle nuts or macadamia nuts and fry them until they are golden brown and aromatic. Remove, drain and slightly cool the nuts, then grind them to a powder in a spice mill or coffee grinder.

4. Add three-quarters of the water to the bowl of flour and spices, and whisk it to form a very thick batter. Fold in the corn, the nut powder, the celery, and the chilies. Adjust the consistency with extra water, if required, to form a thick but spoonable batter.

5. Place oil in a 22.5cm (9-inch) frying pan to a depth of 1.25cm (½-inch) over moderate heat. When the oil is fairly hot, carefully spoon in 6–8 heaped tablespoons of batter, flattening them into circular fritters. Fry them for 3 or 4 minutes, or until the undersides of the fritters are golden brown. Turn the fritters over with kitchen tongs and fry them until the other side is also golden brown. Remove and place on absorbent paper towels to dry. Repeat for all the fritters, and serve hot.

CHEESY VEGETABLE TART

This is a firm, vegetable-laden tart with a pleasant cheesy flavour. It is first baked "blind". This entails baking the shell of the tart lined with paper and filled with dried beans, rice or pasta. When the pastry case is fully cooked, the paper and beans are then removed, and the tart is then filled and finished off in the oven. Serve hot for brunch, a casual meal or as a delightful addition to a picnic lunch.

PASTRY PREPARATION TIME: about 10 minutes
PASTRY CHILLING TIME: 30 minutes
PASTRY BAKING TIME: 20 minutes
FILLING PREPARATION TIME: 20 minutes
FINAL BAKING TIME: 20 minutes
YIELD: 1 deep 22.5cm (9-inch) tart

The pastry:

1¼ cups (310ml) unbleached plain flour
1 teaspoon (5ml) salt
½ cup (125ml) chilled butter
2 tablespoons (40ml), or more, cold water

The filling:

2 tablespoons (40ml) olive oil
½ teaspoon (2ml) yellow asafetida powder
½ cup (125ml) each green and red capsicum pieces, cut 1.5cm (½-inch)
1½ cups (375ml) pumpkin pieces, cut 1.5cm (¾-inch)
1½ cups (375ml) potato pieces, cut 1.5cm (¾-inch)
2 cups (500ml) broccoli florets
½ cup (125ml) carrot rings
3 tablespoons (60ml) butter
¼ cup (60ml) flour
1 cup (250ml) milk
¼ teaspoon (1ml) nutmeg
¼ teaspoon (1ml) freshly-ground black pepper
1 cup (250ml) grated cheddar cheese
¼ cup (60ml) grated parmesan cheese
2 tablespoons (40ml) chopped continental parsley leaves
1 teaspoon (5ml) salt
¼ cup (60ml) sour cream
½ cup (125ml) extra grated cheddar cheese

To prepare the pastry case:

1. Place the flour and salt in a food processor. Cut the butter into large chunks and drop them in.

Process, using rapid on/off pulses until the mixture resembles coarse meal. Add 1 tablespoon (20ml) of water and process for a couple of seconds, then repeat with another spoon of water, processing with 3 or 4 quick pulses. Feel the dough. If it's damp enough to form into a rough mass, take it out or else add a few more drops of water, process, then remove.

2. Gather the dough into one lump. Roll out the pastry on to a lightly floured surface and line a deep 22.5cm (9-inch) fluted tin. Refrigerate for 30 minutes.

3. Pre-heat the oven to 180°C/355°F. Line the base of the tart pastry with a circle of greaseproof baking paper. Cover it with an even layer of beans. Bake the pastry for 10 minutes, remove from the oven, discard the paper and beans, then return it to the oven and cook for another 10 minutes or until lightly golden brown. Remove the pie shell and set aside to cool. Leave the oven on.

To prepare the filling:

1. Heat the olive oil in a large, deep non-stick frying pan over moderate heat. Sprinkle in the yellow asafetida powder. Drop in the capsicum pieces and stir-fry them for 5 minutes or until slightly blistered. Remove the pan from the heat.

2. Bring a few cups of water to the boil in a medium-sized saucepan over high heat. Individually steam or boil the pumpkin, potato, broccoli and carrot pieces until just tender. Drain the vegetables well, then add them to the frying pan with the capsicums, and stir to coat them with the fragrant oil.

3. Warm the butter in a 1-litre/quart saucepan over low heat. When melted, add the flour, raise the heat slightly and stir for 2 minutes, or until the flour mixture is lightly golden. Gently whisk in the milk, and stirring constantly bring the mixture to a boil. Cook for 1 minute or until very thick. Remove from the heat. Sprinkle in the nutmeg, black pepper, the two cheeses, the parsley and the salt. Mix well and fold in the sour cream.

4. Gently fold the cheese sauce into the cooked vegetables, combining thoroughly. Carefully spoon the mixture into the cooled pie crust, sprinkle with the extra cheese, and bake for 20 minutes, or until the top is golden brown. Serve hot, warm or at room temperature.

COCONUT MILK AND RICE FLOUR CRÊPES STUFFED WITH SEASONED POTATOES (MASALA DOSA)

Most cuisines of the world offer some type of unleavened thin pancake. India is no exception, and each of its regions has a favourite version, all noticeably different. The traditional *masala dosa* served in South India uses a semi-fermented batter of spiced ground rice and *dal* wrapped around a potato stuffing. This recipe combines the traditional seasoned potato filling from South Indian *dosas* wrapped in an untraditional but delightfully silky soft crêpe-like pancake made instantly from two flours and thin coconut milk. The batter can be successfully refrigerated for several days so that the pancakes can be cooked just before serving. The pancakes themselves are also very user-friendly and can also be refrigerated or frozen if stored between layers of non-stick kitchen paper.

FILLING COOKING TIME: 10–15 minutes
BATTER PREPARATION TIME: a few minutes
CRÊPE COOKING AND ASSEMBLY TIME:
5–7 minutes per pancake
YIELD: 10–12 dosas

The potato filling:

1½ tablespoons (30ml) ghee or oil
1 tablespoon (20ml) minced fresh ginger
1 tablespoon (20ml) minced seeded green chilies
½ teaspoon (2ml) black mustard seeds
15 curry leaves
3 cups (750ml) par-boiled, peeled potatoes, about 400g, diced 0.5cm (¼-inch)
1 teaspoon (5ml) coriander powder
½ teaspoon (2ml) cumin powder
½ teaspoon (2ml) chat masala
½ teaspoon (2ml) turmeric powder
½ teaspoon (2ml) salt
½ cup (125ml) water
2 teaspoons (10ml) lemon juice
2 tablespoons (40ml) chopped fresh coriander leaves

The crêpe batter:

¾ cup (185ml) rice flour
1 cup (250ml) plain cake flour
1 teaspoon (5ml) salt
2⅔ cups (665ml) thin coconut milk, or 1⅓ cups (335ml) coconut milk and 1⅓ cups (335ml) water

To prepare the potato stuffing:

1. Heat the ghee or oil in a large frying pan over moderate heat. When the ghee is hot, drop in the minced ginger and chilies and fry for 1 or 2 minutes, or until they are translucent and fragrant. Add the mustard seeds and fry them until they sputter and pop. Immediately add the curry leaves, then the diced potatoes and stir well. Sprinkle in the four powdered spices and the salt. Sauté for 1 minute, then pour in the water, lower the flame and cook for about 5–10 minutes or until the potatoes are tender and dry.

2. Remove the pan from the heat and fold in the lemon juice and fresh coriander leaves. Set aside to cool.

To prepare the crêpes:

1. Whisk together the two flours and salt in a bowl. Add most of the coconut milk or half coconut milk and half water, whisking to form a smooth pourable batter with a consistency of medium-thin pouring cream. Add a little more coconut milk if required.

2. Heat one or two 22.5cm (9-inch) non-stick frying pans over medium heat until a drop of water sprinkled on will dance and sputter. Lightly oil the pan and, using a ⅓ cup measure, pour a portion of batter onto the pan, immediately spreading it into a thin 22.5cm (9-inch) round, starting from the centre and spiralling outwards. Add more water to the batter if it doesn't easily spread. Cook the crêpe for about 1½–2 minutes, or until lightly golden brown, then turn it over. Cook for 1 or 2 minutes, or until lightly golden brown on the other side. If you want the crêpe to be a little crispy, then add a little ghee or oil to the pan while cooking.

3. Remove the crêpe from the pan and place it on the plate. Spread about 2 tablespoons (40ml) potato stuffing on one half, and fold the crêpe in half, or place the filling in a line on the bottom portion of the pancake and roll it into a tube. Alternatively, you may prefer to cook all the crêpes first and then fill them. Be sure to stack them with non-stick paper between them, then count the number of pancakes, divide the stuffing into that many portions, and stuff them as described above.

Note: If you cannot serve your *Masala Dosa* piping hot, you can keep them warm in a pre-heated warm oven. Serve *Masala Dosa* hot with a few spoonfuls of *South Indian Coconut Chutney*.

HERBY PAN-FRIED POTATO CAKES (HASH BROWNS)

Hash browns are a well-known American breakfast food. Although generally quite plain, this version is spiked with fresh thyme, lemon zest and *Dijon* mustard, and, you guessed it, a little yellow asafetida powder. I've discovered that 7.5cm (3-inch) "egg rings" keep hash browns from disintegrating in the frying pan. They're inexpensive metal rings available from kitchenware or hardware stores — you'll need five for this recipe.

PREPARATION AND COOKING TIME:
about 40 minutes
YIELD: 10 hash browns

5 medium-sized baking-type potatoes, 750g
1 teaspoon (5ml) salt
2–3 teaspoons (10–15ml) fresh thyme leaves, chopped
1–2 tablespoons (20–40ml) Dijon mustard
1 teaspoon (5ml) finely-grated lemon rind
¼ teaspoon (1ml) freshly-ground black pepper
4 tablespoons (80ml) butter
½ teaspoon (2ml) yellow asafetida powder

1. Boil the potatoes in a large saucepan of lightly salted water until just cooked. Drain them, allow to cool slightly, then coarsely chop them. Place the potatoes in a bowl, and add the salt, pepper, thyme, mustard and lemon zest.

2. Heat 1 tablespoon (20ml) of the butter in a small pan over low heat. Sprinkle in the yellow asafetida powder and sauté momentarily. Add this seasoned butter to the potatoes. Combine the mixture well.

3. Melt the remaining butter in a large, non-stick frying pan over moderate heat. Place 5 lightly oiled, 7.5cm (3-inch) egg rings on the pan, and spoon the potato mixture evenly into the rings. Fill the rings to the top, and press down firmly to form flat cakes. Fry the rings of potato for 5–7 minutes, or until a crust forms on the underside. Shake the pan occasionally to avoid sticking.

4. Turn the potato cakes over with a spatula, and carefully remove the rings with tongs. Fry them for another 4–5 minutes, or until crusty on the second side. Remove the hash browns and place them to drain on paper towels. Repeat the procedure for the second batch and serve hot.

JUICY CURD "STEAKS"

Homemade curd cheese, *panir*, is unique. In one sense, the word "cheese" conjures up the wrong impression when describing *panir*. Unlike all other cheeses, you can pan-fry or deep-fry *panir* into succulent golden-brown chunks, and it will soak up whatever flavours you combine it with. It's probably one of the most versatile cooking ingredients in my kitchen, and is especially impressive when used as a "faux" meat. I recall how my spiritual master, Srila Prabhupada, showed us how to prepare a "meaty" dish without meat, but using *panir*, in Melbourne in 1974.

I first tasted these "stick-to-your-ribs" vegetarian curd "steaks" at the Hare Krishna Farm in northern New South Wales many years ago. Rich milk, fresh from Jersey cows, was quickly transformed into curd, briefly pressed, pan-fried and basted in a tasty tomato glaze. Here is my version of these juicy, protein-rich favourites. I have replicated the creamy Jersey milk by adding cream. If you are using creamy fresh milk straight from the cow, leave out the 300ml cream.

CURD PREPARATION TIME: 10 minutes
CURD RESTING TIME: 5–10 minutes
COOKING TIME: about 30 minutes
YIELD: six 160g "steaks"

The curd "steaks":

4 litres whole, fresh milk
300ml double cream
800ml to 1 litre cultured buttermilk

Frying the "steaks":

4 tablespoons (80ml) butter
1 teaspoon (5ml) yellow asafetida powder
½ teaspoon (2ml) coarsely-ground black pepper

The tomato glaze:

¼ cup (60ml) tomato paste (or more for saucier steaks)
2 tablespoons (40ml) soy sauce
¾ cup (185ml) water
1 teaspoon (5ml) sugar

1. Pour the milk and cream into a heavy-based 5-litre/quart saucepan. Bring to the boil over moderate to high heat, stirring often to prevent scorching or sticking. Lower the heat and pour in a little over 3 cups (750ml) buttermilk, or an alternative curdling agent, such as yogurt or lemon juice (you'll need a smaller quantity of yogurt than buttermilk, and a much smaller quantity of lemon juice). Stir the milk gently until it curdles, then remove the saucepan from the heat. If the liquid is not clear but is still milky, return the saucepan to the heat and add more buttermilk.

2. When the curds have completely separated from the whey, pour or scoop the solids into a colander lined with cheese cloth. Gather the corners and hold the bag under lukewarm water for 10 seconds. Squeeze the bag, place it back into the colander, push it into a flat shape and press it under a heavy weight for 5–10 minutes, or just slightly firm. The secret of juicy curd "steaks" is to press the curd for the very minimum amount of time.

3. Unwrap the cloth and carefully remove the curd cheese. Transfer to a flat surface and cut it into 15cm (6-inch) "steaks".

4. Set 2 large non-stick frying pans over low heat. If you only have one, cook the curd in two batches. Place 2 tablespoons (40ml) butter in each pan. When melted, sprinkle ½ teaspoon (2ml) yellow asafetida powder and ¼ teaspoon (1ml) black pepper in each pan.

5. Place the curd in the seasoned butter, increase the heat slightly and pan-fry the curd "steaks", turning when needed, for 3 or 4 minutes or until they are slightly golden brown on each side.

6. Meanwhile, whisk together the glaze ingredients in a small bowl. When the "steaks" are evenly golden brown, pour half the tomato mixture over each batch. Increase the heat slightly and cook, turning often for another 3–4 minutes, or until the liquid has reduced and the "steaks" are well-coated.

7. For optimum results, remove the pans from the heat and cover them, allowing the curd "steaks" to marinate for 15 minutes in the hot glaze. Return the pans briefly to the heat and serve the "steaks" hot.

MAYAPUR-STYLE STUFFED VEGETABLE PASTRIES (SAMOSA)

Someone once said, "there are as many variations for vegetable *samosas* as there are stars in the sky", and I would agree. I've eaten many types of *samosas* over the years, but the tastiest and flakiest ones I've ever encountered are from the kitchens of the Mayapur Chandrodaya Temple in the holy pilgrimage city of Shree Mayapur in West Bengal. The crust for these bite-sized golden-brown triangular pastries is thin, crisp, light and flaky. They are stuffed with a semi-dry filling of buttery potato, a little fried cauliflower, and peas, and supported by a delectable combination of hot, sweet, sour and spicy tastes.

Samosas are usually fried just before serving as a snack or meal savoury. They are also delicious at room temperature in a lunch box or on a picnic. *Samosas* can be successfully reheated in the oven, or partially fried — about two-thirds cooked — cooled, frozen, and then defrosted, air-dried and fried again with stunning results.

PREPARATION TIME: about 1 hour
PASTRY RESTING TIME: 30–60 minutes
FRYING TIME: about 30–40 minutes
YIELD: 24 bite-sized samosas

The filling:

2 cups (500ml) potatoes diced 0.5cm (¼-inch)
1 cup (250ml) green peas
1 teaspoon (5ml) cumin seeds
1 teaspoon (5ml) fennel seeds
1 teaspoon (5ml) fenugreek seeds
one 3.75cm (1½-inch) cinnamon stick
1 teaspoon (5ml) coriander powder
⅓ cup (85ml) ghee or oil
1 teaspoon (5ml) turmeric powder
1½ cups (375ml) tiny cauliflower florets, 0.5cm (¼-inch)
2 tablespoons (40ml) finely chopped, seeded green chilies
2 teaspoons (10ml) finely shredded ginger
2 tablespoons (40ml) shredded coconut
½ teaspoon (2ml) yellow asafetida powder
½ teaspoon (2ml) cayenne pepper
1 teaspoon (5ml) garam masala
1 teaspoon (5ml) chat masala
2 teaspoons (10ml) salt
2 teaspoons (10ml) sugar
1 tablespoon (20ml) lemon juice
2 tablespoons (40ml) finely chopped roasted peanuts
2–3 tablespoons (40–60ml) chopped fresh coriander leaves
ghee or oil for deep-frying

The pastry:

3 cups (750ml) unbleached plain flour
2 teaspoons (10ml) salt
½ cup (125ml) melted ghee or butter
up to ¾ cup (185ml) warm water

To prepare the filling:

1. Place the potatoes and peas in separate small saucepans of water and boil until soft. Drain and reserve the vegetables.

2. Combine the cumin, fennel, fenugreek and cinnamon in a spice mill or coffee grinder. Grind to a fine powder. Add the coriander powder, and set it aside.

3. Pour the ⅓ cup (85ml) ghee in a 3-litre/quart saucepan, deep-frying pan or small wok over moderate heat. When fairly hot, drop in half the turmeric powder, and half the cauliflower pieces. Fry the cauliflower, stirring once or twice until tender and a light golden colour. Remove with a slotted spoon and place in a small bowl. Fry the rest of the cauliflower pieces.

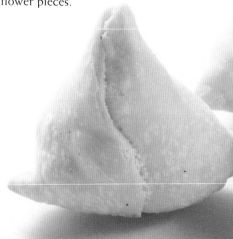

Figure 1

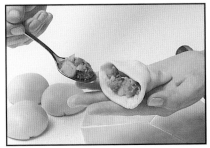

Figure 2

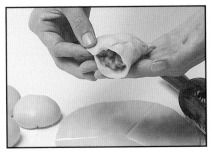

Figure 3

4. Reduce the heat under the hot ghee that remains in the pan. Drop in the chili and ginger, and sauté for 1–2 minutes or until fragrant. Add the shredded coconut and stir-fry it until lightly golden brown. Drop in the yellow asafetida powder and immediately remove the pan from the heat. Sprinkle in the reserved ground spices plus the cayenne, the remaining turmeric, *garam masala*, *chat masala*, the salt, sugar, lemon juice, peanuts, and coriander leaves. Mix well, then carefully add the peas, potatoes and fried cauliflower pieces. Carefully combine everything until well mixed. Set the *samosa* filling aside to cool.

To prepare the pastry:

Combine the flour and the salt in a large mixing bowl. Add the melted ghee or butter and rub it with your fingertips until it is fully incorporated and the mixture resembles breadcrumbs. Add three-quarters of the warm water and work it into the flour. Add the remaining water in dribbles until the pastry can be gathered into a non-sticky, kneadable, medium-soft dough. Knead the dough on a clean surface for about 8 minutes, or until silky-smooth and pliable, cover with a cloth, and set it aside for 30–60 minutes.

To prepare and cook the samosas:

1. Divide the filling into 24 tablespoon-sized mounds.

2. Knead the pastry briefly, and roll it into a rope about 40cm (16-inches) long. Cut it into 8 equal pieces. Shape each piece of pastry into a smooth ball. Working on one piece of pastry at a time, flatten the ball into a patty, then roll it out on a lightly floured surface into a thin disc of pastry 16.5cm (about 6½-inches) round. Cut the round in thirds to form three, even-sized triangular shaped segments (one side of the triangle will be rounded). Dip a fingertip in water and moisten all around the edges of the pastry. Lift a section of the pastry, and bring the two straight edges together to form a cone (see Figure 1). It is essential that the seal is very secure, or else the filling will empty out during the frying. Place a portion of the filling inside the cone, filling it to three-quarters full (see Figure 2). Bring the two open edges of the pastry together and pinch together to seal very securely (see Figure 3). You should have a pyramid-shaped pastry. Form all 24 *samosas* in the same way.

3. Heat 6.5–7.5cm (2½ to 3-inches) ghee or oil to 185°C/365°F in a deep sauté pan or wok over moderate heat. Slip 4 or 6 (or more if your frying vessel and heat source allows) into the oil and fry them for 4 or 5 minutes, or until a light golden brown. Drain the *samosas* on paper towels. Repeat for all the *samosas* and serve hot or warm.

SUCCULENT SATAY STICKS WITH PEANUT SAUCE

This recipe represents a delicious fusion of South-East Asian and Mediterranean cuisine. An assortment of chunky segments of roasted, barbecued, or deep-fried vegetables along with tofu, *tempe* and gluten are threaded onto skewers and served with an irresistible peanut sauce. Allow about two satay sticks per person, and serve hot with salad, pickles and rice.

PEANUT SAUCE PREPARATION TIME: about 10 minutes
SATAY STICK COOKING AND ASSEMBLY TIME: about 30–50 minutes, depending on your choice of ingredients
YIELD: 12 satay sticks, and about 3½ cups (875ml) peanut sauce

The peanut sauce:

inner white section of 2 stalks lemon grass, finely sliced into rings
1 hot green chili, minced
3 teaspoons (15ml) coriander powder
2 teaspoons (10ml) cumin powder
3 tablespoons (60ml) oil
1½ tablespoons (30ml) finely-minced fresh ginger
20 fresh curry leaves, torn
½ teaspoon (2ml) yellow asafetida powder
1½ cups (375ml) water
1 teaspoon (5ml) cayenne pepper
1½ cups (375ml) crunchy peanut butter
1½ tablespoons (30ml) lemon juice
2 tablespoons (40ml) soy sauce
1 tablespoon (20ml) treacle or molasses
½ cup (125ml) thin coconut milk

The satay sticks:

Select 6 or 7 items from the following list. I suggest at least 4 items from Category I coupled with at least 2 items from Category II.

Category I

½ large zucchini
1 large red or green capsicum
1 large eggplant
½ small, ripe pineapple
3 large firm tomatoes, or 12 cherry tomatoes
3 large potatoes

Category II

300g gluten (for instructions how to prepare gluten, see Special Ingredients section)
375g firm tofu
300g tempe
panir cheese from 2 litres milk

To prepare the peanut sauce:

1. Combine the lemon grass and chili in a blender with a few spoons of the water. Process to a purée. Add the coriander powder and cumin powder and process again. Remove the spice paste and set it aside.

2. Pour the oil into a 3-litre/quart saucepan over moderate heat. When hot, drop in the ginger and fry it for 1 or 2 minutes, or until fragrant. Add the curry leaves and fry them for a few moments. Add the yellow asafetida powder, sauté momentarily, then pour in the spice paste. Fry, stirring, until the water evaporates and the oil oozes out of the frying spices.

3. Carefully pour the water into the spice paste, then add the cayenne pepper, the peanut butter, lemon juice, soy sauce and sweetener. Cook, stirring for about 6 or 8 minutes, or until the mixture boils and thickens into a smooth sauce. Add the coconut milk and stir to incorporate it well with the sauce. The peanut sauce should be fairly thick, but slightly runny. Adjust the consistency with water, if necessary.

To prepare and assemble the satay stick ingredients:

1. Select what you would like to thread on to your satay sticks and prepare as described below.

2. Thread your selection of cooked ingredients onto bamboo skewers. Serve with the satay sauce. As an alternative, thread the raw ingredients onto metal skewers, or bamboo skewers soaked in water for 1 hour, and then grill or barbecue them.

Category I:

For the zucchini, capsicum, eggplant or potato: Cut the vegetables into 12 chunks. Grill, deep-fry, or barbecue until done.

For the pineapple or tomato: Cut into 12 chunks. If using cherry tomatoes, thread them whole.

Category II:

For the gluten: Combine gluten flour with 1 cup (250ml) water. Prepare the gluten by following the directions in *Special Ingredients section.* Cut the gluten

into twelve 2.5cm (1-inch) chunks. Boil in lightly salted water for 20 minutes, drain, then squeeze dry. Marinate the chunks of gluten in 2 tablespoons (40ml) soy sauce, then pan-fry in 2 tablespoons (40ml) oil along with ¼ teaspoon (1ml) yellow asafetida powder for 3–5 minutes, or until golden brown.

For the tofu: Cut the tofu into 12 chunks. Deep-fry or pan-fry it in very hot oil until golden brown, then marinate in 2 tablespoons (40ml) soy sauce for 10 minutes.

For the tempe: Cut the *tempe* into 12 chunks. Pan-fry it in 2 tablespoons (40ml) oil with ¼ teaspoon (1ml) yellow asafetida powder until golden brown. Marinate it in 2 tablespoons (40ml) soy sauce for 10 minutes.

For the panir cheese: Prepare *panir* cheese from 2 litres of milk as per the method described in *Special Ingredients.* Cut the *panir* into 12 chunks and pan-fry in 2 tablespoons (40ml) oil mixed with ¼ teaspoon (1ml) yellow asafetida powder until golden brown.

PAN-WARMED WHEAT TURNOVERS STUFFED WITH GOAT'S CHEESE AND SUNDRIED TOMATOES (QUESADILLAS)

Wheat *tortillas* are flatbreads made from wheat flour. As well as being served as breads, they form the basis of numerous Mexican dishes, such as these very quick and delicious appetisers, called *quesadilla*. Wheat *tortillas* are available at Mexican and specialty stores, or well-stocked supermarkets. If *tortillas* are not available, you can use whole wheat *chapatis* or thin wheat *pita* breads. If you are not a fan of goat's cheese, substitute with cream cheese.

PREPARATION AND COOKING TIME:
15–20 minutes
YIELD: 8 appetisers, enough for 4 persons

¾–1 cup (185–250ml) goat's cheese (chevre) or cream cheese
¼ teaspoon (1ml) coarsely-ground black pepper
½–1 green jalapeño chili, seeded and minced
12 large oil-packed sundried tomatoes, drained and sliced 0.5cm (¼-inch)
four 20 cm (8-inch) wheat tortillas
¼ cup (60ml) sour cream
fresh coriander sprigs for garnish

1. Combine the cheese, black pepper, minced chilies and sundried tomatoes in a bowl.

2. Lay out the 4 *tortillas* on a flat surface. Spread a quarter of the cheese mixture over half of each one, leaving 2.5cm (1-inch) border.

3. Heat 1 or 2 non-stick frying pans over moderate heat. Spray with a light film of cooking oil. Lift a *tortilla* onto the pan, fold the uncovered half over to cover the cheese mixture. Press down with a spatula. Cook the *quesadilla* for 2 minutes or until lightly browned. Turn it over and cook the other side, occasionally pressing down with a spatula.

4. Remove the *quesadilla*, transfer to a cutting board and cut it in half to make 2 triangles. Cover with foil, or place in a warm oven while you cook the remaining 3 breads. Serve warm *quesadilla* wedges on a serving platter with sour cream, and coriander leaves for garnish.

SPINACH AND CURD CHEESE PATTIES (KOFTA)

There are innumerable varieties of *koftas* popular in regional cuisines throughout India. They are made from raw or cooked vegetables, and some, like this succulent version, are combined with homemade fresh cheese, *panir*. Drizzled with lemon juice, a light sauce, or served with a dab of chutney, *Spinach and Curd Cheese Patties*, with their thin, crisp crust and moist interior, are simple to prepare and highly delicious.

PREPARATION TIME: about 25 minutes
KOFTA FRYING TIME: 6–8 minutes per batch
YIELD: 18 *koftas*

300g spinach leaves (about 1 medium-sized bunch of spinach), washed and dried
2 teaspoons (10ml) ajowan seeds
2 teaspoons (10ml) kalonji seeds
2 hot green chilies, seeded and minced
¾ teaspoon (3ml) yellow asafetida powder
¼ teaspoon (1ml) nutmeg powder
1½ teaspoons (7ml) salt
¼ cup (60ml) chickpea flour (if the koftas are a little too moist, add 1–2 tablespoons (20–40ml) more)
fresh curd cheese (panir) made from 2 litres milk, hung or pressed for just a few minutes
ghee or oil for deep-frying

1. Gather half the spinach leaves together, roll them into a tube and slice them thinly. Cut these julienned slices of spinach once across and place the shredded spinach in a large bowl. Repeat for the remaining spinach.

2. Set a small saucepan or frying pan over moderate heat. Sprinkle in the *ajowan* and *kalonji* seeds, and dry-roast the spices, shaking the pan occasionally, until the *ajowan* darkens a few shades and becomes fragrant. Remove the pan from the heat and sprinkle the roasted seeds into the bowl of spinach. Drop the chilies, yellow asafetida powder, nutmeg, salt and chickpea flour into the spinach mixture.

3. Heat 6.5–7.5 cm (2½–3 inches) of ghee or oil in a wok or deep-frying vessel to 175°C/345°F.

4. Crumble the hot curd cheese into small pieces and spread it on a clean bench-top. Knead the cheese until it forms a smooth paste. Gather up all the curd cheese and place it into the spice, spinach and chickpea flour mixture. Gently knead the *kofta* mixture until it is well combined. It should be moist enough to pinch into balls. Divide the mixture into 18 lumps. Form each lump into a smooth patty, about 3.75cm (1½ inches) in diameter. Place all the patties on a plate.

5. Slip 6–8 patties into the hot oil. Once they bob to the surface, gently turn them with a slotted spoon. Continue turning them until they are evenly browned and crisp, about 6–8 minutes. Remove and drain on paper towels. Fry the remaining *koftas* and serve piping hot, or keep warm in a pre-heated moderate oven.

VEGETARIAN CORNISH PASTIES

The Cornish pastie was originally a working man's lunch. The traditional shape had a practical purpose — it was designed to fit into his pocket. Here's a vegetarian version of this English country classic, using minced gluten and vegetables — a hearty lunch for a hard-working vegetarian.

PASTRY PREPARATION TIME: 10 minutes
PASTRY RESTING TIME: 30 minutes
FILLING PREPARATION TIME: 15–20 minutes
BAKING TIME: 30–40 minutes
YIELD: 12 pasties

The pastry:

3 cups (750ml) plain flour
1 teaspoon (5ml) salt
185g softened butter
½ cup (125ml) water
a little milk for brushing

The filling:

3 tablespoons (60ml) butter
1 teaspoon (5ml) yellow asafetida powder
250g gluten, minced or chopped fine (see Special Ingredients section for instructions how to prepare gluten)
2 tablespoons (40ml) soy sauce
1 carrot, coarsely grated, about ½ cup (125ml)
1 small turnip, coarsely grated, about ¼ cup (60ml)
2 medium-sized potatoes, steamed until just tender, peeled and cut into 0.5cm (¼-inch) cubes
½ teaspoon (2ml) black pepper
½ cup (125ml) chopped parsley leaves

To prepare the pastry:

Sift the flour and salt into a large mixing bowl. Rub in the butter until the mixture resembles coarse meal. Add most of the water, mix well and add the rest of the water if required. Mix well to form a soft dough. Knead the dough lightly for 2 or 3 minutes, and set it aside, covered, to rest for 30 minutes.

To prepare the filling:

Melt the butter in a heavy frying pan over moderate heat. Sprinkle in the yellow asafetida powder, stir momentarily, then add the gluten. Increase the heat slightly and stir-fry the gluten in the seasoned butter for about 10 minutes, or until it is lightly browned. Add the soy sauce, stir-fry, then remove the pan from the heat and stir in the carrot, turnip, potatoes, black pepper and parsley. Mix well to combine, transfer to a plate or dish and allow the filling to cool.

To assemble and bake the pasties:

1. Roll out the pastry thinly on a floured surface, and cut into 12 rounds using a 12.5–15cm (5–6-inch) pastry cutter or saucepan lid. Alternatively, divide the pastry into 12 even-sized lumps, roll them into balls, flatten them into patties and roll them on a floured surface into 12.5–15cm (5–6-inch) discs of pastry. Pre-heat the oven to 220°C/430°F.

2. Place approximately ½ cup (125ml) cold filling across the centre of each disc of pastry. Dampen the edges of the pastry and lift the two sides of the disc, joining them together at the top and pinching together to form a "cock's comb" frill. As an alternative, fold the pastry over in a half circle and seal the edges by pressing them with fork tines.

3. Stand the well-sealed pasties, seals upwards, on lightly oiled baking trays. Brush the pasties with milk, and bake in the hot oven for 30–40 minutes, or until the pasties are golden brown. Serve warm or at room temperature.

Note: As an alternative filling suggestion, add cubes of cooked pumpkin, sweet potatoes, or green peas, or add a few teaspoons of grated cheese.

FRIED TOFU WITH SESAME SAUCE

Tofu, the soft white cake of pressed soy bean curd is bland in taste, but absorbs the flavour and aroma of the ingredients with which it is mixed. It is a low-cost source of protein, low in saturated fats and calories and free of cholesterol. It is featured in this tasty Cantonese dish served with chunks of cucumber and fried peanuts, and topped with a tasty sesame sauce. Serve it as part of a multi-course dinner or as an entrée.

TOFU PRESSING TIME: 30 minutes
PREPARATION AND COOKING TIME: 15 minutes
YIELD: enough for 4 persons

300g firm tofu
oil for deep-frying
1 cup (250ml) raw peanuts
1 teaspoon (5ml) oil
¼ teaspoon (1ml) yellow asafetida powder
2 tablespoons (40ml) celery, diced fine
½ large cucumber (unpeeled), cut into 1.5cm (¾ inch) cubes

The sauce:

1½ tablespoons (30ml) toasted and powdered sesame seeds
3 tablespoons (60ml) Chinese sesame oil
3 tablespoons (60ml) light soy sauce
1 tablespoon (20ml) brown sugar
2 tablespoons (40ml) lemon juice
½ teaspoon (2ml) Chinese chili oil

1. Press the tofu under a heavy weight for 30 minutes to drain off any excess water. Remove the weight and cut the tofu into 2.5cm (1-inch) cubes.

2. Pour the oil into a small saucepan and set it over moderate heat. When the oil is hot, deep-fry the peanuts until golden brown. Remove and drain them. Increase the oil temperature to 185°C/365°F, and deep-fry the tofu until golden brown. Remove and drain.

3. Heat the 1 teaspoon (5ml) oil in a small pan, and sauté the yellow asafetida powder until it becomes fragrant. Add the diced celery and sauté for 1 minute. Remove from the pan and set aside. Combine the powdered sesame seeds, sesame oil, soy sauce, brown sugar, lemon juice and chili oil in another small pan, and warm, stirring over very low heat, until sauce-like, smooth and well-mixed. It should be a thin, pouring consistency — add water if necessary. Remove from the heat.

4. In a pre-warmed serving dish, decoratively combine the drained cubes of deep-fried tofu, fried peanuts and the cucumber. Spoon the sauce on top, garnish with the sautéed diced celery and serve immediately.

POTATO NUGGETS

As the name conjures up, these are bite-sized, spiced chunks of potato, batter-fried to crispy perfection. I've fine-tuned the recipe for these delicious savouries over the years, since I've cooked them so often. In fact they have quite a "cult following". I've been told they're known as *KFP* — *Kurma's Fried Potatoes*, amongst their aficionados. Old potatoes make the best nuggets, and ghee, with its delicious flavour, is the recommended frying medium. Serve potato nuggets with *Bush Tomato Chutney*, *Kurma's Tomato Ketchup*, or any other pickle, sauce or chutney of your choice.

POTATO PREPARATION TIME: 15 minutes
BATTER PREPARATION TIME: 10 minutes
BATTER RESTING TIME: 10–15 minutes
FRYING TIME: 3–5 minutes per batch
YIELD: about 36 medium-sized nuggets

1kg old potatoes

The batter:

½ cup (125ml) chickpea flour
½ cup (125ml) fine rice flour
½ cup (125ml) self-raising flour
4½ teaspoons (22ml) salt
1½ teaspoons (7ml) kalonji seeds
2 teaspoons (10ml) yellow asafetida powder
1½ teaspoons (7ml) turmeric
2 teaspoons (10ml) cayenne pepper
1½ teaspoons (7ml) ground coriander
½ teaspoon (2ml) ginger powder
1 teaspoon (5ml) bay leaf, powdered in a spice mill
1 teaspoon (5ml) fennel powder
¼ teaspoon (1ml) cinnamon powder
2 teaspoons (10ml) green chilies, seeded and finely chopped
a little over 2 cups (500ml) cold water, or enough to make a fairly thick, smooth batter
ghee or oil for deep-frying

To prepare the potatoes:

Wash the potatoes, and place them whole and unpeeled in a 5-litre/quart saucepan of cold water with 2 teaspoons (10ml) of salt. Bring the water to the boil, and cook the potatoes until they are completely cooked but not falling apart. Drain, cool and peel the potatoes and cut them into bite-sized chunks, about 2.5cm (1 inch). Set them aside.

To prepare the batter and fry the nuggets:

1. Combine all the batter ingredients except the water. Mix well with a wire whisk. Slowly add cold water while whisking the batter until it reaches a consistency of thick, unwhipped cream. Test it by dipping a piece of potato in it. The batter should completely coat the potato and should only drip off after being shaken gently. Have extra rice flour and water on hand to adjust the consistency as required. Let the batter sit for 10–15 minutes.

2. Heat fresh ghee or oil to a depth of 6.5–7.5 cm (2½–3 inches), in a wok or deep-frying vessel until the temperature reaches about 180°C/355°F.

3. Test the oil temperature by dropping a drip of batter into it; the drip should sink, then immediately rise to the surface and begin to fry. Dip 5 or 6 chunks of potato in the batter, and, one at a time, carefully slip them into the hot oil. The temperature may fall, but try to maintain it at 180°C/355°F throughout the frying. Fry the nuggets for about 3–5 minutes, or until they are crisp and golden brown, turning them to cook evenly on all sides. Remove them with a slotted spoon and drain on paper towels set in a colander. Continue frying until all the nuggets are done. Serve immediately, or keep them warm, uncovered, in a pre-heated oven for up to half an hour.

SAVOURY LENTIL DOUGHNUTS (VADAI)

These crunchy, lentil-based and cabbage-laced finger foods from India can be served as light-meal entrées, or as an accompaniment or snack at just about any time — for breakfast, lunch, afternoon tea or supper. They are always served with some kind of freshly-made chutney — usually coconut in South India, and mint, coriander or tamarind in the North. The ingredients are few — split *urad dal* lentils, cabbage, fresh coriander and fresh chilies — but their taste is stunning.

URAD DAL SOAKING TIME: 2 hours
PREPARATION AND COOKING TIME: 45 minutes
YIELD: 15–20 vadais

1 cup (250ml) split urad dal
1 teaspoon (5ml) yellow asafetida powder
4 medium-sized green chilies
1 teaspoon (5ml) salt
½ cup (125ml) finely-chopped cabbage
finely-chopped leaves from one small bunch coriander
oil for deep-frying

1. Place the *dal* on a plate and sort out and discard any foreign matter. Transfer the *dal* to a bowl, cover with water, and rub the *dal* between your palms. When the water is cloudy, drain and rinse the *urad dal*. Repeat this procedure until the water is clear, then cover the *dal* with 3 cups (750ml) water and leave to soak for 2 hours.

2. Drain the *dal* completely, and place it in a food processor with a metal blade. Add the yellow asafetida powder, chilies and salt, and process into a thick batter. Transfer the batter to a bowl, add the cabbage and coriander leaves and mix well.

3. Heat 6.5–7.5 cm (2½–3 inches) oil to 170°C/340°F in a wok or deep frying pan. Divide the thick batter into 15–20 lumps on a large plate. Take a lump of batter and place it on the palm of your hand. Moisten your other hand with water, and press to flatten the batter into a round patty. Make a hole in the centre of the patty. It should resemble a small doughnut. Slip the *vadai* gently into the oil. Repeat quickly and fry the *vadais* in 2 or 3 batches, without crowding the pan. When they float to the surface, fry them, turning them to ensure even cooking, for about 4–5 minutes, or until they are reddish-brown and crisp. Remove and drain them on paper towels, and serve hot with a chutney of your choice.

TENDER POTATO POCKETS (KNISHES)

Knishes are a heavy-duty Jewish savoury favourite from New York. In my version, potatoes are folded with tender vegetables and sour cream and baked in individual flaky pastry cases. Divinely rich already!

PREPARATION TIME: 15–60 minutes
COOKING TIME: 35–40 minutes
YIELD: 10 knishes

The pastry:

2¼ cups (560ml) plain flour
¾ teaspoon (3ml) salt
¾ cup (185ml) cold butter
about 6 tablespoons (120ml) cold water

The filling:

2 large potatoes, about 700g
2 tablespoons (40ml) butter
1½ teaspoons (7ml) ground caraway seeds
½ teaspoon (2ml) yellow asafetida powder
½ cup (125ml) grated cabbage
⅓ cup (85ml) grated carrot
⅓ cup (85ml) finely-chopped green capsicums
⅓ cup (85ml) finely-chopped celery stalks and leaves
3 tablespoons (60ml) minced fresh continental (flat-leaf) parsley
1 teaspoon (5ml) sweet paprika powder
½ teaspoon (2ml) black pepper
2 teaspoons (10ml) salt
1 teaspoon (5ml) sugar
⅓ cup (85ml) sour cream

To prepare the pastry:

1. Place the flour, salt and butter in a food processor with a metal blade. Process with 12–15 on/off pulses, or until the mixture resembles breadcrumbs. Sprinkle in 4 table-spoons (80ml) cold water and process again with 6 short pulses.

2. Add another 2 tablespoons (40ml) water, and process with another 3 short pulses. Feel the dough. If damp enough to cling together, remove it and form it into a ball and place it onto a lightly-floured surface. If a little dry, add a few drops more water. If you are not using the pastry immediately, wrap it in plastic wrap and refrigerate.

To prepare the filling:

1. Scrub the potatoes, and place them whole in a large saucepan of lightly-salted water. Boil until tender. Drain, peel and mash the potatoes. You should have about 2¾ cups (685ml).

2. Warm the butter in a heavy frying pan or small saucepan over moderate heat. Sprinkle in the caraway seed powder and the yellow asafetida powder and sauté very briefly. Add the cabbage, carrot, capsicum, celery and parsley. Raise the heat and sauté the vegetables for 5–7 minutes, or until they are tender. Add the paprika powder, black pepper, sugar and salt, mix well and remove from the heat.

3. Combine the mashed potatoes, sautéed vegetables and the sour cream. Set aside to cool.

To assemble the knishes:

1. Pre-heat the oven to 190°C/375°F. Form the pastry into a rope and cut it in half. Roll out half the pastry to about 0.25cm (⅛-inch) thick on a floured surface. Cut out 5 discs of pastry 12.5cm (5 inches) in diameter. Repeat for the other half of the pastry.

2. Divide the cooled filling into 10, and place a portion of filling in the centre of each disc of pastry. Gather the edges of the pastry up over the filling to enclose it completely. Pinch the seams together until thoroughly sealed and smooth to form a sphere shape, then flatten the spheres slightly. You may need a few drops of water to help close the seal.

3. Place the sealed *knishes*, seam-side down, on a lightly buttered baking sheet. Bake for 35–40 minutes, or until they are golden brown. Serve warm or at room temperature with sour cream.

Party Pizzas

The following recipe produces six small 22.5cm
(9-inch) pizza bases. I have suggested a selection of
six different toppings, each one sufficient to cover
one small pizza. The dough recipe yields a not-too-
thick and not-too-thin crust that's slightly crisp on
the outside and tender on the inside.

DOUGH PREPARATION TIME: 15 minutes
DOUGH RISING TIME: 30 minutes
ROLLING AND TOPPING TIME: 10 minutes per pizza
BAKING TIME: 15–20 minutes
YIELD: six 22.5cm (9-inch) or three 30cm (12-inch)
pizzas

The pizza dough:

4½ teaspoons (22ml) dried yeast
3 teaspoons (15ml) sugar
1½ cups (375ml) warm water
4½ cups (1125ml) plain bread flour
3¼ teaspoons (16ml) salt
6 tablespoons (120ml) oil

The tomato sauce:

(This is sufficient for six small pizzas, although one
of the suggested toppings contains no tomato
sauce.)

3 tablespoons (60ml) olive oil
¾ teaspoon (3ml) yellow asafetida powder
4½ cups (1125ml) tomato purée
3 tablespoons (60ml) fresh basil leaves, chopped
3 tablespoons (60ml) tomato paste
1½ teaspoons (7ml) salt
2 teaspoons (10ml) sugar

The toppings:
Pizza 1: Margherita

3 tablespoons (60ml) tomato sauce
⅓ cup (85ml) fresh basil leaves, chopped
150g grated mozzarella cheese
extra olive oil

Pizza 2: Potato and Rosemary

200g new potatoes, sliced 0.5cm (⅛ inch)
3 tablespoons (60ml) olive oil
½ teaspoon (2ml) yellow asafetida powder
1½–2 teaspoons (7–10ml) fresh or dried rosemary leaves
salt and pepper

Pizza 3: Baby Spinach, Cottage Cheese, Tomato, Pine Nuts & Parmesan Cheese

2 teaspoons (10ml) butter
½ teaspoon (2ml) yellow asafetida powder
75g baby spinach
3 tablespoons (60ml) tomato sauce
150g cottage cheese, or fresh ricotta cheese
2 or 3 medium tomatoes, sliced thickly
2–3 tablespoons (40–60ml) toasted pine nuts
3 tablespoons (60ml) freshly-grated parmesan cheese
sprinkle dried basil

Pizza 4: Tricoloured Peppers, Cherry Tomatoes, Olives and Fresh Bocconcini

2 tablespoons (40ml) olive oil
½ teaspoon (2ml) yellow asafetida powder
3 tablespoons (60ml) tomato sauce
100g sliced red, yellow and green peppers (capsicum)

2–3 tablespoons (40–60ml) fresh basil leaves, chopped
150g bocconcini, sliced
100g halved cherry
tomatoes
handful kalamata olives
salt and pepper

Pizza 5: Fresh Fennel with Sundried Tomatoes and Fresh Oregano

2 tablespoons (40ml) olive oil
½ teaspoon (2ml) yellow asafetida powder
100g fresh fennel root, sliced against the grain into thin strips
3 tablespoons (60ml) tomato sauce
⅓ cup (85ml) sliced oil-packed sundried tomatoes
1–2 teaspoons (5–10ml) fresh oregano leaves
salt and pepper
sprinkle dried oregano
1 tablespoon (20ml) flavoured oil from the sundried tomatoes

Pizza 6: Artichoke Hearts, Sundried Tomatoes, Bocconcini, Rocket Pesto and Parmesan Cheese

3 tablespoons (60ml) tomato sauce
150g sliced bocconcini
200g oil-packed artichoke hearts, sliced
⅓ cup (85ml) chopped oil-packed sundried tomatoes

*2–3 tablespoons (40–60ml) rocket pesto
(see Hot Roasted Jacket-baked Pototoes with Angula Pesto)*

*2–3 tablespoons (40–60ml) freshly grated
parmesan cheese*

To prepare the pizza dough:

1. Combine the yeast, sugar and a few spoons of the warm water in a small bowl. Allow the mixture to stand in a warm place for 10 minutes, or until frothy. Sift the flour and salt into a bowl. Make a well in the centre and pour in the oil, the yeast mixture and the remaining water. Mix to form a firm dough, and knead the dough on a lightly floured surface for 8–10 minutes or until smooth and elastic. Place it in a lightly oiled bowl, cover the bowl with oiled plastic wrap, and leave in a warm place for 30 minutes or until doubled in size.

2. Punch down the dough with your fist, knead briefly, then divide into 6 pieces. Flatten the dough with your fingers and gently pull it into the required size, or use a rolling pin. Place the dough carefully on lightly oiled baking sheets, or pizza trays. Set the dough aside while you prepare your sauce and toppings.

To prepare the tomato sauce:

Place the olive oil in a 3-litre/quart saucepan over moderate heat. When fairly warm, sprinkle in the yellow asafetida powder and sauté momentarily. Add the remaining sauce ingredients, bring to the boil, reduce the heat, then simmer for 10 minutes or until the sauce is slightly reduced. Remove from the heat.

To prepare the toppings and assemble the pizzas:

Pizza 1

1. Spread the tomato sauce over the pizza base, leaving a little border uncovered. Sprinkle on half the basil leaves, the mozzarella cheese, and then the remaining basil leaves. Sprinkle with a little olive oil.

2. Bake in a pre-heated hot oven (220°C/430°F) for 15–20 minutes, or until the crust is golden brown.

Pizza 2

1. Boil the potato slices in lightly salted water for 5–10 minutes, or until just tender. Remove and drain.

2. Trickle the olive oil into a medium-sized frying pan over moderate heat. Sprinkle in the yellow asafetida powder and add the potato slices. Pan-fry the potatoes until golden brown and fully cooked.

3. Arrange the potato slices on the pizza base, sprinkle with the rosemary, salt and pepper, drizzle over the olive oil that remains in the pan and bake in the pre-heated hot oven as in the previous pizza recipe.

Pizza 3

1. Melt the butter over moderate heat in a medium-sized frying pan. Drop in the yellow asafetida powder and remove the pan from the heat. Add the spinach leaves, stirring them into the hot butter to slightly wilt them.

2. Spread the tomato sauce over the pizza base, leaving a little border uncovered. Cover with half the spinach leaves, half the cottage cheese, the remaining spinach, the remaining cottage cheese, then the tomato rings. Sprinkle with the pine nuts, drizzle with the butter in which you wilted the spinach, sprinkle with the parmesan cheese and the dried basil. Bake in the pre-heated hot oven as per *Pizza 1*.

Pizza 4

1. Pour the olive oil into a medium-sized frying pan over moderate heat. Sprinkle in the yellow asafetida powder, drop in the peppers and pan-fry them for 3 or 4 minutes, or until they are slightly wilted.

2. Spread the tomato sauce over the pizza base, leaving a little border uncovered. Arrange half the basil leaves, half the cheese and most of the sautéed peppers. Arrange the cherry tomatoes, the olives, the remaining cheese, basil and sautéed peppers, and sprinkle with salt and pepper. Bake in the pre-heated oven as per *Pizza 1*.

Pizza 5

1. Set the oil in a medium-sized frying pan over moderate heat. Sprinkle in the yellow asafetida powder and drop in the sliced fennel. Fry for 3 or 4 minutes or until the fennel is lightly golden on the edges.

2. Spread the tomato sauce over the pizza base, leaving a little border uncovered. Arrange the fennel, fresh oregano and the sundried tomatoes. Sprinkle with salt and pepper and the dried oregano. Drizzle with the sundried tomato oil. Bake in the pre-heated oven as per *Pizza 1*.

Pizza 6

Spread the tomato sauce over the pizza base leaving a little border uncovered. Arrange half the bocconcini, the artichoke hearts, sundried tomatoes, the remaining bocconcini, dabs of *pesto* and gratings of fresh parmesan cheese. Bake in the pre-heated oven as per *Pizza 1*.

SAVOURY FRESH CHEESE BALLS IN CREAMY TOMATO SAUCE (MALAI KOFTA)

Malai kofta is a rich and tasty addition to a special or formal dinner. The main ingredient is *panir*, or homemade curd cheese. Although cottage cheese, ricotta cheese or "farm" cheese appear similar to *panir*, they will not work as a substitute, because *panir* is the only cheese that can be successfully deep-fried.

PREPARATION AND COOKING TIME:
50–55 minutes
YIELD: 35–40 small *kofta* balls

The kofta balls:

curd cheese, panir, from 3 litres/quarts milk, hung or pressed for 1 hour (see Special Ingredients for manufacturing details)
1 tablespoon (20ml) flour
3 tablespoons (60ml) sultanas
3 tablespoons (60ml) slivered almonds
1 or 2 green chilies, seeded and chopped, about 2 teaspoons (10ml)
1 teaspoon (5ml) salt
¼ teaspoon (1ml) black pepper
½ cup (125ml) chopped fresh coriander leaves
ghee or oil for deep-frying

The malai sauce:

1 tablespoon (20ml) ghee
1 teaspoon (5ml) finely-minced fresh ginger
¼ teaspoon (1ml) yellow asafetida powder
4 cups (1 litre) tomato purée
1 teaspoon (5ml) salt
2 teaspoons (10ml) sugar
½ cup (125ml) evaporated milk
1 teaspoon (5ml) garam masala
3 tablespoons (60ml) chopped fresh coriander leaves

To make the kofta balls:

1. Knead the curd cheese thoroughly on a bench top until smooth and creamy. Better still, place it in a food processor and process until creamy smooth.

2. Add the flour, sultanas, almonds, chilies, salt, pepper and fresh coriander and knead or process until very smooth.

3. Roll the cheese mixture into 35–40 1.5cm (¾-inch) smooth balls. Heat the ghee or oil in a wide pan to a depth of 5cm (2 inches) over moderate heat. When the temperature reaches 160°C/320°F or a slight haze appears over the ghee, gently place in a quantity of cheese balls. Fry the balls gently, stirring with a slotted spoon to evenly cook them, for 5–7 minutes, or until they turn a rich, dark brown. Lift them out and drain them. Repeat for all the *kofta* balls.

To make the sauce and combine with the kofta:

1. Place 1 tablespoon (20ml) ghee in a wide mouthed 5-litre/quart saucepan and apply moderate heat. When the ghee is hot, add the ginger and stir for a few moments. Sprinkle in the yellow asafetida powder, stir momentarily, then add the tomato purée, salt and sugar. Bring the sauce to the boil, then reduce the heat and simmer for 2 or 3 minutes.

2. Mix in the *garam masala*, stir in the evaporated milk, then gently add the *kofta* balls. Simmer them gently in the sauce for 5–10 minutes. For optimum results, plan to serve the *kofta* balls within 30 minutes of soaking them in the sauce. Just before serving, sprinkle with the chopped, fresh coriander.

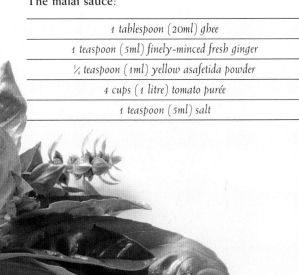

GRAINS, BEAN & PASTA DISHES

Fresh Polenta with Melted Butter and Parmesan Cheese
(Polenta Fresca al Burro e Parmigiano)

Mauritian-style Dal Rissoles (Gateaux-Piments) with Home-style Tomato Chutney

Fettucine Pasta with Tender Spring Vegetables (Pasta Primavera)

Chickpea Flour Dumplings in Creamy Karhi Sauce (Pakora Karhi)

Egyptian Broad Bean Croquettes with Tahini Sauce (Ta'ameya)

Pasta Ears with Fresh Rocket Leaves (Orecciette con Arugule)

Turkish Bulgur Wheat Pilaf (Bulgur pilavi)

Mexican Spicy Bean and Cheese Stuffed Flatbreads (Burras)

Cannelloni Stuffed with Garden Vegetables and Ricotta Cheese

Crispy Fried Gluten with Sweet and Sour Sauce

Savoury Chickpeas in Tomato Glaze

Curried Malay Noodles (Laksa)

Cashew Nut Curry

Spaghetti with Roasted Capsicums, Sunflower Seeds and Sundried Tomatoes

Rich and Tasty Lasagna with Grilled Vegetables and Sundried Tomatoes

Sago Pilaf (Sabudana Khichari)

Punjabi Red Bean Curry (Rajma)

Soft, Savoury Chickpea Swirls (Khandvi)

Pumpkin Dumplings with Sage-scented Butter and Parmesan Cheese
(Gnocchi di Zucca)

Sautéed Sprouted Mung Beans (Vadu)

FRESH POLENTA WITH MELTED BUTTER AND PARMESAN CHEESE (POLENTA FRESCA AL BURRO E PARMIGIANO)

Polenta, yellow cornmeal, is northern Italy's staple food. This hearty, ultra-simple dish is Italy's answer to mashed potatoes. Although *polenta* is easy to prepare, it is essential that you put aside 30–40 minutes of your time to stir the *polenta* to avoid sticking as it slowly cooks. Serve *Polenta Fresca* as a side dish or entrée.

PREPARATION AND COOKING TIME:
50 minutes
YIELD: enough for 4–6 persons

4 cups (1 litre) water
1 teaspoon (5ml) salt
1 cup (250ml) polenta
3 tablespoons (60ml) butter
freshly-ground black pepper
3 tablespoons (60ml) freshly-shaved parmesan cheese, or more if desired

1. Place the water and salt in your most heavy 2-litre/quart saucepan, preferably non-stick, over high heat. When the water boils, add the *polenta* in a slow and steady stream, stirring constantly with a wooden spoon or better still a wire whisk. Reduce the heat to low and simmer gently, scraping any grains down from the sides of the pan. Be careful because it may "spit". Stir, almost constantly, for 30–40 minutes, or until the graininess of the *polenta* has all but disappeared.

2. When ready, divide the *polenta* between 4 or 6 bowls, and serve hot, topped with knobs of butter, freshly-ground black pepper and generous shavings of parmesan cheese.

Note: For variety, warm 2 teaspoons (10ml) each of fresh herbs, such as thyme leaves, oregano leaves and rosemary sprigs in a little olive oil, and add them to the *polenta* just before serving.

MAURITIAN-STYLE DAL RISSOLES (GATEAUX-PIMENTS) WITH HOME-STYLE TOMATO CHUTNEY

When Indians first came to Mauritius, they brought with them their own traditional cuisine. *Gateaux-Piments* (literally "chili-cakes") are a good example of the strong Indian influence still existing in Mauritian cooking today. Sold by vendors on street corners all over the island, these crunchy savouries are wholesome and tasty. For a delicious combination, serve with fresh bread and the accompanying tomato sauce which, although not generally sold on the streets, would be served if preparing *Gateaux-Piments* at home.

SOAKING TIME: overnight
PREPARATION AND FRYING TIME:
about 45 minutes
YIELD: 25–30 patties

2 cups (500ml) chana dal, soaked overnight in 6 cups water
½ teaspoon (2ml) yellow asafetida powder
½ teaspoon (2ml) coriander powder
2 long green chilies, finely chopped
40 fresh curry leaves, torn
leaves from 1 small bunch of fresh coriander, finely chopped
2 teaspoons (10ml) salt
oil or ghee for deep-frying

1. Drain the soaked *dal* and place it in a food processor along with the yellow asafetida powder and coriander powder. Process the *dal*, adding a few teaspoons of cold water, to form a fairly smooth paste. Remove the blended mixture and place in a large bowl. Add the chopped chilies, curry leaves and fresh coriander leaves and combine well. Mix in the salt just before you are ready to start frying.

2. Heat ghee or oil to a depth of no less than 5cm (2 inches) in a large wok or pan over a moderately high heat. Take heaped table-spoons of the mixture and form them into balls. Carefully press them flat and make a slight depression in their centre with your finger. Continue forming the patties until all the mixture is used.

3. When the ghee or oil is hot, carefully lower in enough patties that will fry comfortably without overcrowding. They will initially fry while sitting on the bottom of the frying vessel. Do not attempt to dislodge them for at least 2 minutes. After about 4½ minutes, the patties will float to the surface of the oil. If they do stick on the bottom slightly, you can dislodge them easily with a slotted spoon after this time. Fry the patties on both sides until golden brown, about 7½ minutes total frying time. Continue to fry the *gateaux-piments* in batches until they are all cooked. Serve hot with *Home-style Tomato Chutney* (recipe follows).

HOME-STYLE TOMATO CHUTNEY

PREPARATION AND COOKING TIME: 15–20 minutes
YIELD: about 3 cups (750ml)

3 tablespoons (60ml) oil
2–3 hot green chilies, seeded and sliced lengthways
½ teaspoon (2ml) yellow asafetida powder
5 cups (1250ml) coarsely-chopped tomatoes, about 1kg
1–1½ teaspoons (5–7ml) salt
2 tablespoons (40ml) fresh coriander leaves

Place the oil over moderate heat in a 3-litre/quart saucepan or frying pan. When the oil is hot, drop in the chilies, and fry them until they start to blister. Sprinkle in the yellow asafetida powder, sauté momentarily, then drop in the chopped tomatoes. Cook the tomatoes, stirring occasionally for 15–20 minutes, or until they are broken down and soft. When the chutney is sufficiently thick and reduced, add the salt and fresh coriander leaves. Serve with the hot *Gateaux-Piments*.

Fettucine Pasta with Tender Spring Vegetables (Pasta Primavera)

In the *Bhagavad-gita*, Krishna says: "Of seasons I am flower-bearing spring." Spring is not only the time that sweet blossoms appear on the trees, but also when many new-season vegetables are at their optimum sweet tenderness.

This barely-seasoned, crisp and delicious pasta dish features fresh, young, spring vegetables cooked separately to preserve their individual delicate textures and colours.

PREPARATION AND COOKING TIME:
about 25 minutes
YIELD: enough for 4–6 persons

100g slender baby green beans
the tender parts of 12 young asparagus stalks, cut into 2.5cm (1-inch) lengths
1½ cups (375ml) broccoli, cut into tiny florets, about 100g
1 cup (250ml) zucchinis, sliced 0.5cm (¼ inch) on the diagonal
½ cup (125ml) fresh baby peas, a little under 100g, about 300g before shelling
1 cup (250ml) baby carrots, sliced thinly on the diagonal, about 100g
400g green fettucine noodles, or green tagliolini pasta
3 tablespoons (60ml) butter
300ml heavy cream
2 teaspoons (10ml) salt
¼–½ teaspoon (1–2ml) coarsely ground black pepper
¾ cup (185ml) freshly-grated parmesan cheese

1. Bring to the boil a few cups of lightly salted water in a 1- or 2-litre/quart saucepan. Cook each vegetable separately for a couple of minutes or until they are just tender. Be careful not to overcook them. Remove the vegetables with a slotted spoon and transfer them to a large bowl of cold water for a few minutes to preserve their colour and crispness.

2. Boil a 5-litre/quart saucepan of slightly salted water, and cook the pasta until it is just tender, *al dente*, according to the directions on the packet.

3. Meanwhile, melt the butter in a 3-litre/quart saucepan over low heat. Drain the vegetables well and stir them into the melted butter. Add the cream, salt and black pepper and warm over very gentle heat for a couple of minutes.

4. When the pasta is fully cooked, drain it, transfer it to a pre-warmed serving dish and toss it with the freshly grated parmesan cheese. Fold in the cream and vegetables and serve immediately.

CHICKPEA FLOUR DUMPLINGS IN CREAMY KARHI SAUCE (PAKORA KARHI)

Karhi is made from yogurt or buttermilk whisked with chickpea flour and simmered into a creamy gravy. The tartness of the yogurt greatly affects the flavour of *karhi*. Fresh, mild yogurt or buttermilk is recommended for a mellow flavoured sauce. If you like a tangier sauce, use a stronger flavoured yogurt. Whereas *karhi* dishes from western India tend to be soup-like with a hint of sweetness, this typical northern Indian *karhi* is a fairly thick, full-bodied sauce. The chickpea flour dumplings, commonly known as *pakoras*, are very simple to prepare and, soaked in the hot *karhi*, they make a classic and delicious combination. *Pakora Karhi* is always served with rice, and usually as a replacement for *dal* dishes.

PREPARATION AND BATTER RESTING TIME: 30–60 minutes
COOKING TIME: 30–40 minutes
YIELD: enough for 4–6 persons

The pakora dumplings:

⅔ cup (165ml) chickpea flour, measured after sifting
½ teaspoon (2ml) salt
½ teaspoon (2ml) cayenne pepper
½ teaspoon (2ml) yellow asafetida powder
¼ teaspoon (1ml) turmeric powder
about ⅓ cup (85ml) slightly warm water
¼ teaspoon (1ml) baking powder
ghee or oil for deep-frying

The karhi:

5 tablespoons (100ml) chickpea flour, measured after sifting
3 cups (750ml) water
2 cups (500ml) plain yogurt or buttermilk
½ teaspoon (2ml) turmeric powder
2 teaspoons (10ml) salt

The seasoning:

2 tablespoons (40ml) ghee
1½ teaspoons (7ml) cumin seeds
one 2.5cm (1-inch) cinnamon stick
6 whole black peppercorns
4 whole cloves
2 or 3 whole dried red chilies or as desired
8–10 fresh curry leaves
½ teaspoon (2ml) yellow asafetida powder
3 tablespoons (60ml) chopped fresh coriander leaves

To prepare the pakora dumplings:

1. Whisk together the chickpea flour, salt, cayenne, yellow asafetida powder and turmeric in a 2-litre/quart bowl. Gradually whisk in sufficient water to make a smooth, light batter, the consistency of medium thick cream. Set aside to rest and thicken for 30 minutes.

2. Pour enough ghee or oil into a 17.5 or 20cm (7- or 8-inch) wide frying pan to fill to a depth of 1.5cm (¾ inch). Place the pan over moderate heat. Meanwhile, whisk the baking powder into the batter.

3. When the oil is hot but not smoking, scoop up scant teaspoonfuls of batter and drop them into the hot oil. Cook no more than 12 at a time. As the spoons of batter hit the oil, they should immediately begin to swell into round, puff-like *pakora* dumplings. Fry the *pakoras*, stirring often with a slotted spoon, for about 5 minutes or until they are evenly crisp and golden. Remove and drain on paper towels. Repeat the procedure until all the *pakoras* are fried.

To prepare the karhi:

1. In a 2-litre/quart bowl, whisk together the 5 tablespoons (100ml) chickpea flour with ¼ cup (60ml) water to form a paste-like batter. Whisk in the remaining water, yogurt, turmeric and salt until smooth and creamy. Set aside near the stove.

2. Place a 3-litre/quart saucepan over moderate heat. Melt the ghee and when quite warm drop in the cumin seeds, cinnamon stick, peppercorns, cloves and whole dried, red chilies. Swirl the pan, allowing the spices to darken a few shades. Tear the curry leaves into pieces and drop them into the sautéing spices, along with the yellow asafetida powder. When the curry leaves crackle and darken, pour the *karhi* mixture into the

spices. Stir to mix, and add half the fresh coriander leaves.

3. While stirring constantly with a wooden spoon, bring the sauce to a gentle boil, and then reduce the heat to low. Simmer the sauce for 20 minutes, stirring frequently, until it thickens to a light, custard-like consistency. Add the chickpea flour dumplings and remaining coriander leaves. Stir, cover, and remove from the heat. Allow the dumplings to soak for a few minutes, then serve piping hot.

EGYPTIAN BROAD BEAN CROQUETTES WITH TAHINI SAUCE (TA'AMEYA)

This is my version of the spicy bean croquettes, made from dried broad beans, called *ful nabed*, that are a national dish of Egypt. The Egyptians say that the recipe was "imported" to Israel, where they became *falafel*. Dried broad beans are available at Middle Eastern grocery shops. Plan ahead when making *Ta'ameya*, since you will have to soak the beans for two days before cooking them. Don't forget to change the water often, especially when the weather is warm. *Ta'ameya* are delicious served with hot *pita* breads, dressed with the tahini sauce and accompanied with a green salad.

BEAN SOAKING TIME: 2 days (if using whole beans)
PREPARATION TIME: about 20 minutes
RESTING TIME: 50 minutes
COOKING TIME: about 5 minutes per batch
YIELD: 25–30 croquettes

2 cups (500ml) dried broad beans, (ful nabed)
½ cup (125ml) chopped fresh continental parsley
1 teaspoon (5ml) yellow asafetida powder
3 tablespoons (60ml) chopped fresh coriander leaves
1½ teaspoons (7ml) salt

½ teaspoon (2ml) freshly-ground black pepper
¼ teaspoon (1ml) cayenne pepper
¼ teaspoon (1ml) bicarbonate of soda
about ⅓ cup (85ml) of sesame seeds
oil for deep-frying

1. Soak the beans in a large bowl of cold water in a cool place for 2 days. Change the water 2 or 3 times.

2. Drain the beans and remove their tough skins by pressing each one between your fingers. The beans should pop out. For the ones that don't pop open, peel back some skin, then squeeze.

3. Place all the ingredients, except the sesame seeds and oil, in a food processor, and blend until well mixed. Scrape the mixture into a bowl and knead it until smooth. Allow the mixture to rest for 30 minutes.

4. Divide the mixture into heaped tablespoon mounds. Form each mound into a thick patty about 3.75cm (1½inch) diameter. Place the sesame seeds on a plate and press both sides of the patty onto the seeds and then place them on a tray. Leave the patties for 20 minutes.

5. Fill a heavy pan or wok with oil to a depth of 6.5–7.5 cm (2½–3 inches). Heat the oil to 180°C/355°F, lower in 6–8 croquettes and deep-fry them, turning when required, for 5 or 6 minutes, or until they are evenly golden brown. Drain the croquettes on paper towels. Repeat the procedure until all the croquettes are cooked. Serve hot, warm, or at room temperature with *Tahini Sauce* (recipe follows).

TAHINI SAUCE

¾ cup (185ml) tahini

4 tablespoons (80ml) lemon juice

¼ teaspoon (1ml) yellow asafetida powder

1 teaspoon (5ml) salt

½ cup (125ml) water, or more for a thinner sauce

½ teaspoon (2ml) cumin powder

¼ teaspoon (1ml) cayenne pepper (optional)

½ cup (125ml) finely-chopped parsley

Place the tahini in a bowl and beat in the lemon juice, yellow asafetida powder and salt. The mixture will become very thick. Gradually whisk in the water until the sauce is a smooth creamy consistency. Add more water as desired. Fold in the cumin, the optional cayenne and the chopped parsley.
Serve with the *Ta'ameya*.

PASTA EARS WITH FRESH ROCKET LEAVES (ORECCIETTE CON ARUGULE)

Orecciette, or "little ears", are a disc-shaped pasta with an indentation, perfect for holding sauce. The ears are made by hand and are unique to southern Italy's fertile Puglia region, an area famous for the excellence and variety of its green vegetables. In this recipe, fresh rocket leaves with their brisk, semi-bitter flavour are combined with the pasta ears in a flavoursome, chili-laced, fresh tomato sauce.

Orecciette are available from good quality Mediterranean produce stores or specialty shops. If unavailable, substitute *conchiglie, penne* or *rigatoni*. Serve *Orecciette con Arugule* hot with crusty bread for a heart-warming meal.

PREPARATION AND COOKING TIME: 35–40 minutes
YIELD: enough for 4–6 persons

500g orecciette pasta

2 tablespoons (40ml) olive oil

2 medium-sized red chilies, seeded and sliced into fine, thin strips

½ teaspoon (2ml) yellow asafetida powder

10–12 juicy large, ripe Roma tomatoes, blanched,
peeled and chopped

1 tablespoon (20ml) tomato paste

1½ teaspoons (7ml) salt

1 teaspoon (5ml) sugar

100g fresh rocket leaves, washed, trimmed and stalks removed

shavings of parmesan cheese

1. Boil the pasta according to directions on the packet in plenty of salted water until *al dente*.

2. Meanwhile, warm the olive oil in a 2-litre/quart saucepan over moderate heat. Drop in the chilies and sauté them for 1–2 minutes or until softened. Sprinkle in the yellow asafetida powder, stir momentarily, add the tomatoes, tomato paste, salt and sugar. Increase the heat and, stirring occasionally, cook for 10–15 minutes or until reduced and saucy.

3. When the pasta is cooked and drained, remove the sauce from the heat. Fold in the fresh rocket leaves. Toss the sauce through the pasta and serve hot, topped with shavings of fresh parmesan cheese.

TURKISH BULGUR WHEAT PILAF (BULGUR PILAVI)

Bulgur wheat is a grain product made by par-boiling and drying whole wheat kernels and crushing them into various sizes. It has a chewy texture, a pleasant nutty taste and is rich in protein, calcium, phosphorus and iron. In this hearty and warming dish, *bulgur* wheat is cooked like rice in a buttery vegetable stock with green capsicum and tomatoes. *Bulgur* wheat is available at health food stores, super-markets and Middle Eastern grocers.

PREPARATION AND COOKING TIME:
30–40 minutes
YIELD: enough for 4–6 persons

4 tablespoons (80ml) butter
½ teaspoon (2ml) yellow asafetida powder
1½ cups (375ml) diced green capsicum (peppers)
¾ cup (185ml) peeled chopped tomatoes
2¼ cups (560ml) vegetable stock
1 teaspoon (5ml) salt
1½ cups (375ml) coarse bulgur wheat

1. Melt the butter in a heavy, non-stick 2-litre/quart saucepan over moderate heat. Sprinkle in the yellow asafetida powder, sauté momentarily, then add the green peppers and tomatoes. Cook the vegetables for 10 minutes or until the tomatoes break down and soften.

2. Add the vegetable stock and salt, raise the heat and bring to the boil. Stir in the *bulgur*, return to the boil and, stirring, allow it to boil for 1 more minute. Reduce the heat to low and simmer with a tight-fitting lid for 5–10 minutes or until all the liquid has been absorbed. Place the saucepan, still covered, on a heat diffuser or some other warm surface, or place it in a warm oven wrapped in a towel for another 15–20 minutes or until the grains are fluffy, fully expanded and firm. Serve hot.

MEXICAN SPICY BEAN AND CHEESE STUFFED FLATBREADS (BURRAS)

Burras, (called *burritos* in the US) are the *tacos* of north-western Mexico, but are made with wheat flour *tortillas* instead of the traditional corn variety. In this delectable recipe, they are filled with spicy refried beans (*frijoles refritos*), cheese, shredded lettuce, sour cream and spicy Mexican tomato sauce, then rolled and served with extra sour cream and tomato sauce. This recipe yields chili-hot *burras* — reduce the chili powder for a milder result.

BEAN SOAKING AND BOILING TIME:
about 2 hours
SAUCE PREPARATION TIME: about 15 minutes
BEAN FRYING TIME: 15 minutes
BURRA ASSEMBLY TIME: about 30 minutes
YIELD: 8 burras

The beans:

1½ cups (375ml) dry beans, such as pinto, black turtle beans or red kidney beans
7–8 cups (1750ml–2 litres) water
2 tablespoons (40ml) butter
½ teaspoon (2ml) yellow asafetida powder
3 teaspoons (15ml) chili powder
1½ teaspoons (7ml) cumin powder

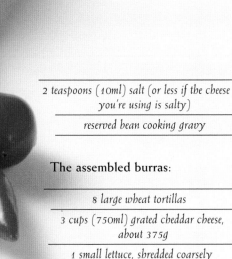

2 teaspoons (10ml) salt (or less if the cheese
you're using is salty)

reserved bean cooking gravy

The assembled burras:

8 large wheat tortillas

3 cups (750ml) grated cheddar cheese,
about 375g

1 small lettuce, shredded coarsely

1 cup (250ml) sour light cream, or crème fraîche

1 quantity Mexican hot tomato sauce (see recipe below)

To prepare the beans:

1. Pick out any stones or foreign matter from the
   beans. Rinse the beans twice in cold water and
   drain them. Place the beans and about 8 cups
   (2 litres) water in a 3- or 4-litre/quart saucepan.
   Bring to the boil over high heat, boil for 1
   minute, then turn off the heat, cover tightly and
   leave for 1 hour.

2. Bring the beans back to the boil over high heat.
   Reduce the heat and simmer the beans, covered,
   for about one hour, or until the beans are
   tender. (Exact cooking time will depend on the
   type of beans you use.) Drain the beans, being
   careful to reserve the entire bean cooking liquid
   — you'll need it later.

To "re-fry" the beans:

1. Set a large, heavy frying pan or 4-litre/quart
   saucepan over medium heat. Melt the butter,
   sprinkle in the yellow asafetida powder, sauté
   momentarily and add a cup of the beans and a
   little bean liquid. Add the chili powder, cumin
   powder and salt. Stir to mix, increase the heat
   to fairly high, and partially mash the beans with
   a masher — I prefer not to purée them — the
   chunky bits add more character.

2. Continue to add more beans and liquid,
   coarsely mashing the beans and simultaneously
   frying and scraping the sides and bottom of the

pan to prevent sticking until all beans are incorporated. Cook until the beans are a thick paste
and you can see the bottom of the pan as you
stir. Remove the *frijoles refritos* from the heat, fold
in 1 cup (250ml) grated cheese, stir to mix well,
cover the pan and set it aside.

To assemble the burras:

1. If the wheat tortillas are pre-cooked, place them
   in a pre-heated fairly hot oven and warm them
   through. Otherwise, bake according to instruc-
   tions.

2. Place about ⅓ cup (85ml) cooked beans on the
   tortilla. Cover with 1–2 tablespoons (20–40ml)
   cheese, a sprinkle of lettuce, a tablespoon of
   sour cream and a couple of teaspoons of hot
   sauce (recipe follows). Fold up the bottom of
   the *tortilla*, then fold in the two sides.

3. Serve *burras* warm with extra sour cream and
   tomato sauce on the side.

MEXICAN HOT TOMATO SAUCE

PREPARATION AND COOKING TIME:
about 10 minutes
YIELD: makes about 1 cup (250ml)

1 tablespoon (20ml) olive oil

1 teaspoon (5ml) minced green chilies

½ teaspoon (2ml) yellow asafetida powder

1 cup (250ml) tomato purée

1 teaspoon (5ml) chili powder

1 teaspoon (5ml) lemon juice

½ teaspoon (2ml) salt

½ teaspoon (2ml) raw sugar

Heat the olive oil in a 2-litre/quart saucepan over
moderate heat. Add the green chilies and sauté for
1 minute. Sprinkle in the yellow asafetida powder
and sauté momentarily. Add the tomato purée,
chili powder and lemon juice, stir to mix and
simmer, uncovered, for 5–10 minutes, or until the
sauce is slightly thickened. Add the salt and sugar,
and remove from the heat.

CANNELLONI STUFFED WITH GARDEN VEGETABLES AND RICOTTA CHEESE

Homemade curd cheese (*panir*) can be successfully used instead of the ricotta cheese in this home-style pasta dish. For something a little different, try using giant pasta shells instead of *cannelloni* pasta tubes.

PREPARATION AND COOKING TIME: about 2 hours
YIELD: enough for 6 persons

The tomato sauce:

4 tablespoons (80ml) olive oil
2 bay leaves
3 tablespoons (60ml) fresh basil leaves, chopped
1 teaspoon (5ml) fresh thyme leaves
¼ teaspoon (1ml) fresh sage leaves, chopped
4 cups (1 litre) tomato purée
½ teaspoon (2ml) salt
½ teaspoon (2ml) dried oregano
1 teaspoon (5ml) raw sugar

The bechamel sauce:

¼ cup (60ml) butter
¼ cup (60ml) plain flour
2 cups (500ml) milk
⅛ teaspoon (0.5ml) nutmeg powder
1 teaspoon (5ml) salt
¼ teaspoon (1ml) black pepper
4 tablespoons (80ml) parmesan cheese

The filling:

1 tablespoon (20ml) olive oil
½ teaspoon (2ml) yellow asafetida powder
1 cup (250ml) cooked corn kernels
1 cup (250ml) carrots, diced small and steamed until soft
1 cup (250ml) cooked green peas
2⅔ cups (665ml) firm ricotta cheese, about 700g
1 teaspoon (5ml) salt
¼ teaspoon (1ml) freshly-ground black pepper
2 tablespoons (40ml) parmesan cheese

The pasta:

twenty-four 10cm (4-inch) tubes instant cannelloni

To prepare the tomato sauce:

Heat 4 tablespoons (80ml) olive oil in a 3-litre/quart saucepan over moderate heat. Add the bay leaves and sauté them in the oil for a few seconds. Add the fresh basil, thyme and sage leaves, sauté briefly, then add the tomato purée, salt, dried oregano and sugar. Mix well, bring the sauce to the boil then reduce the heat and simmer for 5 minutes, or until the sauce is slightly reduced.

To prepare the bechamel sauce:

Melt the butter in a 2-litre/quart saucepan, stir in the flour and cook over gentle heat for 2 minutes. Gradually add the milk, bringing the sauce to the boil while stirring the mixture constantly with a wire whisk. Let the mixture bubble gently for 2 minutes. Remove from the heat and whisk in the nutmeg, salt and pepper, and half the parmesan cheese.

To prepare the filling:

1. Heat the olive oil in a 3-litre/quart saucepan over low heat. When the oil is warm, sprinkle in the yellow asafetida powder. Stir momentarily, and add the cooked corn, carrots and peas. Increase the heat to moderate and sauté the vegetables for 2 or 3 minutes.

2. Remove the saucepan from the heat and fold in the ricotta cheese, salt, pepper and parmesan cheese.

To assemble the dish:

1. Pre-heat the oven to 220°C/430°F.

2. Carefully stuff all the *cannelloni* tubes with the filling. Spread half the tomato sauce on the bottom of a 25cm x 35cm (10-inch x 14-inch) casserole dish or deep baking tray. Arrange the stuffed *cannelloni* on top of the sauce. Pour the rest of the tomato sauce on top of the *cannelloni*. Carefully pour and spread the *bechamel* sauce on top, and sprinkle with the remaining cheese.

3. Bake for 40–45 minutes, or until the *cannelloni* tubes are cooked and soft enough to be easily pierced with a knife. Serve hot.

CRISPY FRIED GLUTEN WITH SWEET AND SOUR SAUCE

Because of the versatile "pseudo-meat" quality of gluten, this dish tastes, feels and looks quite a lot like *Sweet and Sour Pork*. It combines beautifully with hot, plain rice and can be appropriately served as part of an Asian-style banquet.

PREPARATION AND COOKING TIME:
about 1–1½ hours
YIELD: enough for 4–6 persons

The fried gluten:

400g raw gluten, made from 1 heaped cup (250ml) gluten flour (see Special Ingredients section for method)
1 cup (250ml) plain flour
1 cup (250ml) cold water
1 tablespoon (20ml) peanut oil
oil for deep-frying

The marinade:

1 tablespoon (20ml) soy sauce
¼ teaspoon (1ml) freshly-ground black pepper
½ teaspoon (2ml) salt
¼ teaspoon (1ml) Chinese five-spice powder

The sweet and sour sauce:

1 tablespoon (20ml) soy sauce
3 tablespoons (60ml) tomato purée
2 tablespoons (40ml) lemon juice or vinegar
2 tablespoons (40ml) sugar
¾ cup (185ml) water
1 tablespoon (20ml) cornflour
1 tablespoon (20ml) water
2 tablespoons (40ml) oil
¾ teaspoon (3ml) minced fresh ginger
½ teaspoon (2ml) yellow asafetida powder
½ cup (125ml) water chestnuts
1 medium-sized red capsicum (peppers), diced into 1.25cm (½-inch) cubes, about ¾ cup (185ml)
1 cup (250ml) pineapple pieces
½ cup (125ml) cooked green peas

To prepare the gluten:

1. Cut the raw gluten into 1.25cm (½-inch) chunks. Drop the pieces into a large saucepan of lightly salted boiling water, and boil vigorously for 30 minutes. Drain the gluten in a colander and when a little cool, squeeze the gluten pieces to extract as much hot water as possible.

2. Combine the marinade ingredients in a medium-sized bowl. Drop in the gluten pieces, combine well and set the bowl aside for 10 minutes.

3. Whisk the plain flour and cold water together to form a smooth batter. Add 1 tablespoon (20ml) oil and whisk again. Set the batter aside for 10 minutes.

To fry the gluten:

1. Heat the deep-frying oil in a wok or deep-frying vessel over fairly high heat. When the oil is hot, dip a few gluten pieces into the batter and lower them into the oil. Fry them, turning occasionally, until the chunks of gluten are an even light golden brown, and crisp. Remove them and drain them in a colander lined with paper towels.

2. Repeat for all the gluten pieces. Don't remove the oil from the stove — the fried gluten will be refried one more time a little later.

To prepare the sauce and complete the dish:

1. Combine the soy sauce, tomato purée, lemon juice, sugar and water in a small bowl. In another small bowl, mix together the cornflour and 1 tablespoon (20ml) cold water. Reheat the deep-frying oil.

2. Warm the 2 tablespoons (40ml) oil in a 5-litre/quart saucepan over moderate heat. When the oil is hot, add the ginger, sauté it for 1 minute, sprinkle in the yellow asafetida powder, stir briefly, then add the water chestnuts and the capsicum pieces. Increase the heat and stir-fry them for 1 or 2 minutes, or until the capsicum pieces are a little softened. Add the pineapple pieces, raise the heat and cook for another 2 minutes, or until the pineapple is soft.

3. Add the cooked green peas, pour in the soy sauce, tomato, lemon, sugar and water combination. Allow the mixture to return to the boil, add the cornflour and the water mixture, and, stirring, cook for 1 or 2 more minutes, or until the mixture thickens. Keep the sauce on a low heat.

4. Re-heat the deep-frying oil. When hot, carefully drop the fried gluten pieces back into the hot oil, and re-fry them for 30 seconds to crisp them. Remove and drain the gluten pieces, place them in a serving dish, pour over the boiling hot sauce and serve the dish immediately.

SAVOURY CHICKPEAS IN TOMATO GLAZE

Chickpeas are rich in good quality vegetable protein — 100g cooked chickpeas contain 20g protein. Chickpeas provide nearly double the amount of iron and more vitamin C than most legumes. They are an important item in a vegetarian's diet, since they help promote muscle building and body growth.

These savoury, butter-soft chickpeas coated with spiced tomato glaze are substantial and delicious. Serve them with fresh wheat breads such as *Super-flaky Wholemeal Griddle-fried Breads*, *Puffed Fried Sesame Breads* or rice for a warm breakfast, brunch or dinner.

CHICKPEA SOAKING TIME:
8 hours or overnight
PREPARATION TIME: 10 minutes
COOKING TIME: 1 hour
YIELD: enough for 4–6 persons

1¼ cups (310ml) dried chickpeas
4–5 cups (1–1.25 litres) water
3 tablespoons (60ml) olive oil or ghee
½ teaspoon (2ml) mustard seeds
1½ teaspoons (7ml) cumin seeds
1½ teaspoons (7ml) minced fresh ginger
1½ teaspoons (7ml) fresh green chilies, seeded and chopped
10 fresh curry leaves
1¾ cups (435ml) ripe, finely-chopped tomatoes, about 5 medium tomotoes
1 teaspoon (5ml) turmeric
¼ cup (60ml) chopped fresh coriander leaves
1½ teaspoons (7ml) chat masala
½ teaspoon (2ml) garam masala
1¼ teaspoons (6ml) salt
1 tablespoon (20ml) butter

1. Place the chickpeas in a large bowl and cover them with 5 or 6 cups (1.25 – 1.5 litres) water. Leave to soak for 8 hours or overnight.

2. Pour the chickpeas into a colander and drain them. Place them in a 3-litre/quart saucepan over high heat with 4 or 5 cups of water and a dab of oil or ghee. Bring the water to the boil, reduce the heat to low and cook for 1 hour or until the chickpeas are butter-soft, but not broken down.

3. Meanwhile, in a 2-litre/quart saucepan, prepare the tomato glaze as follows: Warm the oil or ghee over moderate heat. When fairly hot but not smoking, drop in the mustard seeds. When they crackle and turn greyish, add the cumin. As the cumin darkens a few shades, drop in the ginger, chilies and curry leaves. Stir-fry the spices for 1 or 2 minutes or until the spices are fragrant. Add the chopped tomatoes, turmeric, half the fresh coriander, the *chat masala* and the *garam masala*. Cook, stirring occasionally for 5–7 minutes, or until the ghee or oil oozes out and the tomatoes are broken down and saucy.

4. Drain the chickpeas, reserving the cooking water. Stir the chickpeas into the sauce, reduce the heat to low and cook for another 10 minutes more, adding a little chickpea cooking liquid, if required, to keep the chickpeas moist.

5. Remove the savoury glazed chickpeas from the heat, add the remaining butter, salt, and the rest of the herbs. Serve hot with wedges of lemon or lime and the breads and accompaniments suggested above.

Curried Malay Noodles (Laksa)

Laksa is a taste sensation — a delicious one-pot soupy combination of mild, chili-hot, rich, aromatic and delicate flavours, and a tantalising combination of crunchy, soft and milky textures. There are many versions of *laksa* served throughout the Malaysian peninsula. This is my hearty vegetarian version.

An essential ingredient for the authentic *laksa* taste is a fresh herb known as *daun laksa* or *daun kesom* — literally *laksa* leaf. It is available from Malaysian food suppliers. It is also available from Vietnamese providores where it is known as *rau ram*, or Vietnamese mint. Although it is not a true mint, it is sold as a popular Vietnamese salad herb.

PREPARATION AND COOKING TIME: 50–60 minutes
YIELD: enough for 6–8 persons

The curry:

2½ tablespoons (50ml) dried tamarind, soaked in 1 cup (250ml) hot water
1 cup (250ml) stringless beans or snake beans cut into 2.5cm (1-inch) lengths
oil for deep-frying
400g tofu, cut into 1.5cm (½-inch) cubes
2 or 3 small thin eggplants, bias cut into 0.5cm (¼-inch) rings
1 tablespoon (20ml) cumin seeds
1 tablespoon (20ml) coriander seeds
5 or 6 large dried red chilies
3 tablespoons (60ml) oil
one 5cm (2-inch) cube fresh peeled ginger, shredded
one 2.5cm (1-inch) cube fresh peeled galangal, shredded
finely sliced white inner stems of 2 or 3 stalks of lemon grass
1½ teaspoons (7ml) yellow asafetida powder
1 teaspoon (5ml) turmeric
5–6 medium tomatoes, peeled and chopped
1 tablespoon (20ml) Malay curry powder
1 teaspoon (5ml) freshly-ground black pepper
2 cups (500ml) potatoes cut into 1.5cm (¼-inch) cubes
1½ cups (375ml) carrots, bias cut into 0.5cm (¼-inch) rings
2 cups (500ml) rich vegetable stock
2–3 tablespoons (40–60ml) palm sugar
2 teaspoons (10ml) salt
4 cups (1 litre) thick coconut milk

The noodles:

1kg fresh rice noodles, or 350g dried rice vermicelli

The garnish:

2 cups (500ml) bean sprouts
2 small seedless green cucumbers, unpeeled, cut into matchstick strips
1 small bunch laksa leaves, finely shredded
coarsely-ground black pepper
2 pink ginger flowers, shredded (if available)
lime wedges
sambal oelek , hot chili paste (optional)

To prepare the curry:

1. Squeeze and strain the soaking tamarind, discarding the seeds and fibres. Set aside the purée.

2. Place the beans and a little water in a small saucepan and steam the beans for 10 minutes or until tender. Drain and set the beans aside.

3. Heat the deep-frying oil in a heavy pan or wok over high heat. When the oil is very hot, add the tofu cubes, a few batches at a time, and deep-fry them until they are dark golden brown.

Remove and drain the tofu on absorbent paper towels. Deep-fry the eggplants in the same hot oil until tender. Drain them and set them aside.

4. Sprinkle the cumin seeds, coriander seeds and dried chilies in a small saucepan or non-stick frying pan over moderately low heat. Dry roast the spices for 5 minutes or until fragrant and slightly dark. Place the spices in a spice mill or coffee grinder and grind them to a powder. Set the powder aside.

5. Pour 3 tablespoons (60ml) oil in a 5-litre/quart heavy-based saucepan over moderate heat. When hot, add the shredded ginger and *galangal*. Fry for 2–3 minutes or until opaque and fragrant. Add the sliced lemon grass, fry for another minute, or until fragrant. Sprinkle in the yellow asafetida powder, and the turmeric, fry momentarily, then add the tomatoes. Stirring occasionally, cook the tomatoes for 5–10 minutes, or until they are soft and broken down, and the oil is visible.

6. Add the dry-roasted spices, the curry powder, black pepper, potato, carrot and vegetable stock. Stir to combine. Cover with the lid, bring to the boil, reduce the heat, and simmer for 5–10 minutes, or until the vegetables are tender.

7. While the curry is cooking, cook the noodles briefly in lightly salted boiling water, or according to directions. Drain and keep hot.

8. Add the tamarind purée to the simmering curry, then add the cooked beans, the sugar, salt, fried tofu, and the coconut milk. Allow the mixture to almost come to the boil, add the fried eggplant, stir through gently, and remove the saucepan from the heat.

To assemble the laksa curry:

Scoop a large handful of hot noodles into each individual pre-warmed serving bowl. Ladle on the curry. Garnish with bean sprouts, cucumber, shredded *laksa* leaves, black pepper and shredded ginger flowers. Serve with wedges of lime and optional *sambal oelek*.

CASHEW NUT CURRY

Cashew nuts, slowly simmered in a coconut milk sauce are one of the more well-known and exotic dishes from the Simhalese cuisine of Sri Lanka. The dish is traditionally prepared using freshly picked cashew nuts. Raw cashews, soaked in hot water are an excellent substitute. Here is my version.

CASHEW SOAKING TIME: 6 hours or overnight
PREPARATION AND COOKING TIME: 45–50 minutes
YIELD: enough for 4–6 persons

250g whole raw cashew nuts
1 tablespoon (20ml) ghee
one 7.5cm (3-inch) cinnamon stick
3 small green chilies, seeded and julienned
20 curry leaves
two 15cm (6-inch) lemon grass stalks, bruised
1½ teaspoons (7ml) grated fresh ginger
¼ teaspoon (3ml) yellow asafetida powder
3 cups (750ml) thin coconut milk
½ teaspoon (2ml) turmeric
1½ teaspoons (7ml) salt
one 15cm (6-inch) strip of fresh or frozen pandan leaf
1 cup (250ml) thick coconut milk

1. Place the raw cashew nuts in a bowl, and cover with plenty of cold water. Leave for at least 6 hours or overnight.
2. Set the ghee or oil in a 3- or 4-litre/quart saucepan over moderate heat. When the oil is hot, drop in the cinnamon stick and sauté it for 1 or 2 minutes, or until it turns a few shades darker and emanates a fragrant smell. Sprinkle in the slivered chilies, curry leaves, the lemon grass stalks and the grated ginger. Sauté for 1 or 2 minutes, or until fragrant. Add the yellow asafetida powder, stir momentarily, then add the thin coconut milk. Add the turmeric, salt and *pandan* leaf. Stirring, bring the sauce to a boil, reduce the heat and simmer uncovered for 10–15 minutes.
3. Drain the cashew nuts, add them to the sauce, and simmer uncovered for another 30 minutes, or until the cashew nuts are tender.
4. Stir in the thick coconut milk, heat through until almost boiling and remove the saucepan from the heat. Take out the cinnamon stick and lemon grass stalks and serve hot with rice.

SPAGHETTI WITH ROASTED CAPSICUMS, SUNFLOWER SEEDS AND SUNDRIED TOMATOES

The flowers of the gigantic, glorious yellow sunflowers that always keep their face towards the sun yield a tightly-packed core of edible seeds. These sunflower seeds can be used to enrich any meal with both flavour and nutrition. They are well above average in protein, phosphorus and iron, and are very rich sources of B-complex vitamins.

Sunflower seeds are great sprinkled over cereals, salads, yogurt dishes and soups; they can be mixed with vegetables and can be used like chopped nuts on desserts, or as a snack food. I discovered quite by accident one day that nutty-tasting toasted sunflower seeds are great in pasta, and serve as a contrast to the flavours and textures of roasted capsicums (peppers) and sundried tomatoes. Any type of pasta can be substituted for the spaghetti.

PREPARATION AND COOKING TIME:
about 45 minutes
YIELD: enough for 4 persons

---

2 large red capsicums (peppers), seeds and membranes removed, and cut into four lengthwise

---

1 tablespoon (20ml) olive oil

¼ cup (60ml) sunflower seeds

½ teaspoon (2ml) yellow asafetida powder

---

2 tablespoons (40ml) oil from the sundried tomatoes

---

3 cups (750ml) tomato purée

¼ cup (60ml) drained, sundried tomatoes (the oil-packed variety, sliced)

1½ teaspoons (7ml) salt

¼ teaspoon (1ml) freshly-ground black pepper

1–2 teaspoons (5–10ml) sugar

½ cup (125ml) packed, fresh basil leaves, chopped

500g spaghetti

---

parmesan cheese

---

extra basil leaves for garnish

---

1. Roast the capsicums under a hot griller for 10 minutes, or until their skins are charred and blistered. Remove them and place them in a plastic bag, tie the bag and leave aside for 10 minutes.

2. Remove the capsicums and slide off the skins while rinsing them under cold, running water. Slice the capsicums lengthwise into long 0.5cm (¼-inch) wide strips and set aside.

3. Set a 2-litre/quart saucepan over moderate heat. Pour in the oil, and when hot add the sunflower seeds. Sauté them carefully until they toast and darken to an even, dark-golden brown. Remove a few seeds from the pan and set them aside for garnish. Sprinkle in the yellow asafetida powder, swirl the pan momentarily, and add the sliced capsicum. Stir briefly, add the sundried tomato oil, the tomato purée, the sundried tomato slices, the salt, pepper, sugar and the basil leaves. Allow the mixture to come to the boil and, still over moderate heat and stirring when required, cook the sauce for 10–15 minutes, or until reduced and a little thickened.

4. While the sauce is cooking, plunge the pasta into a large saucepan of lightly salted water, and cook until *al dente.*

5. Combine the cooked pasta with the sauce, and serve hot, sprinkled with the parmesan cheese, garnished with the extra chopped fresh basil leaves and the reserved toasted sunflower seeds.

RICH AND TASTY LASAGNA WITH GRILLED VEGETABLES AND SUNDRIED TOMATOES

I allowed my imagination to run wild when I mentally constructed this multi-layered, deep-dish lasagna before embarking on my test kitchen procedures. You may like to substitute different vegetables in some of the layers. Thin slices of butternut pumpkin can be successfully grilled and added, as can slices of zucchini. Select a casserole dish 25cm x 35cm x 8cm (10-inches x 14-inches x 3½-inches) deep for this "Queen of Lasagna".

PREPARATION AND COOKING TIME:
1 hour 40 minutes to 1 hour 50 minutes
YIELD: 1 deep-dish of lasagna

The vegetables:

1 large eggplant (about 400g), sliced into 0.5cm (¼-inch) rings
3 large red capsicums (peppers), about 500g, cut into quarters lengthwise, cored and de-veined
the leaves from ½ bunch English spinach (about 250g), stalks removed
½ cup (125ml) sundried tomatoes, about 100g, sliced into strips

The tomato sauce:

¼ cup (60ml) olive oil
½ teaspoon (2ml) yellow asafetida powder
1 cup (250ml) fresh basil, chopped
2 teaspoons (10ml) dried oregano
6 cups (1.5 litres) tomato purée
1 teaspoon (5ml) salt
¼ teaspoon (1ml) black pepper
1 teaspoon (5ml) raw or brown sugar
2 tablespoons (40ml) tomato paste

The bechamel sauce:

125g butter
¼ teaspoon (1ml) nutmeg powder
¼ teaspoon (1ml) black pepper
½ cup (125ml) plain flour
4 cups (1 litre) warmed milk

The cheese:

3½ cups (875ml) grated cheddar cheese, about 375g
2 cups (500ml) grated mozarella cheese, about 250g

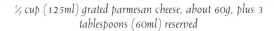

½ cup (125ml) grated parmesan cheese, about 60g, plus 3 tablespoons (60ml) reserved

The pasta:

500g instant lasagna sheets

To prepare the vegetables:

1. Lay the slices of eggplant on an ovenproof flat tray. Spray both sides of the eggplant slices with a light coating of olive oil. Place them under a hot griller and cook on both sides for 5–8 minutes, or until the eggplants are fairly tender. Remove and set aside.

2. Set the capsicum slices under the grill, skin side up. Grill them for 10 minutes or until their skins are blackened. Remove and place them in a plastic bag, and seal the bag. When the capsicums are cool, peel the blackened skin off and set the capsicums aside.

To prepare the tomato sauce:

Pour the olive oil into a large, heavy-based saucepan and set it over moderate heat. When the oil is hot, sprinkle in the yellow asafetida powder, sauté momentarily, then add the basil leaves and oregano, and sauté for another 30 seconds. Pour in the puréed tomatoes, stir to mix and bring to the boil. Add the salt, black pepper, sugar and tomato paste, reduce the heat slightly and cook, uncovered, stirring often for 10–15 minutes, or until it reduces and thickens.

To prepare the bechamel sauce:

Melt the butter in a 2-litre/quart heavy saucepan over low heat. Stir in the nutmeg, black pepper and flour, and sauté, stirring constantly, for about half a minute or until the mixture loosens. Remove the saucepan from the heat, and gradually pour in the warm milk, stirring with a whisk until it is all incorporated and the sauce is smooth. Return the sauce to moderate heat and bring to the boil, stirring. Reduce the heat and simmer for about 5 minutes, stirring constantly, until the sauce develops a thick custard-like consistency.

To assemble the lasagna:

1. Combine all three cheeses (except the reserved parmesan). Divide the cheese into 2 portions, the tomato sauce into 3 portions, the *bechamel* sauce into 4 portions, and the pasta into 5.

2. Spread one portion of the tomato sauce on the bottom of the oven-proof casserole dish. Place a portion of the pasta on top. Layer the eggplant slices on top of the pasta sheets. Spread on a portion of the *bechamel* sauce, then another of the pasta. Sprinkle on half the grated cheese.

3. Continue layering as follows: a portion of the tomato sauce; the sundried tomatoes; the capsicum slices; another portion of the pasta; another of the *bechamel*; another of the pasta, then the remaining cheese. Layer the spinach leaves on top of the cheese.

4. Spread on the remaining tomato sauce, top with the last pasta sheets and the remaining double portion of *bechamel* (this white sauce layer needs to be thicker than the others). Sprinkle the top with the reserved parmesan cheese, place the lasagna in the top half of a pre-heated 200°C/390°F oven and cook for 45–60 minutes, or until the top is slightly golden and the pasta yields easily to a knife point. If the lasagna is darkened on top but does not yield fully to a knife point, cover the lasagna with brown paper or aluminium foil in the last 15 minutes of cooking. When the lasagna is done, leave it in the oven with the door ajar for at least 30 minutes more to allow the lasagna to "plump" up and set. Cut and serve as required.

SAGO PILAF (SABUDANA KHICHARI)

It was difficult to choose a chapter in which to feature this dish. I decided on placing it alongside grain recipes, although sago is not a grain. Known as *sabu* or *sabudana*, sago and tapioca are both used similarly and inter-changeably in Indian cooking, especially as a light-meal choice for Ekadasi grain-fasting days. There is sometimes confusion about which is which because the white beads of sago and tapioca can look identical. But they are from quite different sources. Tapioca is processed from the tubers of the cassava plant, while sago is obtained from the sago palm.

To make things more confusing, packaging and distribution companies sometimes refer to sago as tapioca, and vice versa. It probably makes no difference if you're making a sticky tapioca pudding, but for this recipe I recommend sago. The main reason is that sago has to be soaked for a longer period of time than tapioca, and is less temperamental to deal with. And in this dish, where every pearl has to be separate, it's essential that you don't over-soak it, or it will turn out like a sticky paste. Another potential problem is that sometimes sago or tapioca is partially pre-cooked, although there is no indication on the packaging. That variety is unacceptable for this recipe.

My advice is to purchase your sago from an Indian grocery supplier. Chances are it'll be the right stuff, and quite suitable for preparing *Sabudana Khichari*. Sago, like tapioca, comes in different grades — small, medium and large pearls. The grade required for this recipe is medium — the pearls should be the size of black peppercorns. If you want to take your chances with tapioca, then note carefully the following differences: Indian sago has to be washed once in cold water, then drained. Hot water (not boiling) is then poured over the sago until the water just reaches the surface of the sago, and is left, covered, for 2 hours. It will completely soak up all the water, double in size, and become separate and fluffy.

If using tapioca, follow the same procedure, but it should not be washed, and just soaked in cold water for half an hour only. There is one other very important thing you should know about preparing this dish. Sago, like tapioca, is very heat-sensitive. If you try to fry the soaked pearls of sago in the hot spiced oil or ghee, it will turn into a sticky, gluggy mass, which is impossible to separate. Instead, fold the sago carefully into the warm seasoned oil after the pan has cooled a little. If you need to re-heat the dish, do so on the lowest possible setting, stirring constantly. Having said all that I invite you to try the recipe.

SAGO SOAKING TIME: 2 hours
PREPARATION AND COOKING TIME: 15–20 minutes
YIELD: enough for 4–6 persons

1¼ cups (310ml) Indian sago
4–6 tablespoons (80–120ml) oil or ghee
1 cup (250ml) potatoes, cut 1.25cm (½-inch) cubes
2 teaspoons (10ml) cumin seeds
12–15 curry leaves
1–2 hot green chilies seeded and minced
¼ teaspoon (1ml) turmeric
2 teaspoons (10ml) salt
½ teaspoon (2ml) sugar
½ cup (125ml) freshly-shredded coconut
1½ cups (375ml) roasted peanuts, very finely chopped
1–2 tablespoons (20–40ml) chopped fresh coriander leaves

1. Wash and soak the sago as described above. It is very important to pour only sufficient hot water to just reach the surface of the sago, otherwise it will become sticky. Leave for 2 hours.

2. Gently rake the fully soaked pearls of sago between your fingers to separate them. Heat the oil in a wok or deep-frying pan over high heat. When the oil is hot, drop in the potatoes and fry them for 3–5 minutes or until they are golden brown and fully cooked. Remove them with a slotted spoon, and set them aside.

3. Reduce the heat to low, and allow the oil to cool a little. Drop in the cumin seeds and fry them until they darken a few shades. Add the curry leaves and green chilies, sauté them for half a minute, then remove the pan from the heat. Allow the oil to cool a little more, then sprinkle in the turmeric. When the pan is fairly cool, but not cold, drop in the sago, salt, sugar, coconut, peanuts and potato. Stir well until the sago is an even yellow colour from the turmeric-flavoured oil. Sprinkle on the coriander leaves, and serve immediately. If you want to re-heat, follow the directions as above.

PUNJABI RED BEAN CURRY (RAJMA)

This is the North Indian equivalent of Mexican chili. Laced with cubes of protein-rich homemade *panir* cheese, it is robust, nutritious, filling and spicy. Although ideal for a winter lunch, *Rajma* can be served successfully with any bread or rice selection and as a part of almost any menu.

BEAN SOAKING TIME: 8 hours or 1 hour by the quick method
PREPARATION TIME: 15 minutes
COOKING TIME: ¾ hour–2 hours (depending on the variety of beans)
YIELD: enough for 6 persons

The beans:

2 cups (500ml) dried red kidney beans
6 cups (1½ litres) water
3 small bay leaves
1½ teaspoons (7ml) turmeric
¼ teaspoon (1ml) cayenne pepper

The spice paste:

2½ tablespoons (50ml) coriander seeds
1½ tablespoons (30ml) cumin seeds
1½ teaspoons (7ml) fennel seeds
½ teaspoon (2ml) ajowan seeds
3 tablespoons (60ml) shredded fresh ginger
1½ teaspoons (7ml) garam masala
1½ teaspoons (7ml) turmeric
2 teaspoons (10ml) cayenne pepper
2–3 teaspoons (10–15ml) salt
2 tablespoons (40ml) freshly squeezed lemon or lime juice

The remaining ingredients:

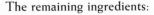

fresh panir cheese, made from 1.5 litres milk, cut into 1.25cm (½-inch) cubes
5 tablespoons (100ml) ghee or oil for frying the panir
4 medium-sized tomatoes, diced into 1.25cm (½-inch) cubes
2 tablespoons (40ml) tomato paste
1 cup (250ml) chopped fresh coriander leaves

To prepare the beans:

1. Sort the beans, removing any stones or foreign matter. Wash the beans twice, then place them in a 3-litre/quart saucepan with 8 cups (2 litres) water. Bring to the boil over high heat, boil for 1 minute, then turn off the heat, cover slightly and set aside for one hour.

2. Bring the beans back to the boil over high heat. Add the bay leaves, turmeric and cayenne, reduce the heat and simmer the beans, covered, for 1–1½ hours, or until the beans are soft and tender, but not broken down. Note that bean cooking time varies immensely for different varieties of kidney beans, so check them carefully.

3. Pour the cooked beans through a colander, being careful to collect all the cooking liquid in a bowl underneath — you'll need it later. Transfer the beans into a bowl. Wash the saucepan and return it to the stove.

4. Separate ½ cup (125ml) cooked beans, mash them to a purée and set them aside in a small bowl.

To prepare the spice paste:

Combine the coriander, cumin, fennel and *ajowan* seeds in a coffee mill or mortar and grind them to a powder. Transfer the powder to a small bowl. Combine the shredded ginger with ½ cup (125ml) water in a blender and process to a smooth liquid.
 Add this ginger

liquid to the bowl of powdered spices. Add the *garam masala*, turmeric, salt and lemon or lime juice, and stir to mix well. The spice paste should have a consistency of thin cream. Add a little water if it is too thick.

To fry the panir cheese:

Place the 5 tablespoons (100ml) ghee or oil in a heavy non-stick frying pan and set it over moderate heat. When the ghee is hot, add the *panir* cheese and stir-fry for 5–7 minutes, carefully turning the cubes with a spoon to brown them on all sides. Remove the pan from the heat and set the *panir* cheese aside.

To assemble the dish:

1. Pour the ghee or oil that remains in the frying pan into the rinsed out 3-litre/quart saucepan in which you cooked the beans. Place the pan over moderate heat, and when the ghee is hot, add the spice paste. Fry the paste for 1 or 2 minutes over moderate heat, or until it begins to stick. Stir in the tomatoes and continue to cook the mixture for 5–8 minutes, or until the tomatoes are reduced to a thick paste, and the ghee starts to separate. Add the water and the reserved mashed beans and stir well until they are fully incorporated.

2. Drop in the cubes of the fried *panir* cheese, the cooked beans, tomato paste and 1½ cups (375ml) cooking liquid, or more if a thinner consistency bean dish is required. Allow the beans to come to the boil, then reduce the heat to low, and simmer for another 10–15 minutes, or until the *panir* cheese cubes are soft and juicy. Stir in the chopped coriander leaves, and serve hot.

SOFT, SAVOURY CHICKPEA SWIRLS (KHANDVI)

The title of this recipe gives only a hint of the unique texture of these tasty savouries from the State of Gujarat on the west coast of India. They're soft and creamy on the tongue, and they feel and look like dainty rolls of fresh pasta. Not only are they mildly seasoned and delicious, they're also highly nutritious. The combination of chickpea flour and yogurt makes a complete protein source ideal for vegetarians. And, to top it off, *khandvi* are low in fat.

Although *Khandvi* are fairly simple to prepare, you have to follow a few important steps. While the mixture cooks, it must be regularly blended with the aid of a hand-held electric cake mixer, or even better a Bamix-type machine. This ensures a smooth, creamy paste without lumps, which is essential for successful *Khandvi*. You must have half an hour of spare time for practically non-stop stirring. You need a fairly large, smooth surface on which to pour the hot mixture; and you should be ready to spread the mixture as soon as it reaches the correct consistency. If you follow all these simple rules, your *Khandvi* will be successful. Serve *Khandvi* as a savoury snack any time.

COOKING TIME: 20–30 minutes
COOLING, CUTTING, ROLLING AND SEASONING
TIME: 15–20 minutes
YIELD: enough for 6–8 persons

The swirls:

1 cup (250ml) yogurt, the more sour the better
1 cup (250ml) chickpea flour
2¼ cups (560ml) water
⅛ teaspoon (0.5ml) turmeric powder
2¼ teaspoons (11ml) salt
¼ teaspoon (1ml) yellow asafetida powder
1 teaspoon (5ml) very finely-minced fresh red or green chilies
1 teaspoon (5ml) minced, fresh ginger root

The garnish:

2 teaspoons (10ml) oil
2 teaspoons (10ml) brown mustard seeds
3 teaspoons (15ml) sesame seeds
½ cup (125ml) coarsely grated-fresh coconut
packed ⅓ cup (85ml) coarsely chopped, fresh coriander leaves

To prepare the swirls:

1. Place the yogurt in a heavy-based 2-litre/quart saucepan. Whisk in the chickpea flour with a hand-held electric beater or Bamix to form a smooth paste. Still whisking, gradually add the water until it is well incorporated. Add the turmeric, salt, yellow asafetida powder, chili and ginger, and whisk again.

2. Set the saucepan over low to moderate heat, and, stirring continuously, bring the mixture to the boil. Reduce to a simmer, and cook, whisking the mixture thoroughly with the beater for another 15–20 minutes, or until the mixture starts to come away from the sides of the pan and resembles a thick custard. Its smell will become more pronounced and it may be approaching the setting point. To test for the setting point, take a small spoon of hot mixture and spread it on the back of a cold, smooth bowl or on a plate. If it is ready, the patch of cold mixture should peel off in one rubbery sheet. If it comes off in shreds, it's not ready. If it's not ready, keep stirring for another 5–10 minutes. If it is ready, proceed to the next step.

3. Pour the mixture quickly over a smooth, cold surface and immediately spread it into a square or rectangle as thinly and evenly as you can with a soft, large rubber spatula. You should be able to almost see through the mixture. Try to cover an area of about 50cm × 75cm (20 inches × 30 inches).

4. Allow the paste to cool for 10 minutes. With a knife, score the paste into a grid, giving you pieces about 10cm x 3.75cm (4 inches × 1½ inches). Vary the size of the pieces if you like.

5. When the paste is scored, carefully lift a piece of the rubbery paste and roll it into a tube. Repeat for all the pieces. Carefully transfer the tubes onto a large tray, with the ends of the tubes tucked under them. As an alternative, roll the paste into thicker tubes and slice them into 2.5 cm (1-inch) sections.

To prepare the garnish:

Place a small saucepan over moderate heat. Add the oil, and when hot sprinkle in the mustard seeds. As they crackle and pop, sprinkle in the sesame seeds, stir momentarily, then remove the pan from the heat. Pour the spices over the *Khandvi* swirls. Sprinkle on the fresh coconut and the chopped coriander leaves. Serve at room temperature.

Note that the *Khandvi* should be consumed within 1 or 2 days — they don't fare too well in the refrigerator.

PUMPKIN DUMPLINGS WITH SAGE-SCENTED BUTTER AND PARMESAN CHEESE (GNOCCHI DI ZUCCA)

Gnocchi makes a refreshing change to pasta. This recipe hails from the north of Italy where the cuisine displays a distinct Germanic influence. The secret of these little delicacies is to first bake the pumpkin rather than boil it. Because baking vegetables allows them to give off some of their water content, the dumplings need less flour to hold them together, and, along with the caramelised flavours that develop in the baked pumpkin, the *gnocchi* have a superior flavour. Choose a flavoursome butternut or *kabocha* pumpkin, or your own choice.

PUMPKIN BAKING TIME: about 1 hour
PREPARATION AND COOKING TIME: 1½ hours
YIELD: enough for 4–6 persons

The dumplings:

800g pumpkin, weighed after peeling and deseeding
200g, a bit less than 1½ cups (375ml), unbleached plain flour
1½ teaspoons (7ml) salt
½ teaspoon (2ml) black pepper

The sage butter:

50g melted butter
2 tablespoons (40ml) chopped fresh sage leaves
5 tablespoons (100ml) parmesan cheese, about 50g

1. Wrap the pumpkin in foil and bake it in a hot oven for about 1 hour or until very tender. Remove and mash thoroughly.

2. Set a large saucepan of salted water over full heat, and bring it to the boil.

3. Melt the butter in another, smaller saucepan. Remove it from the heat and mix in the chopped sage. Set it aside.

4. Meanwhile, combine the mashed pumpkin with the flour, salt and pepper. Work the mixture into a paste. It will be a little sticky, but do not add more flour. Form the paste into 40 balls, and divide them between 2 plates. Take 1 plate of balls to the boiling water. Dip the prongs of a fork in the water and press a ball. It will simultaneously flatten slightly and be marked with ridges. Repeat for all the balls, dipping the fork back into the water between dumplings. When you've completed pressing the dumplings, transfer half the plate of dumplings, one at a time, with the fork, into the water. They will probably stick to the fork, so submerge the dumpling and the end of the fork momentarily in the water, and the dumpling will slide off.

5. The dumplings will sink, then gradually float to the surface. Make sure the water stays boiling. When the last dumpling has fully risen to the surface, allow them to cook for another 2 minutes, then remove the dumplings from the pan with a slotted spoon and drain them.

6. Repeat this procedure until the remaining dumplings have been cooked. Serve hot, drizzled with the warmed, herbed butter and a sprinkling of the grated cheese. As an alternative serving suggestion, serve *Gnocchi di Zucca* with a lightly herbed tomato sauce and a topping of parmesan cheese. You'll need about 2 cups (500ml) of sauce.

SAUTÉED SPROUTED MUNG BEANS (VADU)

Sprouting of grains and legumes is a miraculous process. It increases the vitamin and mineral contact of the grains, simultaneously enhancing the mineral's ability to be absorbed by the body. The process of sprouting also reduces naturally occurring metabolic poisons in the grains.

Sprouting does not take much effort: a little water, one day's soaking time, up to 2 days sprouting time, and only a few moments of attention. Ideally the sprouted beans should barely measure 1.25cm (½ inch). This Gujarati specialty requires home-sprouted mung beans in order to be authentic because the shop-bought variety are too water-logged.

Vadu is a popular dish served with rice and creamy *karhi* sauce. It is also adaptable to any season and is great served as part of a light breakfast. In winter, try accompanying it with a hot herb-tea or *Filipino Ginger Tea*, and a fruit *compôte*. In summer serve with fresh fruits, and a glass of *Chilled Papaya Refresher* or *Lemon Yogurt Shake*.

BEAN SOAKING TIME: 24 hours
BEAN SPROUTING TIME: 24–48 hours
PREPARATION AND COOKING TIME: about 40 minutes
YIELD: enough for 4 or 5 persons

2 cups (500ml) whole green mung beans
1¼ teaspoons (6ml) cumin seeds
3 teaspoons (15ml) coriander powder
1½ tablespoons (30ml) ghee
¼ teaspoon (1ml) mustard seeds
½ teaspoon (2ml) yellow asafetida powder
20 curry leaves
2 teaspoons (10ml) minced ginger
2 teaspoons (10ml) minced green chilies
up to ¾ cup (185ml) hot water
1½ teaspoons (7ml) salt
½ teaspoon (2ml) turmeric powder
2 teaspoons (10ml) sugar
½ teaspoon (2ml) garam masala
chopped fresh coriander leaves, for garnish

1. Wash the mung beans in plenty of cold water. Rinse them, then place them in a large glass jar. Fill the jar with water, cover and set the jar aside in a cool place for 24 hours.

2. Drain the water from the jar of beans, then lay the jar on its side and leave it for another 24 hours. The small amount of moisture left with the beans after draining them will enable the beans to sprout. After 24 hours the sprouts will probably be about 0.5cm (¼ inch) long. Use them now, or set them aside for another 24 hours, after which the sprouts will most probably have increased to 1.25cm (½ inch) in length. This is the optimum time for use. Carefully wash and drain the sprouted mung beans.

3. Grind 1 teaspoon (5ml) of the cumin seeds to a powder in a spice mill or coffee grinder. Combine this powder with the coriander powder. This is known as *dania-jeera* powder, and is well-known in Gujarati cuisine.

4. Pour the ghee into a 3-litre/quart saucepan over moderate heat. When the ghee is hot, add the mustard seeds. When they crackle and pop, sprinkle in the cumin seeds, yellow asafetida powder, curry leaves, ginger and chili. Stir-fry the spices until the cumin seeds are a darker shade of brown and fragrant.

5. Add the sprouted mung beans, stir for a few moments to combine with the spices, then pour in half the water, sprinkle in the *dania-jeera* powder, the salt, turmeric and sugar. Stir briefly to mix, allow the water to boil, then reduce to a simmer and cover the saucepan. Cook the sprouts for 30–40 minutes, or until the sprouted beans are soft when squeezed between the thumb and forefinger. Add a little extra water if the pan runs dry or you prefer a more moist dish.

6. Remove the saucepan from the heat, stir in the *garam masala*, sprinkle on the coriander leaves and serve hot.

ACCOMPANIMENTS

DIPS, SAUCES & DRESSINGS

Sicilian Eggplant Appetiser (Caponata)

Sweet Chili Sauce

Dynamite Dressing

Chili and Cream Cheese Dip

Korean Sesame Sauce

Fresh Coriander and Macadamia Pistou

Kurma's Tomato Ketchup

Sweet and Sour Plum Sauce

Herbed Kalamata Olive Dip

Hot Chili Relish (Sambal Bajek)

Avocado and Sour Cream Dip

Tomato Relish (Salsa Mexicana)

CHUTNEYS, JAMS & PICKLES

Green Mango, Mint and Coriander Chutney

Malini's Tomato Pickle

Blueberry Jam

Quick and Easy Creamy Cashew Chutney

Kumquat Marmalade

Raisin Chutney

Indonesian Yellow Pickle (Acar Kuning)

Green Tomato Chutney

South Indian Coconut Chutney

Fresh Peach Chutney

Homemade Apricot Jam

Bush Tomato Chutney

Fresh Fig Conserve

Spicy Guava Jam

Tender Eggplant Pickles

Rhubarb Chutney

Sweet and Sour Tamarind Chutney

Urad Dal Chutney

SICILIAN EGGPLANT APPETISER (CAPONATA)

Capers are the floral buds of the wild plant *Capparis spinosa* that is cultivated in the southern arid regions of Spain and the Mediterranean basin as a companion crop to olives. Capers are well-loved in Spanish, Greek and Italian cuisine for their unmistakably pungent and strong flavour. Capers vary from tiny currant-size to the size of small olives, and are most commonly available pickled in vinegar or brine. They're great on pizzas, and particularly lend themselves to the famous *caponata*, a popular addition to *antipasto* platters. Serve *caponata* with crusty bread for a delicious meal.

PREPARATION AND COOKING TIME:
20–25 minutes
YIELD: enough for 4–6 persons

¼ cup (60ml) virgin olive oil
½ teaspoon (2ml) yellow asafetida powder
1 large eggplant, about 400g, cut into 1.25cm (½-inch) cubes
1 large red capsicum (pepper), about 200g, cored, de-veined and cut into 1.5cm (½-inch) chunks
1 cup (250ml) celery pieces, cut into 1.25cm (½-inch) chunks, about 2 or 3 blades of celery
1 cup (250ml) tomato purée
1 teaspoon (5ml) salt
1 tablespoon (20ml) chopped fresh basil leaves
¼ cup (60ml) halved, pitted black olives
1 tablespoon (20ml) sugar
¼ teaspoon (1ml) black pepper
2 tablespoons (40ml) brine-packed capers, rinsed and drained
basil leaves for garnish

1. Heat the olive oil in a heavy, 3-litre/quart non-stick saucepan over moderate heat. When the oil is hot, sprinkle in the yellow asafetida powder, stir momentarily, then drop in the eggplant cubes. Stir-fry the eggplants for 2 or 3 minutes, then add the capsicum and celery pieces, and stirring often fry the vegetables for another 15 minutes or until the eggplants are soft.

2. Pour in the tomato purée, sprinkle in the salt and basil, and stir to mix. Allow the tomato purée to come to the boil, then reduce the heat and simmer, covered, for about 5 minutes, or until the sauce is slightly thickened.

3. Remove the pan from the heat, fold in the olives, sugar, black pepper and capers. Mix well and serve warm or cold with a garnish of fresh basil leaves.

SWEET CHILI SAUCE

This sauce is a perfect accompaniment to a variety of savoury dishes, especially fried ones. Choose your chilies carefully; the hotter the chili, the hotter the sauce.

PREPARATION TIME: about 1 hour
SAUCE SITTING TIME: overnight
COOKING TIME: about 1 hour
YIELD: a little over 2 cups (500ml)

125g fresh hot red chilies, weighed after removing the ends
1½ cups (375ml) sugar
1½ cups (375ml) fresh lemon juice
1 tablespoon (20ml) finely-minced fresh ginger
1½ teaspoons (7ml) salt
1 cup (250ml) sultanas, about 175g

1. Slice the chilies in half lengthways and remove the seeds. It is advisable to wear rubber gloves and use a spoon for this.

2. Place all the sauce ingredients in a 3-litre/quart stainless steel saucepan. Bring to the boil over moderate heat, and reduce the heat to very low. Simmer gently with a tight lid for about 1 hour, or until the chilies are very soft. Allow the sauce to cool, preferably overnight.

3. Carefully scrape the sauce mixture into a blender or food processor and process to a very smooth purée. Rinse out the saucepan. Pour the purée through a non-metal fine sieve, collecting the sauce in the rinsed out saucepan underneath. Squeeze and rub until

all you have left in the sieve is a very dry residue. Return the saucepan to moderate heat, bring to the boil, remove from the heat, and pour into hot, dry, sterilised jars. Use as required.

DYNAMITE DRESSING

The Hare Krishnas of Denver, Colorado, run a very popular restaurant, *Govinda's*, on Cherry Street. One of their salad dressings particularly appeals to me; as the name suggests, it's packed with strong flavours. Nutritional or brewers yeast is available at health food stores.

PREPARATION TIME: a few minutes
YIELD: 2 cups (500ml)

1 cup (250ml) blanched almonds
1 cup (250ml) cold water
1 cup (250ml) olive oil
3 tablespoons (60ml) freshly-squeezed lemon juice
3 tablespoons (60ml) tamari or soy sauce
3 tablespoons (60ml) nutritional yeast or brewers yeast

Place all the ingredients in a blender and process until completely smooth. That's it.

CHILI AND CREAM CHEESE DIP

The woodsy, heady flavour of maple syrup gives a subtle sweetness to this delicately flavoured dip. The bite of red chilies and the tang of fresh lime juice add further dimensions of taste.

PREPARATION TIME: a few minutes
YIELD: 1½ cups (375ml)

¾ cup (185ml) cream cheese
½ cup (125ml) yogurt
½–1 teaspoon (2–5ml) seeded and finely-chopped red chilies
1 tablespoon (20ml) maple syrup
1 tablespoon (20ml) fresh lime juice
½ teaspoon (2ml) salt
¼ teaspoon (1ml) freshly-ground black pepper

Combine all the ingredients in a small bowl and whisk until thoroughly mixed.

KOREAN SESAME SAUCE

This piquant sauce is an ideal accompaniment to a platter of raw or blanched vegetable crudités. Obtain unhulled sesame seeds from health food stores.

PREPARATION TIME: 5–10 minutes
YIELD: about 1½ cups (375ml)

¾ cup (185ml) sesame seeds, preferably unhulled
1½ tablespoons (30ml) raw sugar
⅓ cup (85ml) vinegar or lemon juice
½ cup (125ml) light soy sauce

1. Sprinkle the sesame seeds into a frying pan and dry-roast them, stirring constantly over moderate heat for 4 or 5 minutes, or until the seeds are a few shades darker and aromatic. Remove the seeds from the pan and crush them to a powder in one or two batches in a spice mill or coffee grinder.
2. Whisk together all the ingredients for the sauce and serve as desired.

FRESH CORIANDER AND MACADAMIA PISTOU

Macadamias, Australia's contribution to the world of fine nuts, have a rich and creamy taste. They are an extremely versatile ingredient in the kitchen, and are especially popular in cakes, pastries and confectionery. This flavoursome savoury *pistou*, the French version of *pesto*, makes a great garnish for soups, and is delicious spread on wedges of toasted flatbreads. For an extra dimension of flavour, toast the macadamia nuts before puréeing.

PREPARATION TIME: a few minutes
YIELD: ¾ cup (185ml)

½ cup (125ml) raw macadamia nuts
1 small hot red chili, seeded and chopped
1 cup (250ml) packed fresh coriander leaves
¼ cup (60ml) cold water
1 tablespoon (20ml) olive oil
½–¾ teaspoon (2–3ml) salt
¼ teaspoon (1ml) freshly-ground black pepper

Place the nuts in a blender or food processor and pulse until finely chopped. Add the remaining ingredients and process until puréed, scraping down the sides when necessary. Serve at room temperature. The *pistou* can be made two days ahead and kept refrigerated. It will thicken as it sits, so thin it with water as necessary and bring to room temperature before serving.

KURMA'S TOMATO KETCHUP

A good, all-round thick and rich ketchup!

PREPARATION AND COOKING TIME:
1½–1¾ hours

YIELD: about 3¼ cups (810ml)

1 large red capsicum (pepper)
2kg ripe tomatoes, coarsely chopped
1 teaspoon (5ml) yellow asafetida powder
¼ cup (60ml) coarsely-grated fresh ginger
2 tablespoons (40ml) whole coriander seeds
20 cloves
1 teaspoon (5ml) whole black peppercorns
2 tablespoons (40ml) dried tamarind
2 tablespoons (40ml) chopped fresh continental parsley leaves
3 tablespoons (60ml) fresh lemon juice
3 tablespoons (60ml) raw or brown sugar
3 tablespoons (60ml) liquid barley malt
1½ teaspoons (7ml) salt
3 teaspoons (15ml) Hungarian sweet paprika

1. Cut the red capsicum in half lengthwise, removing the core and seeds. Roast the capsicum halves over an open flame, or roast them under a griller for 5–7 minutes or until evenly charred. Seal the capsicum pieces in a plastic bag for 5–10 minutes. This makes peeling easier. Remove the capsicum from the bag, rub and peel off the skin under cold running water and coarsely chop the capsicum.

2. Combine the tomatoes, roasted chopped capsicum, the yellow asafetida powder, the ginger, coriander, cloves, peppercorns, tamarind and parsley in a non-reactive 5-litre/quart saucepan or preserving pan. Bring the mixture to the boil over moderate heat. Reduce the heat and simmer, covered, stirring occasionally for 25 minutes, or until the tomatoes are completely soft and broken down.

3. Remove the saucepan from the heat. Press the mixture through a large sieve or food mill, discarding the dry residue. It is important to extract as much purée as possible. Return the purée to the rinsed-out saucepan. Place over moderate heat, bring to the boil, reduce to a simmer and cook for another 30 minutes, or until the purée has reduced in volume by half. You'll need to stir the saucepan almost constantly at this stage.

4. Remove the purée from the heat. Add the lemon juice, sugar, barley malt, salt and paprika. Mix well. Return to the heat and simmer, stirring frequently for another 15 minutes or until reduced and thick. Pour the ketchup into hot sterilised jars and seal.

SWEET AND SOUR PLUM SAUCE

This is a richly coloured and highly flavoured sauce. It will appear quite tangy when first made, but the flavours will mellow with age. Yellow-fleshed, red-skinned plums, damsons, or blood plums are all suitable.

PREPARATION AND COOKING TIME:
30–40 minutes
YIELD: about 4 cups (1 litre)

1kg ripe red plums, halved and pitted
3 cups (750ml) lemon juice
1 tablespoon (20ml) salt
1 teaspoon (5ml) cayenne pepper
12 whole cloves
1 teaspoon (5ml) ground black pepper
1 teaspoon (5ml) ground allspice (pimento)
3 teaspoons (15ml) shredded fresh ginger
3¾ cups (935ml) sugar, about 750g

1. Place the plums in a heavy 3-litre/quart saucepan over moderate heat with all the ingredients except the sugar. Bring to the boil and simmer, covered, for 20 minutes, or until the plums are broken down and soft. Remove the pan from the heat and set aside to cool for 15 minutes.

2. Transfer the mixture to a bowl, and rinse the saucepan. Press the mixture through a sieve or food mill, collecting the plum purée in the saucepan and discarding the dry residue.

3. Return the saucepan to moderate heat, stir in the sugar until it dissolves, raise the heat and boil vigorously for about 10 minutes, or until the sauce coats a spoon. Remove the sauce from the heat, allow it to cool a little, then pour it into hot dry sterilised jars. Use as required.

HERBED KALAMATA OLIVE DIP

Kalamata olives, the thin, pointy hearty-flavoured olives from Kalamata in Greece are the basis of this rich-tasting dip. As well as a great dip for crackers, breads and other crunchy finger goods, it is also excellent spread thinly on toasted bread, in pasta, or as a pizza base. If kalamata olives are not available, other black, good quality Greek or Sicilian olives may be used as a substitute, although I do not recommend canned pitted olives. Note that no salt is required in this dip as kalamata olives are already quite salty.

PREPARATION TIME: 15–20 minutes
YIELD: about 1¼ cups (310ml)

1 cup (250ml) kalamata olives
½ teaspoon (2ml) yellow asafetida powder
¼ cup (60ml) packed, chopped continental parsley
½ teaspoon (2ml) sprigs fresh rosemary
1 teaspoon (5ml) fresh thyme leaves
3 tablespoons (60ml) virgin olive oil
½ teaspoon (2ml) freshly-ground black pepper
extra continental parsley for garnish

Squeeze the stones out of the olives and discard them. Combine all the ingredients in a food processor, and blend to a smooth paste. Garnish with reserved continental parsley leaves or serve as suggested.

HOT CHILI RELISH
(SAMBAL BAJEK)

This fiery relish is from Bandung, the capital of West Java Province. Bandung is situated in the middle of the Priangan Plateau, surrounded by a ring of mountains, many of which are active volcanoes! You can vary the heat of this very delicious condiment by the type of chilies you use. Milder chilies temper the heat considerably. Serve *Sambal Bajek* with any meal containing rice, or with fried savoury finger-foods.

PREPARATION AND COOKING TIME:
about 40 minutes
YIELD: about 2 cups (500ml)

½ cup (125ml) peanut or olive oil
6 candlenuts or 12 macadamia nuts
5 large hot red chilies and 5 large hot green chilies, ends removed and cut across into 1.25cm (½-inch) sections
3 large firm tomatoes, about 300g, peeled and coarsely chopped
2½ tablespoons (50ml) crushed palm sugar, about 50g
1½–2 teaspoons (7–10ml) salt

1. Set the oil in a frying pan or wok over moderate heat. When the oil is fairly hot, drop in the candlenuts or macadamia nuts. Deep-fry them, turning often, until they turn a light golden brown. Remove the nuts and drain them on paper towels. When they are a little cool, place them in a spice mill or coffee grinder and grind them to a powder.

2. Drop the chili sections into the hot oil and fry them for 3–5 minutes or until they go a little brown around the edges. Add the tomatoes, raise the heat, and cook with the chilies until the tomatoes are very soft and broken down, and the oil starts to ooze out. Add the palm sugar, powdered nuts and salt, and mix well. Cook for a few minutes more, then remove from the heat. Serve at room temperature.

AVOCADO AND SOUR CREAM DIP

The avocado contains more fat than any other fruit except the olive. Having said that, I should add that the fat that it contains is of the highest quality, free of the unpleasant butyric acid with which many fats are contaminated.

The protein found in avocado is also of the finest quality and is much superior to the protein found in breads and cereals. For purity, wholesomeness, ease of digestibility and adaption to human needs, avocado has few rivals.

This avocado and sour cream dip is also great served as a topping for baked potatoes.

PREPARATION TIME: about 10 minutes
YIELD: 1¾ cups (435ml)

1 medium avocado, 300g
¾ cup (185ml) sour cream
1 tablespoon (20ml) lemon juice
¾–1 teaspoon (3–5ml) salt
¼ teaspoon (1ml) freshly-ground black pepper
½ teaspoon (2ml) finely-minced seeded fresh green chilies
1 teaspoon (5ml) olive oil
¼ teaspoon (1ml) yellow asafetida powder
1½ tablespoons (30ml) very finely-diced celery
½ teaspoon (2ml) semi-ground roasted cumin seeds

1. Halve the avocado and remove the seed. Scoop out the flesh and place it in a food processor along with the sour cream, lemon juice, salt, black pepper and green chili. Process to a smooth sauce-like consistency. Remove and place in a bowl.

2. Warm the oil in a small saucepan or frying

pan over fairly low heat. Drop in the yellow asafetida powder and the celery. Sauté the celery for 1 or 2 minutes, or until slightly translucent. Scrape the celery and fragrant oil into the avocado mixture, sprinkle on the cumin seeds, and mix well. Serve immediately or refrigerate.

TOMATO RELISH (SALSA MEXICANA)

Literally meaning "sauce", the term *salsa* can be applied to any kind of sauce in Latin American cuisine. Elsewhere, it is used to describe the sauce or relish made with freshly chopped uncooked ingredients. The basic *salsa* consists of tomatoes, a herb, fresh chilies and sometimes a little lime or lemon juice. This Mexican *salsa* fits the above description. To keep its freshness, prepare *Salsa Mexicana* no more than 2 hours before serving.

Prepare this simple uncooked relish with the freshest, reddest, ripest tomatoes available and consume within a few hours for optimum flavour. The *salsa* is mildly hot. Increase the quantity of chilies for more heat.

PREPARATION AND COOKING TIME:
a few minutes
YIELD: 1½ cups (375ml)

1½ cups (375ml) very finely-chopped, unskinned ripe tomatoes
½ cup (125ml) loosely packed, finely-chopped coriander leaves
¼ teaspoon (1ml) yellow asafetida powder
2 large green chilies (preferably serranos), seeded and finely chopped, about 2 tablespoons (40ml)
1 teaspoon (5ml) salt
a little water, if required
1 teaspoon (5ml) lime or lemon juice (optional)

Combine all the ingredients and mix well. If the tomatoes are dry, you may need to add a few tablespoons of water. The finished product should be loose and pulpy. Set aside the *salsa* for about 30 minutes before serving.

GREEN MANGO, MINT AND CORIANDER CHUTNEY

Mangoes are used as a food in all stages of development. Green or unripe, mangoes contain a large portion of starch which gradually changes into glucose, sucrose and maltose as the fruits begin to ripen, and disappears completely when the fruits are fully ripe. Raw mangoes are a valuable source of vitamins C, B1, B2, and are also a well-known remedy for heat stroke, diarrhoea, bilious disorders and blood disorders.

Green mangoes are also one of the most well-loved ingredients in Indian cuisine. They have a pleasantly sour, fruity taste which features in innumerable dishes, especially pickles and chutneys. Every Indian housewife has a favourite recipe for green mango chutney. This version requires no cooking, is a perfect partner for fried savoury dishes, and makes a pleasant contrast when served in meals featuring *dals* or soups.

PREPARATION TIME: about 20 minutes
YIELD: about 1½ cups (375ml)

packed ⅓ cup (85ml) mint leaves, about 1 small bunch
packed ¼ cup (60ml) coriander leaves, about 1 small bunch
2 medium-sized green mangoes, about 500g total, peeled, seeded and chopped
1–2 hot, green chilies, chopped
one 2.5 cm (1-inch) cube peeled fresh ginger
2 teaspoons (10ml) cumin seeds, dry-roasted and powdered
2 tablespoons (40ml) raw sugar
½–1 teaspoon (2–5ml) salt

1. Carefully clean and wash the mint and coriander, removing all traces of dirt and grit.
2. Place all the ingredients for the chutney in a food processor and blend until very fine. Remove the chutney and serve at room temperature.

MALINI'S TOMATO PICKLE

This delicious spicy pickle contains no sugar. It keeps in a well-sealed jar in a refrigerator for two weeks.

PREPARATION AND COOKING TIME:
50–60 minutes
YIELD: 3 cups (750ml) of pickle

2½kg ripe tomatoes (they should not be too soft)
1 tablespoon (20ml) tamarind pulp, soaked in ¼ cup (60ml) hot water and squeezed to extract all the pulp
2½ tablespoons (50ml) minced fresh ginger
2½ tablespoons (50ml) minced fresh chili
3 teaspoons (15ml) salt
2 teaspoons (10ml) turmeric
½ teaspoon (2ml) yellow asafetida powder

The extra seasoning:

¾ cup (185ml) sesame oil (not the roasted Chinese variety)
3 teaspoons (15ml) mustard seeds
6 large dried red chilies, broken
1 teaspoon (5ml) fenugreek seeds
½ teaspoon (2ml) yellow asafetida powder
2 teaspoons (10ml) dry-roasted fenugreek seeds, powdered

1. Plunge the whole washed tomatoes into a large saucepan of boiling water. Leave for a few minutes until the skins start to blister. Remove the tomatoes, peel them and chop them coarsely.
2. Place the tomatoes in a heavy 5-litre/quart saucepan over moderate to high heat along with the tamarind, ginger, chili, salt, turmeric and yellow asafetida powder. Allow the mixture to boil, and, stirring often, cook for about 20 minutes, or until the mixture is thick and reduced.
3. Prepare the seasonings as follows: In another smaller pan, heat the sesame oil over moderate heat. When hot, sprinkle in the mustard seeds. When they crackle, add the chilies and fenugreek. When the fenugreek darkens slightly, sprinkle in the yellow asafetida powder and quickly pour the contents of the pan into the tomatoes.
4. Cook the tomato pickle for a further 15–20 minutes, or until it becomes a thick paste that gives off its oil. Finally stir in the dry roasted fenugreek powder. Cool the pickle and pack it into a sterilised jar.

BLUEBERRY JAM

In Australia, where blueberries have been successfully grown now for a number of years, the season runs from around September to April. These deliciously sharp-sweet berries are grown mainly on the northern New South Wales coast and in southern Queensland.

When selecting blueberries, note that the blue-grey bloom is natural and is actually a sign of freshness. Choose firm, plump berries with no sign of softness or withering, and store for up to 2–3 days, covered, in the refrigerator crisper.

This recipe yields a soft-set jam. It's great as a topping for cheesecakes, a filling for sponge cakes or as a spread for your favourite crusty bread.

PREPARATION AND COOKING TIME:
25–30 minutes
YIELD: about 1 cup (250ml), 375g jam

250g blueberries
250g sugar
1 tablespoon (20ml) water
juice of half small lemon

1. Place the berries, sugar, water and lemon juice in a heavy 2-litre/quart saucepan. Bring to the boil slowly over moderate heat, stirring to dissolve sugar. Reduce the heat and simmer for about 10 minutes.
2. Increase the heat and boil the jam for another 15–20 minutes, or until the setting point is reached. To test for the setting point, place a spoonful on a plate or saucer that has been chilled in the freezer. If the jam is ready, it should set.
3. Remove the saucepan from the heat and allow the jam to settle for a few minutes. Spoon it into a hot sterilised jar, and seal.

QUICK AND EASY CREAMY CASHEW CHUTNEY

This wholesome and delicious mild-tasting chutney from South India requires no cooking and practically no preparation time. Its velvety-smooth texture lends itself as an excellent raw-food dip for fresh vegetables. Thinned with a little water, it becomes an elegant salad dressing. Select good quality cashews (bits or halves are fine) for best results.

PREPARATION TIME: 10 minutes
YIELD: about 1¼ cups (310ml)

1 cup (250ml) raw cashews, bits or halves, about 140g
½ teaspoon (2ml) lemon juice
1 teaspoon (5ml) salt
one 1.25cm (½-inch) piece of fresh ginger, sliced
1 hot green chili, seeded and chopped
up to ⅓ cup (85ml) water
2 tablespoons (40ml) chopped fresh coriander leaves

Combine the cashews, lemon juice, salt, ginger and chili bits with ¼ cup (60ml) water in a food processor. Process until smooth, adding a little more water if required to produce a loose, smooth purée. You may need to remove the lid once or twice to scrape the sides with a spatula. Transfer the cashew chutney to a bowl, add the fresh coriander and serve.

KUMQUAT MARMALADE

Kumquats look like miniature oranges, and although they are closely related to the citrus species, they belong to a different genus altogether. Whereas most citrus fruits are considered sub-tropical, kumquats are very hardy and grow easily in Melbourne where I live. In fact, I just picked a small bucket off our tree in the backyard. The round, ornamental variety of kumquats are common, but I prefer to cook the more firm, oval variety. Nevertheless, all kumquats yield a delicious marmalade which is both refreshing and tangy. It is a favourite with those who don't like their marmalade too sweet.

STANDING TIME: overnight
PREPARATION AND COOKING TIME:
about 1¼ hours
YIELD: about 4 cups (1 litre)

250g kumquats
3 cups (750ml) water
sugar

1. Wash the kumquats and slice them as finely as possible. Remove the seeds, if any, and reserve them. Combine the sliced fruit and water in a bowl or jug and leave overnight.

2. Next day, place the fruit and water mixture in a non-stick 3-litre/quart saucepan. Gather the reserved pips and tie them in a square of muslin to form a little bag. Drop the bag into the kumquat and water mixture and bring the mixture to a boil over high heat. Reduce the heat, and simmer, tightly covered, for about 1 hour. By this time the fruit will be tender. Remove the saucepan from the heat.

3. Discard the muslin bag of pips. Pour the mixture into a bowl, measuring exactly how many cups there are. Add an equal volume of sugar and return the mixture to the saucepan.

4. Stir over low heat to dissolve the sugar. Return the mixture to the boil, and cook without stirring for 10–15 minutes, or until a spoon of the marmalade sets on a cold plate. You may like to keep the plate in the freezer for a quick set test.

5. Remove the marmalade from the heat. Skim off any scum from the surface and let the marmalade rest for 15 minutes. Spoon it into hot, sterilised jars. Cover immediately, and seal when cold.

RAISIN CHUTNEY

The intense sweetness of raisins is balanced by tart lime juice in this almost uncooked chutney. The nip of fresh chilies and ginger rounds out the flavour combination. Dark raisins, especially seeded muscatels, are a delicious choice.

Try a dab of this sweet and hot chutney with *Super-flaky Wholemeal Griddle-fried Breads, Spinach and Curd Cheese Patties,* or *Mayapur-style Stuffed Vegetable Pastries.*

PREPARATION AND COOKING TIME:
15 minutes
YIELD: about ¾ cup (185ml)

1 teaspoon (5ml) cumin seeds
¾ cup (185ml) seeded raisins, about 150g
4 small red or green chilies, seeded and chopped
one 1.25cm (½-inch) cube peeled fresh ginger
1 tablespoon (20ml) lime juice
½ teaspoon (2ml) salt

1. Set a small non-stick pan or small cast-iron frying pan over gentle heat. Add the cumin seeds and stir until the seeds dry-roast, darkening slightly, giving off their distinctive aroma. Remove the seeds from the pan and grind them to a powder in a spice mill or mortar.

2. Combine all the chutney ingredients in a large mortar or food processor. Grind to a uniformly smooth paste. Add a few drops of water if you prefer your chutney more moist. Remove and serve. Note that the chutney's flavour improves as it sits, and it tastes even better the next day.

INDONESIAN YELLOW PICKLE (ACAR KUNING)

This pickle is from Java. It is usually taken with rice and often served at a marriage feast or dinner for a religious festival or party. Obtain fresh turmeric root at well-stocked Asian grocers. If unavailable, replace with turmeric powder.

PREPARATION AND COOKING TIME:
25–35 minutes
YIELD: enough for 6–8 persons

one 3.75cm (1½-inch) cube of peeled fresh turmeric root, or 1 teaspoon (5ml) turmeric powder
3 large red chilies, seeds removed
12 raw candle nuts or macadamia nuts
one 3.75cm (1½-inch) cube fresh ginger
3 tablespoons (60ml) oil
one 3.75cm (1½-inch) cube galangal root, cut into large slices
500g carrots, cut into batons, 6.5cm × 0.5cm × 0.5cm (2½-inches × ¼-inch × ¼-inch)
500g continental cucumbers, peeled, cut in half lengthways, seeded and cut into batons the same size as the carrots (weigh them after peeling and trimming)
2 tablespoons (40ml) sugar
2 teaspoons (10ml) salt
3 tablespoons (60ml) lime juice, about two fresh limes

1. Place the turmeric, chilies, candle nuts or macadamia nuts, along with the ginger, in a mortar or food processor and process to a purée. You may need to add a few teaspoons of water. Scrape out the spice paste into a small bowl.

2. Heat the oil in a large wok or pan over moderate to high heat. When a haze appears over the surface of the oil, throw in the sliced galangal root and fry it for 2 or 3 minutes or until aromatic. Add the spice paste and fry, stirring, for 3 or 4 minutes, or until the oil oozes from the yellow sauce.

3. Pour in 2 cups (500ml) water to the fried paste and bring it to the boil. Add the carrots, mix well, cover with a lid and reduce the heat a little. Cook for 10 minutes or until the carrots are almost soft.

4. Add the cucumbers, mix well, and cook for 5 minutes, or until they soften. Remove the lid, increase the heat slightly and add the sugar, salt and lemon juice. Cook, stirring often, for a further 3–5 minutes, or until the pickle is almost dry. Remove from the heat and serve it at room temperature.

GREEN TOMATO CHUTNEY

Bengalis love green tomato chutney. It is traditionally cooked by frying the seasoning in mustard oil, a rather strong-tasting medium made more docile by heating it to smoking point for 5 seconds. If using ghee, don't allow it to smoke at all. I find the chutney has a tendency to stick, so use a non-stick pan or stir it often.

PREPARATION AND COOKING TIME:
30–35 minutes
YIELD: about 1¼ cups (310ml)

500g green tomatoes
2 tablespoons (40ml) mustard oil or ghee
1 tablespoon (20ml) fresh green chilies, chopped
½ teaspoon (2ml) mustard seeds
8–10 fresh curry leaves
½ teaspoon (2ml) turmeric powder
2 tablespoons (40ml) sultanas
½ teaspoon (2ml) salt
2 tablespoons (40ml) chopped fresh coriander leaves
1 teaspoon (5ml) shredded ginger
¼ cup (60ml) jaggery or raw sugar

1. Plunge the whole tomatoes into a large saucepan of boiling water. When the tomato skins split, remove the tomatoes from the water, peel them, and chop into 1.25cm (½-inch) cubes. You should have approximately 2½ cups (625ml) tomatoes.

2. Heat the mustard oil in a non-stick 2-litre/quart pan over fairly high heat until smoking hot. Hold it at smoking point for 5 seconds, then lower the heat, allow the oil to cool a little and sprinkle in the mustard seeds. When the mustard seeds cease popping, add the chilies, ginger and curry leaves. Stir the spices in the hot oil for a minute or two or until they are fragrant and slightly soft. Add the tomatoes and turmeric and cook over medium to high heat for 10 minutes or until the tomatoes soften. If you like, you can sprinkle in a little water to assist with the cooking.

3. Drop in the sultanas and salt and cook the chutney for another 5–10 minutes, or until the tomatoes are pulpy and broken down.

4. Add the sweetener, cook for another minute or two, sprinkle in extra water if required, then remove from the heat. Add the chopped fresh coriander and serve at room temperature.

SOUTH INDIAN COCONUT CHUTNEY

South Indian savouries such as *dosas* and *iddlis* are practically never served without some type of fresh, uncooked coconut chutney. This semi-moist variety has the consistency of *pesto*, and a pale yellow-green colour. Fried *chana dal* is added to the chutney to give it "body" and to hold the coconut together. Fried *chana* is available at well-stocked Indian grocers where it is known as *puttu kadalai*. If unavailable, use raw *chana dal* and prepare as directed. Coconut chutney is traditionally served with *masala dosa*.

PREPARATION TIME: 8–10 minutes
YIELD: about 3 cups (750ml)

1 tablespoon (20ml) oil
4 small hot green chilies cut into 2.5cm (1-inch) lengths
1 tablespoon (20ml) fried chana, or chana dal
1 teaspoon (5ml) mustard seeds
6–8 curry leaves
¼ teaspoon (1ml) yellow asafetida powder
⅛ teaspoon (0.5ml) turmeric
2 cups (500ml) freshly-grated coconut or dried coconut reconstituted by soaking it in ½ cup (125ml) boiling hot water for 10 minutes
the purée from one 3.5cm (1½-inch) cube of tamarind soaked in ½ cup (125ml) hot water for 10 minutes
2 teaspoons (10ml) salt
1 teaspoon (5ml) sugar
1 tablespoon (20ml) fresh coriander leaves

1. Pour the oil into a small saucepan or frying pan over moderate heat. When the oil is hot, drop in the chili sections. Fry them for 2 or 3 minutes or until blistered. Remove them with the slotted spoon and place them on a plate.

2. In the hot oil that remains in the saucepan, fry the raw *chana dal* for 1 or 2 minutes, or until golden brown. Remove and drain. If using fried *chana dal* (*puttu kadalai*) omit this step.

3. Drop the mustard seeds into the remaining hot oil. When they crackle, drop in the curry leaves, fry momentarily and remove the pan from the heat. Sprinkle in the yellow asafetida powder and the turmeric. Stir to mix, then set the pan of seasonings aside.

4. Place the *chana dal* in a spice mill or coffee grinder and process to a fine powder. Put this powder, along with the fried chili sections, the coconut, tamarind purée, the salt, sugar and coriander leaves into a food processor. Process until smooth. You will probably need to add cold water — at least 2–3 tablespoons (40–60ml) — to reach the desired consistency, which is "just pourable".

5. Scrape the chutney into a bowl, pour in the seasonings and oil, and mix well. Your chutney is ready to serve.

FRESH PEACH CHUTNEY

Choose peaches that are a little under-ripe for this chutney. Vary the chili content according to taste. Nectarines or apricots can be used instead of peaches with equally successful results.

PREPARATION AND COOKING TIME:
about 45 minutes
YIELD: about 3 cups (750ml)

2 teaspoons (10ml) ghee
½ teaspoon (2ml) cumin seeds
2 teaspoons (10ml) minced fresh ginger
3 small fresh green chilies, seeded and cut into thin julienne strips, (or red ones for a hotter chutney)
750g peaches, peeled, stoned and cut into wedges after weighing

¼ teaspoon (1ml) cinnamon powder
¼ teaspoon (1ml) nutmeg powder
¼ teaspoon (1ml) turmeric powder
¼ teaspoon (1ml) cayenne pepper
¼ teaspoon (1ml) clove powder
¼ teaspoon (1ml) fennel powder
¼ teaspoon (1ml) cardamom powder
¾–1 cup (185–250ml) sugar

1. Melt the ghee in a heavy 2-litre/quart saucepan over medium heat. When the ghee is hot, sprinkle in the cumin seeds and fry them until they darken a few shades. Add the ginger and chilies and sauté them for 1 minute. Add the peaches, powdered spices and ⅓ cup (85ml) water.

2. Reduce the heat to low. Place a lid on the saucepan and steam the peaches for about 15–30 minutes, depending on their ripeness, until they are soft.

3. Remove the lid and allow the remaining water to evaporate. Add the sugar and continue to cook the chutney uncovered for about 30 minutes, or until it thickens. Serve the chutney at room temperature, or cover and refrigerate for up to one week.

HOMEMADE APRICOT JAM

Using dried fruit is a convenient way to make jam when stoned fruits are out of season. I've found that Australian dried apricots make a richer-tasting jam than the imported variety. Even better are sun-dried, unsulphured dried apricots, available from selected natural food stores. The jam will be dark-coloured but delectable. You may need to soak the fruit a little longer.

APRICOT SOAKING TIME: at least 24 hours
PREPARATION AND COOKING TIME: about 45 minutes
YIELD: 4 cups (1 litre)

250g dried apricots
3¾ cups (935ml) cold water
3¾ cups (935ml) sugar
1 tablespoon (20ml) lemon juice

1. Wash the apricots thoroughly. Place them in a basin with the water and allow them to soak for at least 24 hours.

2. Place the fruit, along with the water in which it has soaked, in a 3-litre/quart saucepan. Add the lemon juice. Bring the fruit mixture to a boil over moderate heat and reduce to a simmer, boiling gently for about 20 minutes, or until the apricots start to break up. If you want your jam to be a smooth purée, stir the fruit during this time. If you prefer a chunkier product, don't stir it.

3. Add the sugar and stir gently until it has dissolved. Increase the heat, and stirring more often, cook the jam for another 15 minutes, or until it thickens. Pour into hot sterilised jars and seal.

BUSH TOMATO CHUTNEY

Bush tomatoes are an indigenous fruit of the Australian outback, growing on small hardy shrubs, particularly in the Central Australian desert. They have a strong savoury flavour with spicy, piquant and caramel overtones. Bush tomatoes can be bitter if not used sparingly. Generally they are cooked with other ingredients in the ratio of one part bush tomatoes to 10 parts of the other ingredients. This allows the flavour of the bush tomatoes to come through without the bitterness.

In this recipe, dried, ground bush tomatoes are combined with fresh tomatoes in a hot, sweet, spicy chutney — an interesting blend of Indian and Australian flavours. Ground, dried bush tomatoes are available at gourmet and specialty stores. Note that dried tomatoes also act as a thickening agent, and will swell and absorb liquid during the cooking process. This chutney is versatile and fits into many menu scenarios. It is especially delicious served as an accompaniment to fried or baked savoury dishes.

PREPARATION AND COOKING TIME:
about 25 minutes
YIELD: about 1 cup (250ml)

1 tablespoon (20ml) ghee or oil
1 teaspoon (5ml) cumin seeds
one 2.5cm (1-inch) cinnamon stick
1 or 2 whole dried red chilies
2 cups (500ml) peeled and chopped ripe tomatoes
2½ teaspoons (12ml) dried, ground bush tomatoes
3 tablespoons (60ml) palm sugar or brown sugar
½ teaspoon (2ml) salt

1. Heat the ghee or oil in a large frying pan over moderate heat. When it is hot but not smoking, add the cumin, cinnamon and chilies. Fry until the cumin seeds darken a few shades.

2. Drop in the tomatoes and cook them, stirring often, for about 10 or 15 minutes, or until they are broken down and soft.

3. Sprinkle in the bush tomatoes, the sugar, and the salt, and cook for another 10 minutes, or until the chutney is thick. Serve warm or at room temperature.

FRESH FIG CONSERVE

Soft, sweet and pulpy, figs occupy a high position amongst fruits. The ripe fresh fruit is juicy, wholesome and delicious. Figs are also a restorative food that help in quick recovery after prolonged illness.

For best results, select figs for this delectable conserve that are all fully mature but not overripe and without rupture or blemish.

PREPARATION AND COOKING TIME:
about 30 minutes
YIELD: 4½ cups (1125ml)

1kg fresh ripe figs
4 scant cups (1 litre) sugar
⅓ cup (85ml) lemon juice, about 2 large lemons
2 teaspoons (10ml) packed lemon zest
2 tablespoons (40ml) water, if required

1. Wash the figs and cut off their tips. If the figs are small, cut them in half; if they are large, cut them in quarters.

2. Spread the sugar on a tray and heat it in a pre-heated hot oven, taking care not to burn it.

3. Place the figs in a 5-litre/quart saucepan along with the lemon zest and lemon juice over moderate heat. Bring them to the boil and cook them for about 10 minutes, or until they soften and the syrup darkens to a rich red colour. Do not stir them, and do not allow the figs to break up. You may need to add a little water.

4. Remove the sugar from the oven, and gently stir it into the figs, being careful not to rupture them. When the sugar has dissolved, bring the mixture to a rapid boil and, without stirring, cook for another 10 minutes, or until the setting point is reached. Carefully ladle the conserve into sterilised jars.

SPICY GUAVA JAM

This thick, hot and sweet delicacy is a cross between a spicy fruit butter and a jam. It was a personal favourite of my spiritual preceptor, His Divine Grace A.C. Bhaktivedanta Swami Prabhupada. The recipe is from my godsister Yamuna devi, a fellow cook and also a disciple of His Divine Grace. It appears in her award-winning cookbook *Lord Krsna's Cuisine — The Art of Indian Vegetarian Cooking*. I tested the recipe using yellow-skinned pink guavas, but any just-ripe guava will yield a delicious result.

PREPARATION AND COOKING TIME:
about 1 hour
YIELD: about 2 cups (500ml)

500g just-ripe guavas
3 whole dried red chilies
6 whole cloves
1 teaspoon (5ml) coriander seeds
¼ teaspoon (1ml) cumin seeds
one 7.5 cm (3-inch) piece of cinnamon stick
½ teaspoon (2ml) cardamom seeds
¼ teaspoon (1ml) kalonji seeds
2 cups (500ml) sugar
1½ teaspoons (7ml) lime or lemon juice

1. Wash the guavas, cut each one into eight pieces and place them in a steamer basket over boiling water. Steam for about 20–30 minutes, or until very soft.

2. Meanwhile, combine the red chilies, cloves, coriander seeds, cumin seeds, cinnamon, cardamom and *kalonji* in a heavy frying pan. Place the pan over low heat, and, stirring often, dry-roast the spices until the cumin seeds darken a few shades. Break up the cinnamon stick into small pieces and grind it, along with all the roasted spices, with a mortar and pestle, or in a spice mill.

3. Transfer the steamed guavas to a heavy 3-litre/quart saucepan and mash them to

a smooth purée. If you don't like the guava seeds, pass the guava paste through a food mill or coarse sieve.

4. Place the guavas over low heat, add the sugar and stir until dissolved. Increase the heat, add the lime or lemon juice, and, stirring often, cook for another 10–20 minutes, or until thick, depending on the variety of guava you've used.

5. Remove the pan from the heat and stir in the powdered spices. Transfer the guava jam to a hot, dry, sterilised glass jar and seal. This jam will last up to two weeks.

TENDER EGGPLANT PICKLES

This tender and delicious pickle from Maharastra in north-west India is simultaneously hot, sweet and sour. Select firm fresh eggplants for best results.

PREPARATION TIME: 10 minutes
COOKING TIME: about 20 minutes
YIELD: about 3 cups (750ml)

450g eggplants, about 3 medium-sized ones
½ cup (125ml) peanut oil or sesame oil (not the toasted Chinese variety)
2 teaspoons (10ml) finely-minced fresh ginger
1 teaspoon (5ml) yellow asafetida powder
2 teaspoons (10ml) salt
2 teaspoons (10ml) chili powder or cayenne pepper
½ cup (125ml) vinegar or lemon juice
1 cup (250ml) sugar
2 teaspoons (10ml) ground, roasted cumin seeds

1. Wash and dry the eggplants. Trim them, then slice them in half down the centre, lengthwise. Cut each section in half again crosswise. Slice each quarter in wedges lengthwise, each one measuring about 7.5cm × 0.5cm (3 inches × ¼ inch). Make sure that each wedge has some black skin on it.

2. Heat the oil over fairly high heat in a small heavy wok or deep sauté pan. When the oil is hot, drop in the ginger and stir it for about 1 minute or until fragrant. Sprinkle in the yellow asafetida powder, stir momentarily, then add the eggplant, salt and chili powder. Stir-fry the eggplants constantly for about 10 minutes, or until they become soft enough to pierce with a knife point.

3. Add the vinegar or lemon juice, and sugar. Reduce the heat slightly and cook for another 10 minutes, or until the eggplants are very tender. Stir in the ground cumin seeds, and remove the eggplants from the heat. Allow the pickle to cool, and store in a glass jar.

RHUBARB CHUTNEY

Commonly thought of as a fruit, rhubarb is in fact a stalk or stem vegetable. But that doesn't change the fact that it makes a great chutney. This one is simultaneously hot, sweet, sour and spicy, and keeps well for about a week, covered and refrigerated. Serve it on a holiday, festival or for a banquet menu.

PREPARATION AND COOKING TIME:
about 25 minutes
YIELD: enough for 6–8 persons

2 teaspoons (10ml) ghee
1 tablespoon (20ml) grated fresh ginger
500g ripe red rhubarb stalks, cut into 1.25cm (½-inch) lengths
½ teaspoon (2ml) powdered allspice
½ teaspoon (2ml) finely-ground coriander powder
½ teaspoon (2ml) chili powder
¼ teaspoon (1ml) cinnamon powder
¼ teaspoon (1ml) clove powder
½ cup (125ml) sultanas
1 teaspoon (5ml) salt
¾ cup (185ml) sugar

1. Place the ghee in a 2-litre/quart saucepan over moderate heat. When the ghee is fairly hot, add the grated ginger and sauté it for about 1 or 2 minutes, or until fragrant. Add the rhubarb, salt, all the spices and 1 tablespoon (20ml) water. Stir to combine everything, then reduce the heat to low and place a tight-fitting lid on the saucepan. Steam the rhubarb for about 10 minutes, or until it is soft.

2. Add the sultanas and sugar, and still over low heat, cook without the lid, stirring occasionally for about 10 minutes, or until the chutney thickens. Remove the chutney from the heat and serve at room temperature.

SWEET AND SOUR TAMARIND CHUTNEY

Tamarind is the fruit contained in the hanging pods of the tamarind tree, *Tamarindus indica*. The pods themselves are between 10–15cm (4–6 inches) long, cinnamon-brown coloured with a fuzzy coating. The pulp from inside the pods is piquant with a sour, date/apricot flavour.

Dried tamarind is available at all Indian and Asian grocers in two main forms — blocks of pressed pulp, and jars of concentrate. The dried pulp, which needs to be reconstituted by soaking it in water, varies immensely from source to source. Some appears full of fibre, and others are relatively fibre-free. But this is not an indication of quality; some of the best tasting tamarind purée comes from soaking very unappealing looking dried tamarind. Shop around, and choose your favourite brand.

There are innumerable variations on this classic chutney. This one is sauce-like and sweetened predominantly with dates. It is very versatile and popular, and especially suited as an accompaniment for fried dishes, such as *samosas, kofta, pakoras* and *vadai*.

PREPARATION AND COOKING TIME:
30–40 minutes
SOAKING TIME: 1 hour
YIELD: about 2 cups (500ml)

⅓ cup (85ml) tamarind pulp
¾ cup (185ml) dried dates
1½ teaspoons (7ml) minced fresh ginger
1–2 fresh green chilies chopped
½ cup (125ml) sugar
1 teaspoon (5ml) salt
1½ teaspoons (7ml) garam masala
½ teaspoon (2ml) cayenne pepper

1. Soak the tamarind pulp in 1⅓ cups (335ml) hot water for 1 hour. Soak the dates in ½ cup (125ml) hot water for 1 hour. Place the soaked dates and their soaking liquid along with the ginger, the green chilies, and another cup (250ml) water in a 2- or 3-litre/quart saucepan. Bring to the boil, then cook, covered, over low heat for 15–20 minutes, or until the dates are very tender. Remove the saucepan from the heat.

2. Meanwhile, squeeze out all the soft pulp from the soaked tamarind, push and squeeze it through a sieve, reserve the purée and discard the stones and roughage. Combine the strained tamarind purée with the tender cooked dates and their cooking liquid in a food processor. Blend to a smooth purée.

3. Pour the purée into the rinsed out saucepan that held the dates. Add the sugar, salt, *garam masala* and cayenne pepper. Bring to the boil over a gentle heat, stirring to dissolve the sugar. Simmer the chutney for 5–10 minutes more, then allow it to cool to room temperature before serving. The flavours of this chutney improve as it sits.

URAD DAL CHUTNEY

Sometimes known as black gram, *urad dal* lentils are a close relative of the well-known mung bean. These lentils are substantially rich in protein — ⅔ cup, 145 grams, of cooked beans yields about 20 per cent of a person's daily requirements. When combined with protein-rich yogurt, as in this tasty dish, the yield is much higher. Although it is called a chutney, this creamy South Indian condiment can be successfully adapted in many ways. It makes a delicious sandwich spread — reduce the chilies if you like. Add a little water and it becomes a tasty dipping sauce, or serve as is with rice. I've even served it as a mayonnaise for salads. It's also quick, cheap and easy to make. Split *urad dal* lentils are available in all Indian grocery stores.

PREPARATION AND COOKING TIME:
15–20 minutes
YIELD: 2 cups (500ml) chutney

½ cup (125ml) split urad dal lentils (the cream-coloured variety, not the unhulled split lentils with the black skin still attached)

4 large dried red chilies, or to taste
2 teaspoons (10ml) ghee
1½ teaspoons (7ml) salt
1½ cups (375ml) yogurt
1 teaspoon (5ml) black mustard seeds
½ teaspoon (2ml) cumin seeds
10 fresh curry leaves, torn in small pieces, or dried ones, crushed

1. Place a wok or large non-stick frying pan over medium heat. Add the *urad dal* lentils, and dry-roast them for about 10 minutes, or until they turn a rich golden brown and emit an aromatic fragrance. When the lentils are halfway done, add the dry chilies. If you like, add 1 teaspoon (5ml) ghee to help the roasting. Avoid over-roasting the lentils.

2. Remove the roasted *urad dal* lentils and chilies to a plate, cool slightly, and transfer to an electric coffee grinder or spice mill. Grind to a very fine powder. You may have to grind them in two batches.

3. Combine the ground *dal* and chili powder, the salt, and the yogurt in a bowl. Mix well with a wire whisk.

4. Reheat the wok or pan again over moderate heat. Add the ghee. When fairly hot, sprinkle in the mustard seeds. As they crackle and pop, add the cumin and curry leaves. When the cumin seeds darken a few shades, remove the pan from the heat and tip the ghee and spices into the yogurt and *dal* mixture. Scrape out all of the spice seeds and flavoured ghee, whisk in the spices and your *urad dal* chutney is ready.

SWEETS & DESSERTS

Greek-style Nut-filled Pastries in Fragrant Syrup (Kataifi)

Creamy Vermicelli Dessert (Kheer Sevian)

Sweet Cheese-filled Pancakes (Blintzes)

Grapefruit Granita

Crispy Fried Batter Spirals in Saffron Syrup (Jalebis)

Carob and Raisin Cake

Apple Kuchen

Pumpkin Pie

Poached Pear and Prune Tart

Danish Pastries

Italian-style Rice Pudding

Indonesian Sweet Coconut-stuffed Pancakes (Dadar)

Ginger, Saffron and Pistachio Kulfi

Indonesian Fruit Platter with Hot and Sweet Dipping Sauce (Rujak Manis)

Pistachio Milk Fudge (Pista Burfi)

Almond Toffee Fudge

Carrot Halava

Macadamia and Blueberry Muffins

Rose-scented Marzipan Half-moon Pastries

Flaked Almond and Saffron Semolina Halava

Quick and Easy Vanilla Ice Cream

Apricot and Walnut Crescents (Rugelach)

Amish Apple Dumplings

Strawberry Cream Shortcake

Fresh Nectarine Pie

Pecan Carob Chip Cookies

Hazelnut and Fruit Granola

GREEK-STYLE NUT-FILLED PASTRIES IN FRAGRANT SYRUP (KATAIFI)

These aromatic stuffed pastries are a well-known sight in sweet shops throughout Greece, Turkey and the Middle East. Known as *kataifi* in Greece and *kadayif* in Turkey, they feature very thin white strands of a vermicelli-like dough that is made by pouring and shaking flour and water batter through a sieve onto a hot metal plate. The raw pastry, also known as *kataifi*, *kadayif* or *konafa*, is available frozen from Greek, Turkish or Middle Eastern stores worldwide, where you will often see the baked pastries arranged for sale on large trays. For best results, pour the hot syrup onto the hot pastries as soon as you remove them from the oven, and serve them the following day.

PREPARATION TIME: 25–35 minutes
COOKING TIME: about 1 hour
COOKED PASTRY SOAKING TIME:
a few hours, or overnight
YIELD: 16 pastries, 5cm × 7.5cm
(2 inches × 3 inches)

The filling:

⅔ cup (165ml) chopped walnuts
⅔ cup (165ml) chopped pistachios
⅔ cup (165ml) chopped blanched almonds
1 teaspoon (5ml) cinnamon
¼ teaspoon (1ml) freshly-grated nutmeg
½ cup (125ml) sugar

The syrup:

2 cups (500ml) sugar
1½ cups (375ml) water
one 10cm (4-inch) cinnamon stick
4 whole cloves
one 10cm × 2.5cm (4-inch × 1-inch) strip lemon zest
2 teaspoons (10ml) lemon juice

The pastry:

250g unsalted butter
500g kataifi pastry

To prepare the filling:
Combine all the filling ingredients in a bowl, and mix well. Divide into 8 portions.

To prepare the syrup:
Place all the syrup ingredients in a small saucepan over low heat. Stir to dissolve the sugar, increase the heat, and bring the syrup to the boil. Reduce the heat, simmer for 10 minutes, then remove the syrup from the heat and set it aside.

To assemble the pastries:

1. Melt the butter. Remove the *kadaifi* pastry from the packet, and carefully separate it on a flat surface into 8 equal-sized portions, being careful not to smash the delicate strands.

2. Take one portion of pastry and tease it into a rectangle measuring 15cm × 22.5cm (6 inches × 9 inches). Try to ensure that the strands are all running the same way. Brush the pastry generously with melted butter.

3. Spoon and spread one portion of filling along the narrow edge of the pastry. Grasp the pastry strands carefully with both hands and carefully and firmly roll the pastry into a tight roll measuring 5cm × 15cm (2 inches × 6 inches). Repeat for all the remaining portions of pastry and filling.

4. Pre-heat the oven to 190°C/375°F. Butter a 20cm × 30cm (8 inches × 12 inches) baking dish. Carefully lift the pastries and place them packed closely together in two rows of four. Brush them with any remaining butter. Bake on one shelf above the centre of the oven for 50–55 minutes, or until the pastries are golden brown. Meanwhile, re-boil the sugar syrup, remove from the heat, and discard the cloves, lemon zest and cinnamon stick.

5. Pour the hot syrup evenly over the hot pastries. Cover the tray with a tea towel and leave to cool. Cut the pastries once across to form 16 even-sized pieces. Leave for a few hours, or overnight, at room temperature. The *kataifi* will be soft and sticky-sweet underneath, but will remain crisp and golden on top.

CREAMY VERMICELLI DESSERT (KHEER SEVIAN)

This quick and easy-to-prepare creamy sweet pudding is well-loved throughout North India and especially in Pakistan and the Punjab. Different names for and versions of the dish abound, and practically every household has its own favourite recipe. It is traditionally prepared using very fine vermicelli noodles available as *seviya* or *sev* at Indian grocers. I use very fine Italian vermicelli or *capellini*, which works wonderfully. Serve *Kheer Sevian* hot or chilled.

PREPARATION AND COOKING TIME: 20–30 minutes
CHILLING TIME (if required): 2 hours
YIELD: enough for 6–8 persons

3 tablespoons (60ml) ghee or unsalted butter
⅓ cup (85ml) slivered raw almonds
⅓ cup (85ml) sliced raw pistachio nuts
6 whole cardamom pods, bruised
¼ cup (60ml) sultanas
5 cups (1250ml) milk

75g fine vermicelli, broken into 3.75cm (1½-inch) lengths
½ cup (125ml) sugar
¼ cup (60ml) double cream
1–2 tablespoons (20–40ml) pure distilled rosewater (not essence or concentrate)

1. Melt the ghee or butter in a heavy-bottomed 3-litre/quart non-stick saucepan over moderate heat. When it is slightly hot, drop in the nuts and cardamom, and sauté them for 3–5 minutes, or until the nuts are golden brown. When the nuts are almost done, drop in the sultanas and fry them until they swell up.

2. Pour in the milk, add the vermicelli, increase the heat, and bring the mixture to the boil. Reduce the heat slightly and simmer, stirring occasionally, for 20 minutes or until the pudding is thickened and creamy. Add the sugar and cream, mix well, cook a little more and then remove from the heat. Stir in the rosewater. Serve hot, or chilled. Note that the pudding thickens considerably in the refrigerator. You may like to cook the vermicelli with extra milk if you plan to serve it cold. Or else you may thin it with extra milk and cream after removing it from the fridge.

Sweet, Cheese-filled Pancakes (Blintzes)

Blintzes are one of the great specialities of the Jewish Ashkenaizic kitchen. Like French crêpes, or Russian *blinis*, which they resemble, *blintzes* are thin pancakes that can be wrapped around sweet or savoury fillings, and can play the role of appetiser, main course or dessert. Other sweet fillings could include apple, rhubarb, pears, blueberries or cherries. Potatoes are popular as the basis for vegetarian savoury fillings. Although I use *neufchatel*, other soft cheeses, such as cottage cheese, curd cheese, cream cheese or quark are all suitable for filling the *blintzes*.

PREPARATION AND COOKING TIME:
1–1¼ hours
YIELD: makes 12–14 pancakes

The pancakes:

¼ cup (60ml) soured buttermilk
1 tablespoon (20ml) sugar
2 tablespoons (40ml) melted butter
¼ teaspoon (1ml) salt
1 cup (250ml) milk
¾ cup (185ml) water
¼ teaspoon (1ml) ground nutmeg
1¼ cups (310ml) self-raising flour

The filling:

250g cottage cheese
250g neufchatel, or a cream cheese type of your choice, or homemade panir cheese
2 tablespoons (40ml) sour cream
3–4 tablespoons (60–80ml) sugar
finely grated outer rind of 2 lemons
¼ cup (60ml) seedless raisins
¼ teaspoon (1ml) cinnamon powder
¼ teaspoon (1ml) nutmeg powder

Pan-frying the blintzes:

2 teaspoons (10ml) butter

Toppings or accompaniments:

2 tablespoons (40ml) brown sugar mixed with ½ teaspoon (2ml) cinnamon powder or 1 cup (250ml) berries such as blueberries, raspberries or strawberries or a combination, poached in a little sugar, or ½ cup (125ml) sour cream

To prepare the pancake batter:

Combine the buttermilk, sugar, melted butter, salt, milk, water and nutmeg in a food processor. Add 1 cup (250ml) of the flour. Process until smooth and creamy. Check the consistency of the batter. It should be slightly thicker than pouring cream. Add some of the remaining flour to adjust as required. Pour out the pancake batter and set it aside.

To prepare the filling:

Drop in all the ingredients for the filling, except the raisins, into the food processor. Process until smooth. Remove, fold in the raisins and set aside.

To cook the pancakes:

1. Heat 1 or 2 shallow, 20cm (8-inch) non-stick frying pans over moderate heat, until a drop of water sprinkled on bounces off their surface.

2. Ladle in 3 tablespoons (60ml) of batter, immediately tilting the pan to evenly distribute the mixture to form pancakes to fill the pan. If the batter doesn't spread easily, add a little more water to it. Cook the pancake for 2 or 3 minutes, or until it sets up, the edges begin to curl and the top of the pancake is dry to the touch.

3. Turn the pancake over, cook for 10 seconds only, then transfer to a plate, undercooked side facing down.

4. Continue to cook the rest of the pancakes in the same manner, stacking them between layers of non-stick paper. You will probably need to allow the pans to cool between pancakes.

To assemble the blintzes:

1. Heap 2 tablespoons (40ml) filling on the bottom half of a pancake. Roll up the pancake, tucking in the sides as you go to form a tight rectangular parcel. Repeat for all the *blintzes*.

2. Melt 1 teaspoon (5ml) butter in a frying pan. Place the *blintzes*, seam down, on the pan. You may need to cook them in two batches. Sauté over moderate heat until the *blintzes* begin to turn golden brown. Carefully turn them over, and cook for a minute or two on the other side.

3. Slide the pancakes on to a hot serving plate and serve them with any of the suggested accompaniments.

GRAPEFRUIT GRANITA

A *granita* is an iced dessert or refreshment resembling a sorbet. The refreshing taste of this *granita* quenches and cools.

PREPARATION AND COOKING TIME:
a few minutes
FREEZING TIME: 3 hours
YIELD: 1 litre

½ cup (125ml) sugar
1 cup (250ml) water
finely grated outer rind of 3 grapefruits
3 cups (750ml) freshly-squeezed grapefruit juice

1. Combine the sugar and water in a small saucepan over low heat and stir to dissolve. Bring to the boil, simmer for 2 minutes, then remove from the heat. You will need only 1 cup (250ml) of this syrup. Combine the cup of syrup with the grapefruit rind, and chill it.

2. Mix the grapefruit juice with the chilled syrup and pour into a shallow metal tray. Place it in the freezer, stirring every hour to prevent separation of the juice and syrup. Allow the *granita* to freeze for 3 hours. To serve, draw a serving spoon across the surface to produce a granular ice. Serve immediately.

CRISPY FRIED BATTER SPIRALS IN SAFFRON SYRUP (JALEBIS)

If I have a favourite sweet, it has to be *jalebis*. They are saffron-coloured, light, juicy and slightly crunchy — and very addictive. They don't take long to make, although the batter does have to sit for at least 18–24 hours to ferment slightly. This fermentation is essential for the *jalebis* to develop the correct texture when fried. A little practice is required to master the uniform shapes of *jalebis*, although even strange-looking squiggles will taste just as good. *Jalebi* batter has to be poured into the hot ghee, formed, fried, removed, then soaked in syrup for only a few seconds, removed, then drained — all in quick succession; so it's useful to cook *jalebis* with a partner, one handling the frying and the other looking after the dipping in syrup.

There are a number of alternative utensils you can use for extruding the batter into the hot ghee: a piping bag or cylinder, a plastic squeeze bottle, a metal cookie "gun", or even a plastic bag with a small hole — are all quite suitable. *Jalebis* are a wonderful dessert to make for a special buffet and will receive rave reviews. Incidentally, I've heard that *jalebis* eaten with hot milk relieves the symptoms of a cold. That sounds like a good enough excuse to eat *jalebis*, doesn't it?

PREPARATION TIME: 15 minutes
BATTER RESTING TIME: 18–24 hours
COOKING TIME: 25–30 minutes
YIELD: enough for 6–8 persons

2 cups (500ml) unbleached plain flour
1½ tablespoons (30ml) rice flour
¼ teaspoon (1ml) baking powder
2 tablespoons (40ml) yogurt
1¼ cups (310ml) warm water
½ teaspoon (2ml) powdered saffron
3 cups (750ml) sugar
2⅔ (665ml) water

1½ tablespoons (30ml) rose water

ghee for deep-frying

1. Mix together the flour, rice flour and baking powder in a glass or ceramic bowl. Add the yogurt, the 1¼ cups (310ml) warm water, and half the saffron, and whisk it into a smooth batter. Cover it, and leave it in a warm place for 18–24 hours. The batter will be ready when it appears somewhat gelatinous and gooey when whisked. It should flow from a spoon in a broad solid band without breaking.

2. Combine the sugar, the remaining saffron and 2⅔ cups (665ml) water in a 3-litre/quart frying pan or sauté pan. Place over moderate heat, stir to dissolve the sugar, raise the heat and boil for 8 minutes. Remove the pan from the heat and stir in the rosewater.

3. Set a cake rack on a tray near the cooking area. Fill a large flat pan with ghee to a depth of 3.75cm (1½ inches) and heat to 180°C/355°F.

4. Pour the batter into your piping bag or squeeze bottle and squeeze the batter out over the surface of the hot ghee. You can form three-ring connecting spirals, loose double-figure eights or a series of loops, joined in a chain. Each piece should be about 5cm × 7.5cm (2 inches × 3 inches) wide. Fry for about 30 seconds on the first side, and 20–30 seconds on the second side, or until they turn crisp and golden brown.

5. Lift the *jalebis* out of the ghee, and drop them carefully in the hot syrup. With another slotted spoon, hold them under the syrup for 15–20 seconds to allow the hot syrup to fill up the hollow centres of the loops. Don't let them languish too long in the syrup lest they become limp. Remove the *jalebis* from the syrup and place them on a cake rack to drain. Continue to shape, fry, soak and drain the remaining *jalebis*. Serve hot.

CAROB AND RAISIN CAKE

You don't need eggs to make a light sponge cake. This recipe is proof.

BATTER RESTING TIME: 30 minutes
PREPARATION AND COOKING TIME: 10 minutes
BAKING TIME: 50–60 minutes
YIELD: one 22.5cm (9-inch) sponge cake

1½ cups (375ml) water
1½ cups (375ml) sugar
1 cup (250ml) raisins
½ teaspoon (2ml) ground cloves
½ teaspoon (2ml) cinnamon powder
¼ teaspoon (1ml) salt
¾ cup (185ml) carob powder
250g butter
3 tablespoons (60ml) water
1 teaspoon (5ml) baking soda
2 cups (500ml) plain flour, sifted

1. Pre-heat the oven to 180°C/355°F. Butter a 22.5cm (9-inch) springform cake tin.

2. In a 3-litre/quart heavy-based saucepan, combine the 1½ cups (375ml) water, the sugar, raisins, cloves, cinnamon and salt. Whisk in the carob powder, add the butter, and place the saucepan over medium heat, bring to the boil, then reduce the heat and simmer the mixture for 5 minutes. Remove the pan from the heat and set it aside for 30 minutes, or until the mixture is cool.

3. Bring to the boil the 3 tablespoons (60ml) water in a small saucepan, and stir in the soda until it is completely dissolved. Add this water along with the sifted flour to the rest of the cooled ingredients, and mix well.

4. Pour the cake mixture into the buttered cake tin. Place in the lower third of the oven, and bake for 50–60 minutes, or until a wooden skewer inserted into the centre of the cake comes out clean and dry.

5. Cool the cake in the pan for 10 minutes. Carefully remove the sides of the spring-form and turn the cake onto a wire rack. Invert onto a second rack, and cool completely, right side up. At serving time, sieve the top of the cake with confectioner's sugar, or split and fill with jam and cream.

APPLE KUCHEN

Tangy apples baked with sultanas and sweet spices under a crispy, buttery topping — highly delectable! This delicious dessert is wonderful served hot with whipped cream or custard. Please note that if the topping browns before the apples are fully cooked, try covering the apple *kuchen* with foil until the apples are done, then uncover and cook for a few minutes more to crisp up the topping.

PREPARATION AND COOKING TIME: about 70 minutes
YIELD: enough for 4–6 persons

5 very large green cooking apples, about 900g
1 tablespoon (20ml) lemon juice
½ cup (125ml) sugar
2 tablespoons (40ml) plain flour
1 teaspoon (5ml) good quality Dutch cinnamon powder
½–¾ teaspoon (2–3ml) nutmeg powder, or 1 teaspoon (5ml) if you like a little more nutmeg flavour
¾ cup (185ml) sultanas
⅔ cup (165ml) plain flour
⅓ cup (85ml) softened butter
⅓ cup (85ml) brown sugar

1. Peel, core and thinly slice the apples, dropping the slices into iced water acidulated with the lemon juice to prevent browning.

2. Combine the ½ cup (125ml) sugar, 2 table-spoons (40ml) flour, the spices and sultanas in a bowl. Pre-heat the oven to 190°C/375°F.

3. Drain the apples and toss with the flour and sugar mixture. Place the mixture in a 22.5cm (9-inch) ovenproof pie dish, mounding the fruit slightly in the middle.

4. Mix together the remaining flour, softened butter and brown sugar, and rub together to form a moist, crumbly topping. Sprinkle this topping over the apples and place the pie dish in the top half of the pre-heated oven. Bake for about 45 minutes, or until the apples are soft and the topping is golden brown. Serve hot with the toppings suggested above.

PUMPKIN PIE

This is a spicy, all-American favourite dessert. Select highly flavoured, dark-fleshed pumpkins for optimum flavour. Butternut, or especially *kobocha*, is highly recommended.

PREPARATION AND BAKING TIME: about 2 hours
YIELD: one 22.5cm (9-inch) pie

The crust:

1 cup (250ml) unbleached plain flour
⅓ cup (85ml) butter
½ teaspoon (2ml) salt
5–7 tablespoons (100–140ml) cold water

The filling:

1 medium-sized pumpkin
one 400g can sweetened condensed milk, 1¼ cups (310ml)
2 tablespoons (40ml) cornflour (cornstarch)
1 teaspoon (5ml) cinnamon powder
½ teaspoon (2ml) salt
2 teaspoons (10ml) freshly-ground whole allspice berries
½ teaspoon (2ml) freshly-grated nutmeg

To prepare the pastry:

1. Combine the flour, butter and salt in a food processor and process with 12–15 short bursts until it resembles coarse breadcrumbs. Sprinkle in 2 table-spoons (40ml) cold water, and process with another 6 short bursts. Add another 1 or 2 tablespoons (20–40ml) water, if required, to form a damp mass.

2. Remove and gather the pastry into a ball, and place it on a floured surface. Roll out the pastry to line a 22.5cm (9-inch) pie dish or tart pan with removable bottom. Trim and crimp the edges and chill while you prepare the filling.

To prepare the filling:

1. Split the pumpkin crosswise. Remove and discard the seeds and fibres. Place the pumpkin, cut side down on a lightly buttered baking sheet. Place in a 160°C/320°F oven and bake for about 1 hour, or until the pumpkin is tender when pierced with a knife.

2. Scrape away the pulp from the skin, discard the skin, and place the pulp in a food processor fitted with a metal blade. Process in batches until smooth.

3. Force the pumpkin purée through a sieve, measure 2 cups (500ml) for the pie and reserve the remainder for other purposes. Combine the measured pumpkin purée with all the other filling ingredients. Beat with a wire whisk until smooth and creamy.

To assemble and bake the pie:

Pre-heat the oven to 200°C/390°F. Pour the filling into the chilled pastry case and smooth it out. It should be barely 2.5cm (1-inch) deep. Bake for 40 minutes or until the filling is set. Cool, cut into wedges and serve with whipped cream.

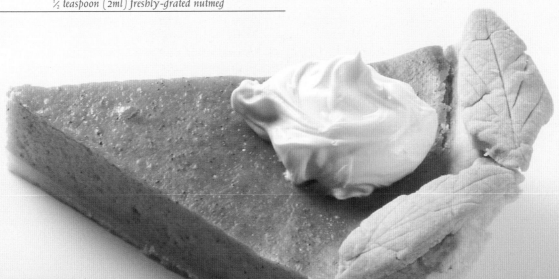

POACHED PEAR AND PRUNE TART

Homer (the ancient, not Bart's dad) called the pear "one of the fruits of the gods". There are usually a good variety to choose from, but all pears are not equal; some are more suited for cooking than others. Silky, aromatic Bartletts and Red Bartletts, Bosc pears with their nutty, firm dense flesh and the fine-grained juicy Packhams are by far the best for poaching.

Coupled with succulent prunes, and flavoured with vanilla bean, orange, cinnamon, and lemon zest, pears display their heavenly qualities in this delectable tart. Serve it warm or at room temperature with thick cream, *crème fraîche*, or vanilla ice cream.

PASTRY PREPARATION AND COOKING TIME: 35–40 minutes
BAKING TIME: 30–40 minutes
YIELD: 1 heaped 22.5cm (9-inch) tart

The pastry:

1 cup (250ml) unbleached plain flour
1 tablespoon (20ml) sugar
⅓ cup (85ml) chilled butter
¼ cup (60ml) iced water

The filling:

½ cup (125ml) sugar
2 tablespoons (40ml) lemon juice
¾ cup (185ml) orange juice
two 7.5cm (3-inch) cinnamon sticks
1 vanilla bean, split lengthwise
1 teaspoon (5ml) lemon zest
300g pitted prunes
4 large fully ripe but firm pears (about 300g each), cored, peeled and cut into eighths, lengthwise

To prepare the pastry:

1. Place the flour, sugar and butter in a food processor fitted with a metal blade. Process 5 or 6 times in short bursts or until the pastry resembles breadcrumbs. Dribble in three-quarters of the iced water, process in short bursts for no more than 10 seconds until the pastry forms a loose ball. Add the rest of the water only if it is required.

2. Turn out the pastry and form into a firm ball. Flatten with flour-dusted hands into a disc, wrap it in plastic and refrigerate it for half an hour.

To prepare the filling:

1. Combine the sugar, ½ cup (125ml) orange juice, the lemon juice, cinnamon sticks, vanilla bean and lemon zest in a 3-litre/quart saucepan and stir over medium heat until the sugar dissolves. Add the prunes and simmer, covered, for 10–15 minutes or until the prunes swell and the syrup thickens.

2. Lift the lid and add the pears, the remaining orange juice and ¼ cup (60ml) water. Simmer without stirring to avoid breaking up the prunes for another 10 minutes or until the pears are tender. Set the filling aside until cool.

To assemble the tart:

1. Pre-heat the oven to 200°C/390°F. Drain the syrup from the filling, remove the cinnamon sticks and vanilla bean and place the syrup in a small saucepan over medium heat. Reduce the syrup for 5–10 minutes or until very thick.

2. Roll out the pastry and line a 22.5cm (9-inch) tart tin with a removable base. Prick all over with the fork, then bake in the pre-heated oven for 15–20 minutes, or until lightly golden.

3. Remove the tart from the oven. Pile on the fruit filling, spoon over 2 or 3 tablespoons (40–60ml) of the reduced syrup, and return the tart to the oven. Bake for another 15–20 minutes, or until the pastry is a rich golden brown.

4. Before serving, warm any remaining syrup and drizzle it over the tart. Serve with the accompaniments suggested above.

DANISH PASTRIES

There are a great number of varieties of Danish pastries. This variety contains no yeast, and is made flaky with the use of ricotta cheese. If you prefer, substitute homemade curd cheese (*panir*) for the ricotta.

PREPARATION TIME: about 35 minutes
PASTRY RESTING TIME: 1 hour
BAKING TIME: 20–25 minutes
YIELD: 16 pastries

The pastry:

2¼ cups (560ml) self-raising flour
2 teaspoons (10ml) powdered cardamom seeds
1 cup (250ml) cold butter
1 cup (250ml) ricotta cheese

The filling:

¼ cup (60ml) sugar
2 teaspoons (10ml) cinnamon powder
⅓ cup (85ml) currants
⅓ cup (85ml) sultanas
⅓ cup (85ml) chopped glacé cherries

The topping:

⅓ cup (85ml) apricot jam, plus 1 tablespoon (20ml) water
2 tablespoons (40ml) hot water
1 cup (250ml) icing (confectioner's) sugar

1. Place the flour, cardamom powder and cold butter in a food processor. Process with several short bursts until the mixture resembles coarse breadcrumbs. Add the ricotta cheese and process until the mixture clumps together. Remove and gather the pastry into a lump, knead it for a few moments, wrap it in foil and chill in the refrigerator for 1 hour.

2. While the pastry is refrigerating, combine the filling ingredients in a bowl and set them aside.

3. Pre-heat the oven to 200°C/390°F. Unwrap the pastry, and sprinkle a little flour on a large, smooth surface. Press and roll out the pastry to a 30cm × 37.5cm (12-inch × 15-inch) rectangle. Sprinkle the filling ingredients evenly over the surface of the pastry rectangle. Grasping the shorter side of the pastry, roll it up into a tight roll. Seal the exposed edge of the roll, then with a sharp knife cut the pastry into 16 slices 1.5cm (¾-inch) in length.

4. Butter a large cookie sheet or pizza tray and place the pastries cut side up. Do not crowd them because they will expand. If necessary, bake on two trays, or in two batches. Place the pastries in the centre of the pre-heated oven and bake for 20–25 minutes or until firm and golden brown.

5. While the pastries are baking, prepare the topping as follows: Heat the jam and water in a small saucepan for a few minutes until smooth, then remove from the heat. Combine the icing sugar and hot water in a small bowl. When the pastries are done, remove them from the oven, and, while still hot, brush them with the apricot glaze. Finally, spread the hot pastries with the icing mixture. Allow the pastries to fully cool and serve at room temperature.

ITALIAN-STYLE RICE PUDDING

This is a simple but delectable dessert. Serve warm or at room temperature.

PREPARATION AND COOKING TIME: about 50 minutes
YIELD: enough for 6–8 persons

¾ cup (185ml) arborio or other Italian superfino rice
6 cups (1½ litres) fresh whole milk
¼ teaspoon (1ml) cinnamon powder
¼ teaspoon (1ml) freshly grated nutmeg
1 teaspoon (5ml) finely grated orange zest (avoid the white pith)
½ cup (125ml) sugar
1 cup (250ml) fresh ricotta cheese
2 teaspoons (10ml) pure vanilla extract
2–3 tablespoons (40–60ml) flaked, sliced or slivered almonds

1. Pour 4 litres water into a 5-litre/quart saucepan and set it over full heat. When it boils, add the rice, return the water to the boil, and boil for 8 minutes. Drain the rice in a strainer, discarding the water.

2. Bring the milk to the boil in another heavy 3-litre/quart saucepan, preferably non-stick, over high heat. When it boils, add the partly-cooked rice, the cinnamon, nutmeg and the orange zest. Reduce the heat to low and simmer, stirring frequently, for 40 minutes or until the dessert reaches a thin pudding consistency. Towards the end you will need to stir the creamed rice dessert constantly to avoid it sticking or scorching.

3. Add the sugar and set the pudding aside for an hour to cool. Fold in the ricotta cheese and vanilla extract. Turn the rice pudding into a serving dish and garnish with the reserved almonds.

INDONESIAN SWEET COCONUT-STUFFED PANCAKES (DADAR)

Versions of these toothsome delicacies appear in many South-East Asian countries. Sweet, coconut-filled pancakes are well-known all over Indonesia, especially Jakarta, where they are served as a snack, often alongside other kinds of cakes. Sometimes *Dadar* can be found on the menu at wedding receptions and other formal functions.

The taste combination of coconut, palm sugar and *pandan*, a popular Asian flavouring, is found in many varieties of Indonesian cakes and sweets. The ingredients in this dish attest to the value of the coconut palm — the coconut milk, fresh coconut and palm sugar are all derived from the palm tree. Fresh or frozen *pandan* leaves or *pandan* flavouring is available at Asian grocers.

BATTER RESTING TIME: 15 minutes
PREPARATION AND COOKING TIME: 40–60 minutes
YIELD: 16–18 pancakes

The filling:

400g palm sugar
grated flesh from one medium-sized coconut, about 2½ packed cups (625ml) or 2½ cups (625ml) desiccated dried coconut
½ teaspoon (2ml) salt
2 pandan leaves or ½ teaspoon (2ml) pandan flavouring

The pancakes:

2 cups (500ml) plain cake flour
2¾ cups (685ml) thin coconut milk
a few drops orange food colouring (optional)

To prepare the filling:

Break the palm sugar into small pieces, combine with the coconut and the salt, and cook it over very low heat in a heavy 3-litre/quart saucepan until the sugar melts. Add the *pandan* leaf, raise the heat slightly and cook, stirring often, for 15 minutes, or until the mixture is sticky and thick. If using *pandan* flavouring, add it at the end of the cooking. Place the filling aside to cool.

To prepare the pancake batter:

1. Whisk together the flour, coconut milk and the optional food colouring. Set the batter aside for 15 minutes, then, if necessary, add up to ½ cup (125ml) cold water, to bring the batter to a pourable consistency — somewhere between light and heavy cream. You should have about 4½ cups (1125ml) batter.

2. Heat one or two non-stick 20cm (8-inch) frying pans over moderate heat. Lift a pan off the heat and pour in 3 tablespoons (60ml) batter. Swirl and tilt the pan to spread the batter to form a thin 15cm (6-inch) pancake. Cook the pancake on both sides for a total of 2 or 3 minutes, or until the pancake is a pale golden colour. Stack each pancake between sheets of non-stick paper. Repeat until all the batter is used.

To assemble the pancakes:

Place a two tablespoon (40ml) strip of filling a little off-centre on a pancake. Fold over the portion of pancake that is filled onto the rest of the pancake. Tuck in the two sides, and roll into a tube. Repeat for all the pancakes. Serve *Dadar* at room temperature.

GINGER, SAFFRON AND PISTACHIO KULFI

Kulfi is traditional Indian ice cream. Unlike Western egg-based ice creams, *kulfi* is thickened by cooking down milk in the time-honoured way, and then adding a little cornflour (cornstarch). This delicious saffron-coloured version is studded with pistachio nuts and glacé ginger and enriched with cream, condensed milk and evaporated milk. *Kulfi* should be served as firm as possible, preferably in cone-shaped, screw top aluminium moulds (available from Indian suppliers), in cubes (from an ice cube tray), or cut into diamond shapes.

PREPARATION AND COOKING TIME:
35–45 minutes
FREEZING TIME: 6 or 7 hours
YIELD: enough for 6–8 persons

---

4 cups (1 litre) full cream milk

1¼ cups (310ml) light, pouring consistency cream

1¾ cups (435ml) evaporated milk

1¾ cups (435ml) sweetened condensed milk

---

seeds from 8 green cardamom pods, crushed

½ teaspoon (2ml) pure saffron strands crushed and dissolved in 2 tablespoons (40ml) hot milk

---

1½ tablespoons (30ml) cornflour (cornstarch)

⅓ cup (85ml) chopped glacé ginger

---

1 tablespoon (20ml) pure distilled rosewater (not concentrate or essence)

¼ cup (60ml) pistachio nuts, blanched, peeled and finely-chopped shredded pistachio nuts for garnish

---

1. Place the milk, cream, evaporated milk, sweetened condensed milk, cardamom and saffron infusion in a wide, heavy 3-litre/quart saucepan over moderate heat. Stir constantly until the milk boils, scraping the bottom of the saucepan to avoid scorching. When the liquid boils, reduce to a simmer, and, leaving the pan uncovered, simmer gently for 30–40 minutes or until the milk reduces in volume.

2. Combine the cornflour with 2 tablespoons (40ml) cold water, and whisk it into the simmering reduced milk. Raise the heat slightly and allow the milk to thicken. Remove the pan and set it aside, occasionally stirring in the skin that forms on the surface of the milk as it cools. When cool, stir in the glacé ginger, the rosewater and pistachio nuts.

3. Stir the mixture well, then pour into moulds, ice cube trays, or a shallow metal freezing container. Cover with foil and freeze 6 or 7 hours, or until set. If serving from the moulds or ice cube trays, dip the moulds or tray into warm water for just long enough to allow the *kulfi* to slip out. Serve immediately.

Indonesian Fruit Platter with Hot and Sweet Dipping Sauce (Rujak Manis)

This is a very popular dish amongst Indonesian women and girls, and especially expectant mothers. *Rujak* means any kind of mixed fruit or vegetable salad with a spicy sauce, sometimes containing ground peanuts, and *manis* means sweet. *Rujak Manis* is often sold door-to-door by street vendors, and is also readily available in the busy city streets. The fruits are freshly cut and the sauce spooned on top, keeping the fresh individual tastes of the fruits intact. When I first tasted this dish, the fruit selection contained rose apple and *bangkwang*, also known as yam bean, or *jicama*. These fruits are sometimes hard to come by in non-tropical countries, so I have suggested some alternatives.

PREPARATION TIME: about 30 minutes
YIELD: enough for 6–8 persons

The dipping sauce:

a walnut-sized lump of soft, seeded tamarind paste, about 50g

½ cup (125ml) hot water

½ cup (125ml) roasted peanuts, about 75g

3 hot green chilies, seeded

1 tablespoon (20ml) fresh lime or lemon juice

250g palm sugar (or less for a less sweet sauce). Substitute with brown sugar if unavailable

1½ teaspoons (7ml) salt

The fruit selection:

500g each of 5 or 6 of the following fruits, cut into large bite-size chunks: pineapple, red or yellow papaya, bangkwang or apple, rose apple, or pear, banana, honeydew melon, cantaloupe, or any other firm fruit

1. Soak the tamarind in the hot water for 10 minutes, or until soft. Mix and squeeze the pulp and then push it through a sieve to collect all the tamarind purée, discarding the pith and seeds.

2. Drop the peanuts into a food processor and grind them until smooth. Add the chilies, tamarind purée, lime juice, palm sugar and salt. Process to a smooth, sauce-like consistency. You may need to add a few drops of water.

3. Set the sauce aside for 10 minutes for the flavours to mingle. Arrange the fruits on a platter with the sauce in a separate bowl, along with skewers or toothpicks, allowing diners to dip the fruits or pour the sauce onto the fruits as they desire.

Pistachio Milk Fudge
(Pista Burfi)

Pistachio *burfi* is a delightful example of a traditional Indian milk sweet, where the milk is reduced gradually until it thickens to a fudge-like paste. Note that, as all *burfis*, pistachio *burfi* will firm up as it sits. If you keep it well covered, you can store it for up to 10 days in the refrigerator.

PREPARATION AND COOKING TIME:
about 1½ hours
YIELD: 36 small pieces of fudge

2 litres fresh whole milk
1¼ cups (310ml) sugar
1 teaspoon (5ml) ghee or unsalted butter
½ teaspoon (2ml) powdered cardamom seeds
1 cup (250ml) raw blanched pistachio nuts, chopped fine
edible pure silver or gold foil (optional)

1. Combine milk, sugar, ghee and cardamom in a 5-litre/quart saucepan, preferably non-stick. Bring the milk to a rolling boil over moderate heat and continue to cook it, stirring occasionally with a wooden spoon for about 45 minutes, or until the milk has reduced to a thick bubbling creamy mass, about half its original volume.

2. Continue to reduce the fudge, stirring continuously with gently rhythmic strokes for a further 10 minutes, or until the mixture resembles a thick paste.

3. Add the pistachio nuts, reduce the heat to medium low, and cook the fudge, stirring and scraping with the wooden spoon for a further 20 minutes or until the mixture becomes a thick dry lump. Remove the pan from the heat and allow the mixture to cool for one minute. You should have about 2½ cups (625ml) fudge.

4. Transfer the fudge to a buttered, shallow tray. As the mixture cools a little more, use a buttered spatula to shape it into a smooth, flat cake, about 15cm (6-inches) square. Allow the fudge to cool for a further one hour.

5. With a minimum of handling, slip the sheets of silver or gold foil over the fudge and press down gently with the backing paper, allowing the foil to adhere to the fudge. Cut the fudge into 36 pieces with a sharp, buttered knife. You may need to wipe the knife clean after each cut. Serve or store as suggested above.

Note: As an alternative, press the semi-cooled fudge into decorative sweet moulds.

ALMOND TOFFEE FUDGE

I can honestly say that I've cooked more fudge than any other one preparation in my quarter-century kitchen career. Different versions of the same basic recipe, often prepared in 2,000–5,000 piece batches, have been devoured with delight at innumerable expos, food fairs, alternative life-style events and catering programs. I've supplied the recipe hundreds of times to "fudgeaholics".

Here's the original almond variety, immortalised in print. You should know that the best-tasting fudge requires top quality unsalted butter, premium quality cream and, most important, full-fat powdered milk. Compared to *Pistachio Milk Fudge*, almond toffee fudge is almost instant.

PREPARATION AND COOKING TIME:
about 30 minutes
YIELD: about 50 pieces of fudge

250g good quality unsalted butter *(I prefer Danish style)*
1½ cups (375ml) raw sugar
1 cup (250ml) pouring consistency pure cream
1 cup (250ml) whole unblanched almonds, oven-roasted or fried, and very coarsely chopped
about 3½ cups (875ml) full cream powdered milk
extra toasted, crushed, slivered, flaked or whole almonds for decorating the surface of the fudge (optional)

1. Gently melt the butter in a heavy 5-litre/quart saucepan over low heat. Add the sugar, increase the heat to moderate and, stirring constantly, cook for about 3 minutes or until the sugar melts into the butter and becomes frothy.

2. Cook for a few minutes more until it develops a light caramel colour. The caramelised sugar will give off a light toffee fragrance. Be careful to avoid over-darkening the sugar at this point; excess caramelisation will give the fudge a bitter flavour. The butter will probably be completely separated from the caramelised sugar at this stage, but that's normal.

3. Remove the pan from the heat and allow it to cool for 2 or 3 minutes. Stir in the cream and nuts. Using a wire whisk, gradually mix in the powdered milk a little at a time, whisking vigorously to avoid forming any lumps. When the mixture just hangs onto the whisk, it is ready. If it reaches this stage before you've added all the powdered milk, don't add any more. If it's still too runny after adding it all, add a little more.

4. Very lightly butter a 25cm × 30cm (10-inch × 12-inch) tray. With a spatula, scrape the hot fudge mixture into the tray. Smooth it out and sprinkle the top with the optional nuts. Allow the fudge to set in a cool place for 1 hour. Cut into approximately 3.75cm (1-inch) squares, and stand back.

CARROT HALAVA

Unlike the Middle Eastern sesame based *halva*, Indian *halavas* are more like fluffy puddings, and can be made with grains, vegetables, fruits, seeds or legumes. In my ultra-simple version of the famous North Indian dish, fresh sweet carrots are shredded and cooked with ghee and sweet spices, then folded with dried fruit and nuts to form an aromatic dense pudding.

Carrot *halava* is delicious, although it is not an everyday dessert. Many strict followers of Vaisnava tradition enjoy it regularly on the Ekadasi grain-fasting day.

PREAPARATION AND COOKING TIME: about 45 minutes
YIELD: enough for 4–6 persons

⅔ cup (165ml) unsalted butter or ghee, about 140g
900g fresh carrots, trimmed, peeled and coarsely shredded (weighed after trimming and peeling)

1 teaspoon (5ml) freshly-powdered cardamom seeds
¾ cup (185ml) sugar
¼ cup (60ml) sultanas
½ cup (125ml) toasted cashew halves or pieces

1. Melt the butter or ghee in a 5-litre/quart non-stick saucepan over low heat. Add the shredded carrots, increase the heat to moderate and, stirring frequently, cook the carrots and butter together for 30 minutes, or until the carrots are very reduced, dry and completely soft.

2. Add the powdered cardamom, sugar, sultanas and cashews, and stirring steadily to prevent scorching, cook for about 10–12 minutes, or until the orange coloured ghee oozes out of the pudding, and the mixture is again nearly dry. Remove the carrot *halava* from the heat and serve hot or warm.

MACADAMIA AND BLUEBERRY MUFFINS

One of the secrets of good muffin making is not to
overdo the mixing. It's sufficient to just stir the
ingredients together until they are all moistened,
and not beat or smooth out the mixture. Lightly
mixed, uncooked muffin mixture actually improves
when kept in the refrigerator for 2–3 days.

PREPARATION AND COOKING TIME:
about 35 minutes
YIELD: 12 medium-sized muffins

¼ cup (60ml) softened butter
½ cup (125ml) sugar
¾ cup (185ml) milk
2 cups (500ml) self-raising plain flour
1 teaspoon (5ml) cinnamon powder
½ cup (125ml) coarsely-chopped, toasted macadamia nuts
1 cup (250ml) blueberries, about 150g

1. Pre-heat the oven to 180°C/355°F. Cream
   together the butter and sugar in a bowl. Mix in
   the milk, then gently fold in the sifted flour and
   cinnamon, and gently stir in the nuts and berries.

2. Butter 12 medium-sized muffin tins, and spoon in
   the muffin mixture. Bake the muffins in the
   middle of the pre-heated oven for 20–25 minutes
   or until the muffins are lightly browned. Remove,
   allow to cool, then serve.

ROSE-SCENTED MARZIPAN HALF-MOON PASTRIES

Marzipan, the smooth but firm confectionery paste based on almonds, has been around for centuries. It was a popular confection in sixteenth century Europe, the origin of these half-moon shaped pastries. If you like marzipan, you'll love these delicate pastries, scented with ginger and rosewater.

PREPARATION AND FRYING TIME: 1–1¼ hours
YIELD: 24 pastries

The filling:

1 cup (250ml) pure marzipan paste, about 300g
2 teaspoons (10ml) pure distilled rosewater
1 teaspoon (5ml) ginger powder

The pastry:

2 cups (500ml) plain cake flour
2 tablespoons (40ml) ghee or butter
5 tablespoons (100ml) buttermilk
1–2 tablespoons (20–40ml) water
olive oil or ghee for frying
caster sugar for dusting

To prepare the filling:

Chop the marzipan into small pieces, and combine with the ginger and rosewater in a bowl. Knead until well incorporated, and set aside.

To prepare the pastry:

1. Sift the flour into a bowl.
2. Melt the ghee or butter and combine it with the buttermilk and 1 tablespoon (20ml) water. Pour the mixture into the flour, stir and gather the mixture into a ball. If a little dry, add the remaining water. Knead the pastry lightly. It should be soft but not sticky. Set it aside.

To assemble the half-moons:

1. Form the marzipan filling into a ball. Roll the ball on non-stick paper with your hands, forming it into a long tube, then cut it into 24 pieces. Roll each piece into a ball and flatten each ball slightly.
2. Place the dough on a smooth, dry working surface and roll it out thinly. With a 7.5cm (3-inch) cutter, cut the pastry into 24 rounds. Alternatively, roll the pastry into a long tube and cut the tube into 24 pieces. With a rolling pin, roll out each piece of pastry into a 7.5cm (3-inch) disc.
3. Position a patty of filling slightly off-centre on a disc of pastry. Dip a finger in water and moisten the edges of the pastry. Fold the disc in half, press to seal the edges carefully, lay the pastry on its side and flatten slightly to form a half-moon shape. Seal the edges with the tines of a fork. Repeat for the remaining pastries.
4. Heat ghee or oil in a wok or deep-frying vessel over moderate heat. When it reaches about 115°C/240°F, slip in 8–12 pastries. Fry, turning to evenly cook them, for 3–5 minutes, or until they are lightly golden brown. Remove and drain them in a colander lined with paper towels. Repeat for the remaining pastries. Sprinkle the half-moons with the sugar and serve at room temperature.

½ teaspoon (2ml) saffron strands, soaked in 1 tablespoon (20ml)
boiling hot milk for 30 minutes

140g unsalted butter

1¼ cups (310ml) coarse grained semolina

⅓ cup (85ml) flaked almonds

1 teaspoon (5ml) ground cardamom

⅓ cup (85ml) sultanas

FLAKED ALMOND AND SAFFRON SEMOLINA HALAVA

To many aficionados of Hare Krishna cooking worldwide, *halava* rates on top of the list of their favourite dishes. It's hot, buttery, sweet, flavoursome and completely satisfying, especially on a cold winter's day. In this recipe, the humble semolina teams up with the world's two most expensive spices — saffron and cardamom. Enriched with milk, sultanas and flaked almonds, serve fluffy, plump grained *halava* hot with cream, custard, or as is for an epicurian experience.

PREPARATION AND COOKING TIME: about 30 minutes.
YIELD: enough for 6–8 persons or 4–6 halava addicts

2¼ cups (560ml) water

½ cup (125ml) milk

1¼ cups (310ml) sugar

1. Combine the water, milk, sugar and the soaked saffron in a 2-litre/quart saucepan. Place over moderate heat, stirring to dissolve the sugar. Bring to the boil, then reduce the heat to very low and cover with a tight-fitting lid.

2. Melt the butter in a 2- or 3-litre/quart saucepan over low heat, stirring occasionally. Add the semolina, and slowly and rhythmically stir-fry the grains for about 20 minutes, or until they darken to a tan colour and become aromatic. Add the flaked almonds to the grains towards the end of the toasting process.

3. Raise the heat under the syrup, add the cardamom and the sultanas, and bring it to a rolling boil. Raise the heat under the semolina for 1 minute, stirring continuously. Remove the saucepan of semolina from the heat, and slowly pour the hot syrup into the semolina, stirring steadily. The grains may at first splutter, but will quickly cease as the liquid is absorbed.

4. Return the *halava* to the stove and stir steadily over very low heat until the grains fully absorb the liquid, start to form into a pudding-like consistency, and pull away from the sides of the pan. Place a tight-fitting lid on the saucepan and cook over the lowest possible heat for 5 minutes. A heat-diffuser works well. Removed the covered saucepan from the heat and allow the *halava* to steam for an additional 5 minutes. Serve hot.

QUICK AND EASY VANILLA ICE CREAM

The vanilla plant is an orchid which grows as a massive vine needing a frame or trellis to support it. The fruit takes the form of a long thin pod, containing a pulp in which is found a mass of minute black seeds. Each of the pods must be handpicked just before they are ripe enough to split open naturally. Then they are fermented to enable the pods to develop their concentration of vanillin crystals which are chiefly responsible for the unique, haunting perfumed flavour of vanilla.

The subtlety and delicacy of vanilla makes it a perpetual favourite. The vanilla required for this most popular ice cream is in the form of pure vanilla extract, available at gourmet food suppliers. Avoid imitation, or alcohol-based essences, usually found on supermarket shelves.

PREPARATION TIME: 10 minutes
CHILING TIME: 2 hours
FREEZING TIME: 6–10 hours
YIELD: about 4 cups (1 litre)

3 cups (750ml) whipping cream (up to 40 per cent milk fat)
1½ teaspoons (7ml) pure vanilla extract
1¼ cups (280ml) sweetened condensed milk, 400g

1. Combine the ingredients in a large bowl. Cover, and chill in the refrigerator for 2 hours.
2. Remove the mixture from the refrigerator. Beat the mixture until it holds firm peaks. Spoon into a metal freezer container and freeze for 6–10 hours, or until firm. Return the ice cream to the refrigerator to soften slightly before serving.

APRICOT AND WALNUT CRESCENTS (RUGELACH)

Rugelach is a well-loved sweet pastry from Jewish cuisine. As an alternative to the ricotta cheese in the pastry, you may prefer to add cottage cheese.

PREPARATION TIME: 35–40 minutes
PASTRY REFRIGERATION TIME: 2 hours
COOKING TIME: 30–35 minutes
YIELD: 16 crescents

The pastry:

¼ teaspoon (1ml) salt
1¼ cups (310ml) unbleached plain flour
120g butter
⅓ cup (85ml) ricotta cheese, or homemade curd cheese (panir)
3 tablespoons (60ml) sour cream

The filling:

a generous ½ cup (125ml) walnuts, very finely chopped
½ cup (125ml) chopped pitted prunes
3 teaspoons (15ml) cinnamon powder
3–4 tablespoons (60–80ml) apricot jam
4 tablespoons (80ml) sugar

To prepare the pastry:

Combine the flour, salt and butter in a food processor fitted with a metal blade. Process with 8–10 short bursts, or until the pastry resembles breadcrumbs. Add the ricotta cheese and process for a few more seconds. Drop in the sour cream and process with another 8–10 quick bursts. The mixture should start to bind. Remove the pastry, gather it into a ball, press it into a thick patty, wrap it in plastic and refrigerate it for 2 hours.

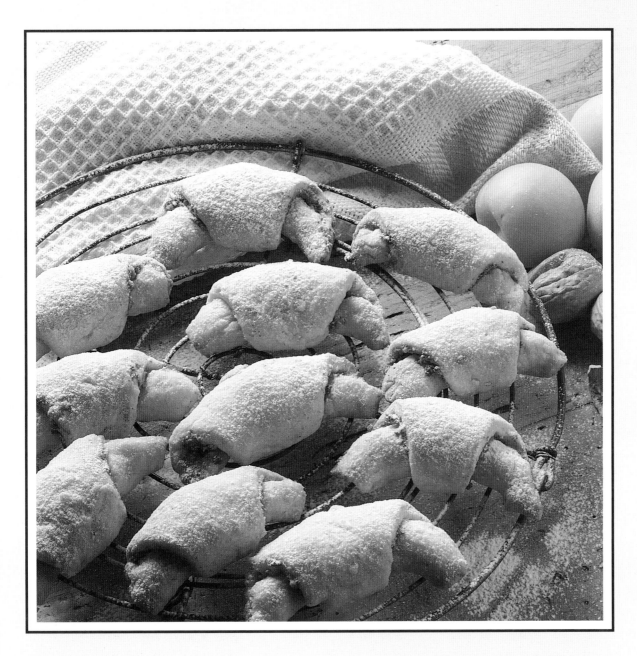

To prepare the filling:

Combine the nuts, prunes, cinnamon and sugar in a small bowl and mix well.

To assemble the pastries:

1. Pre-heat the oven to 180°C/355°F. Divide the pastry into two. Sprinkle a little flour on a large, smooth surface and roll out each half of the pastry into a 25cm (10-inch) wide circle. Spread each circle with the apricot jam, and sprinkle on the nuts, prunes and cinnamon mixture.

2. Cut each circle of pastry into 8 wedge-shaped sections with a sharp knife. Carefully remove one section. Holding the outer edge of the wedge, roll it tightly towards the centre point. Lift up the pastry and bend it slightly into a crescent. Repeat for all the pastries. Place the crescents on a large baking tray covered with baking paper, taking care to sit them with their centre points tucked underneath them. Bake the crescents for 30–35 minutes, or until they are golden brown. Serve at room temperature.

AMISH APPLE DUMPLINGS

In this monumental dessert, sweet red apples are wrapped in a rich pastry and then baked in an even richer sauce. This recipe, originally from the Amish people of Pennsylvania, is definitely not diet food. The Amish are famous for their hard work. If you've been building barns or ploughing the fields all day, you won't feel guilty returning home to these deliciously saucy, individually packaged apple pies.

PREPARATION TIME: 15–20 minutes
COOKING TIME: 40–50 minutes
YIELD: 8 apple dumplings

The apples:

3 cups (750ml) plain flour
1 teaspoon (5ml) salt
1¼ cups (310ml) cold butter
2 tablespoons (40ml) buttermilk
2 tablespoons (40ml) cold water
1 tablespoon (20ml) vinegar or lemon juice
8 sweet red apples, peeled and left whole

The sauce:

½ cup (125ml) butter
1 cup (250ml) brown sugar
4 tablespoons (80ml) water

1. Sprinkle the flour and salt into a bowl. Cut the butter into small pieces and rub it into the flour until the mixture resembles coarse meal. Combine the buttermilk, water and vinegar or lemon juice, and stir it into the flour mixture to form a soft pastry. Knead the dough briefly, then set it aside for a few minutes.

2. Roll out the pastry on a large floured surface until it's big enough to cut into 8 squares, each big enough to completely fit around an apple. Cut the pastry into 8 squares, place an apple on one square and wrap it, lightly sealing the pastry on top. Repeat for all the apples. Place the apples on a lightly buttered 22.5cm × 32.5cm (9-inch × 13-inch) baking pan. Pre-heat the oven to 180°C/355°F.

3. Combine the butter, sugar and water in a small saucepan and bring this sauce to the boil over moderate heat. Pour the sauce over the apple dumplings, place the pan in the oven and bake for 40–50 minutes, or until the dumplings are golden brown and the apples yield easily to a knife. The Amish like to pour cold milk over their warm

dumplings. Try cream or ice cream. Happy ploughing.

STRAWBERRY CREAM SHORTCAKE

This cake is actually somewhere between a shortcake and a sponge. It's enriched with ground walnuts or hazelnuts topped with strawberry jam, piled with rich vanilla-flavoured cream and studded with vine-ripened straw-berries. Irresistible!

PREPARATION AND BAKING TIME:
about 45 minutes
CAKE COOKING TIME: at least 30 minutes
YIELD: enough for 6–8 persons

The cake:

1¼ cups (310ml) self-raising plain flour
pinch salt
4 tablespoons (80ml) butter, about 60g
3 tablespoons (60ml) sugar
⅓ cup (85ml) ground walnuts, or ground toasted hazelnuts
about ⅓ cup (85ml) buttermilk

The cream topping:

300ml double cream
1 tablespoon (20ml) sugar
1 teaspoon (5ml) pure vanilla extract
1 tablespoon (20ml) milk powder
a little cold milk if required to thin the cream

The remaining topping ingredients:

3–4 tablespoons (60–80ml) strawberry jam
250g ripe, sweet strawberries, whole or cut in half lengthwise

1. Pre-heat the oven to 200°C/390°F.
2. Mix together the flour and salt in a large bowl. Rub in the butter until the mixture resembles breadcrumbs, then stir in the sugar and ground nuts.
3. Pour in three-quarters of the buttermilk and gather the mixture into a soft manageable dough. If too dry, add some more buttermilk. Press the cake mixture into a buttered 20cm (8-inch) fluted cake tin with removable base, taking care to evenly work the mixture up the sides of the tin. Place the cake in the oven and bake for 25 minutes, or until pale golden brown all over. Remove from the oven and allow it to cool. Carefully remove the cake from its tin.
4. Combine the cream, sugar, vanilla and powdered milk in a mixing bowl and beat it until the cream stands in soft peaks. If you plan to pipe the cream through a pastry bag, beat it until it stands in stiff peaks. If the cream is too thick to start with, add a little cold milk and then whip it.
5. Spread the strawberry jam over the surface of the cake, pipe or spread the cream, then top with the straw-berries. Cut into wedges and serve.

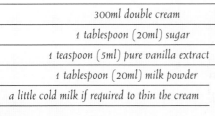

FRESH NECTARINE PIE

Slices of flavoursome, peak-of-the-season fresh nectarines, baked in crisp, double-crust golden flaky pastry — nectarine! Don't forget the three golden rules of successful pastry making: Be careful not to over-mix the butter and flour, add enough cold water for a soft pastry, and only handle the pastry as much as necessary.

As an alternative to a solid pie crust top, cut the top pie crust into strips and weave into a lattice-topped design, working from the centre of the pie to the edges. Seal the lattice to the sides of the base after the weaving is complete. If the nectarines are very juicy, the filling may boil over during the baking process. I suggest you place a cookie sheet or a large sheet of aluminium foil on the rack directly underneath the pie to ensure a clean oven. Try peaches as an alternative to nectarines.

PREPARATION TIME: about 35 minutes
BAKING TIME: about 50 minutes
YIELD: one 22.5cm (9-inch) double crust pie

The pastry:

2¼ cups (560ml) plain flour
¾ teaspoon (3ml) salt
¾ cup (185ml) butter
about 6 tablespoons (120ml) cold water

The filling:

6 cups (1.5 litres) peeled, pitted and slices nectarines, about 800g
2 tablespoons (40ml) fresh lemon juice
¼ cup (60ml) plain flour
⅔ cup (165ml) sugar
¼ teaspoon (1ml) salt
⅛ teaspoon (0.5ml) nutmeg powder
2 tablespoons (40ml) unsalted butter

To prepare the pastry:

1. Combine the flour, salt and the butter in a food processor. Process the mixture with 12–15 on/off pulses. The mixture will be crumbly. Sprinkle in 4 tablespoons (80ml) cold water, and process again with 6 rapid on/off pulses.

2. Add 2 more tablespoons (40ml) water and process again, this time only 3 quick pulses. Remove the lid of the processor and feel the dough. It should be damp enough to cling together. Add a few more sprinkles of cold water only if it is too dry, pulsing momentarily, otherwise don't add any more water. The mixture should not be a ball, but at this stage simply a rough, unmixed mass. If you are making the pastry by hand, use your fingertips or a hand-held pastry blender to combine the butter, flour and salt with a minimum of handling. Carefully stir in the water with a fork in stages, as with the food processor method.

3. Remove the pastry with floured hands, and transfer onto a lightly floured surface. Pat the pastry into two smooth cakes, one slightly larger than the other. If you are not using the pastry immediately, wrap it in plastic wrap and refrigerate it.

To prepare the filling and assemble the pie:

1. Pre-heat the oven to 220°C/430°F. If using a glass pie dish, you may have to increase the heat to 230°C/450°F.

2. Place the nectarines in a large bowl, sprinkle with lemon juice, toss to coat well and set aside.

3. Roll out the slightly larger ball of dough on a lightly-floured surface to a circle, 5cm (2 inches) larger than the diameter of the pie dish. Carefully lift the pastry into the dish, patting it into place. Trim the dough with kitchen scissors leaving a 2.5cm (1-inch) overhang. Roll out the top crust to the same thickness as the base.

4. Combine the flour, sugar, salt and nutmeg in a small bowl. Add this mixture to the nectarines and toss to combine. Pile the fruit mixture into the pastry-lined pie dish and dot with pieces of butter.

5. Brush the rim of the bottom crust with water. Lay the rolled-out top crust over the pie and trim the pastry, leaving a 1.25cm (½-inch) overhang. Press firmly to seal the crusts together. Fold the overhang under itself to make an upstanding edge. Hold your thumb on top of the rim of the pie and forefinger underneath. Flute the edge by pinching together the dough edges while pressing down your thumb. Repeat at close intervals. Alternatively, press with the tines of a fork to seal. With a small knife, cut 4 or 5 slits in the top crust to allow steam to escape during baking.

6. Place the pie in the pre-heated oven and bake for 25 minutes, then reduce the heat to 180°C/355°F and bake until the top is browned, about 25 minutes more. When the pie is fully baked, remove it from the oven, allow to cool a little and serve as desired.

PECAN CAROB CHIP COOKIES

Cookies or biscuits — the name varies from country to country — are always good to have on hand for unexpected guests. Pecan carob chip cookies are always popular and are quick and easy to make. If you choose to use sweetened carob chips, you may want to slightly reduce the sugar content of the cookie mixture.

PREPARATION TIME: 20 minutes
BAKING TIME: 15–20 minutes
YIELD: 24 medium-sized cookies

¾ cup (185ml) softened butter
½ cup (125ml) raw or brown sugar
1 tablespoon (20ml) buttermilk or yogurt
1½ cups (375ml) self-raising flour
¾ cup (185ml) pecan nuts, coarsely chopped
1½ cups (375ml) unsweetened carob chips or coarsely chopped carob buttons

1. Pre-heat the oven to 180°C/355°F. Beat the butter and sugar together in a bowl until light and fluffy. Add the buttermilk or yogurt and beat thoroughly.

2. Fold in the flour, nuts and carob chips, and combine well. Form the mixture into 24 balls. Flatten into patties and place slightly apart on an ungreased baking tray. Bake for 15–20 minutes, or until the cookies are lightly browned. Remove and allow the cookies to fully cool before serving or storage.

HAZELNUT AND FRUIT GRANOLA

Here's a crisp, crunchy cereal for those of you that need a quick, nutritious and sustaining breakfast but haven't got a lot of time to cook.

PREPARATION AND COOKING TIME:
55–60 minutes
YIELD: 1.6kg

5 cups (1250ml) rolled oats (not instant oats)
1 cup (250ml) rolled barley or rolled rye
1 cup (250ml) coarse oat bran
¾ cup (185ml) hazelnuts, about 90g
½ cup (125ml) sunflower seeds
¼ cup (60ml) sesame seeds, preferable unhulled
⅓ cup (85ml) corn oil
½ cup (125ml) barley malt
½ cup (125ml) raw sugar
3 cups (750ml) assorted dried fruit (sultanas, raisins, chopped apricots, apple, peaches, pears and nectarines)
½ cup (125ml) shredded (ribbon) coconut

1. Combine the rolled oats, rolled rye or barley, and the oat bran in a large bowl. Place the hazelnuts on a tray and toast them in a pre-heated 180°C/355°F oven for 15 minutes, or until they are aromatic. Remove the nuts and rub them in a dry tea towel to remove the crispy, brown skin. Crush or chop roughly. Leave the oven on.

2. Toast the sunflower seeds in a dry frying pan, tossing and stirring constantly. When the seeds are half done, sprinkle in the sesame seeds. When both seeds are toasted, darker and aromatic, turn out onto a plate to cool.

3. Gently warm the oil, malt and sugar in a small saucepan over moderate heat to dissolve the sugar. When the mixture is runny, remove the saucepan from the heat, and pour it into the bowl of mixed oats and bran. Mix thoroughly with both hands. Turn half the mixture into a large lightly-oiled roasting pan and place in the pre-heated oven. Bake for 15 minutes, stirring once or twice, to prevent it browning too much around the edges and on top.

4. Turn the roasted grains into a large bowl to cool. They will appear sticky but will go crisp on cooling. Meanwhile, roast the remaining half of the mixture and cool it in a similar fashion. Separate any large clumps of toasted grain.

5. When fully cool, thoroughly combine the toasted grains and seeds, the dried fruits, nuts and the coconut, and store in an airtight container.

DRINKS

Kumquat and Passionfruit Refresher

Vietnamese Avocado Smoothie

Lemon Verbena Punch

Turkish-style Fragrant Milk (Sahlep)

Filipino Ginger Tea (Salabat)

Chilled Papaya Refresher (Refresco de Papaya)

Malted Peanut Milkshake

Iced Vegetable Cocktail

Mango Nectar

Lemon Yogurt Shake (Nimbu Lassi)

Iced Tamarind Soda

Old Fashioned Homemade Lemonade

KUMQUAT AND PASSIONFRUIT REFRESHER

Squeezing kumquats for a drink may seem daunting, but you don't need many and the results are stunning.

PREPARATION AND COOKING TIME:
about 35 minutes
YIELD: enough for 4 persons

250g ripe kumquats, preferably the round variety
(about 2 dozen medium sized)

8–10 large, juicy passionfruits

½ cup (125ml) sugar

about 4 cups (1 litre) iced water

crushed ice

1. Cut the kumquats in half and hand-squeeze them to remove their juice. Strain out any pips. You'll need about ⅓ cup (85ml) juice.

2. Remove the seeds and pulp from the passionfruits — you should have about ¾ cup (185ml). Combine this pulp with the kumquat juice and sugar in a small saucepan.

3. Bring the juice to a boil over moderate heat, stir to dissolve the sugar, and simmer for 10 minutes. Remove from the heat and allow to cool.

4. Push and rub the fruit syrup through a coarse metal sieve until only the passionfruit pips remain. Scrape the underside of the sieve to capture all the fragrant fruit pulp. Discard the pips. Place the syrup in a 1-litre jug and top it up with iced water to the 1-litre mark. Serve over crushed ice in chilled glasses.

VIETNAMESE AVOCADO SMOOTHIE

If you've only ever tasted avocados in a savoury context, this drink will be a pleasant surprise. My first encounter with an avocado drink was in the highlands outside of Jakarta; I found it both comforting and filling.
This is a popular version from Vietnam where it is known as *sinh to bo*. It is traditionally served very thick — you may prefer to add a little extra iced water.

PREPARATION AND COOKING TIME:
15–20 minutes
YIELD: enough for 4–6 persons

½ cup (125ml) sugar

½ cup (125ml) water

5 small or 2 large ripe avocados, about 800g

2–3 cups (500–750ml) iced water

⅔ cup (165ml) sweetened condensed milk

1 cup (250ml) crushed ice

extra crushed ice

extra iced water (optional)

1. Combine the sugar and ½ cup (125ml) water in a small saucepan. Bring the syrup to the boil over moderate heat and simmer for 5 minutes. Remove the syrup from the heat and allow it to cool.

2. Cut the avocados in half and remove the stones with a sharp knife. Spoon the flesh into a blender or food processor, add the sugar syrup and 2 cups (500ml) iced water and blend to a smooth purée. Add the condensed milk and ice and process again. If you find the consistency a little too thick for your taste, add a little more iced water and blend again. Serve in tall, chilled glasses with the extra crushed ice.

LEMON VERBENA PUNCH

Lemon verbena is a small deciduous shrub originally from Chile, with strongly perfumed fragrant lemony leaves. The leaves can be successfully used as a substitute for lemon grass in Asian recipes, and are best gathered from the time the flowers begin, either picking individual leaves off by hand, or by cutting and pruning to shape the bush. The leaves also dry well, become very crisp, and store well.

Lemon verbena makes a great tea, and couples well with other fruit juices, as in this chilled lemon verbena-scented fruit punch.

PREPARATION AND COOKING TIME: 1 hour
YIELD: enough for 8–10 persons

5 cups (1.25 litres) water
½ cup (125ml) packed fresh lemon verbena leaves
½ cup (125ml) sugar
1 cup (250ml) orange juice
½ cup (125ml) lemon juice
1½ cups (375ml) apricot juice
1½ cups (375ml) unsweetened pineapple juice
ice
orange rings, lemon rings, pineapple pieces and a few chopped lemon verbena leaves for garnish

1. Bring the water to the boil in a large saucepan. Drop in the lemon verbena leaves and sugar. Dissolve the sugar, then remove the saucepan from the heat, and set it aside for one hour to cool, allowing the fragrance of the leaves to infuse.

2. Strain the infusion and chill it. Combine it thoroughly with all the other ingredients, and serve with ice and the fruit garnishes.

TURKISH-STYLE FRAGRANT MILK (SAHLEP)

Sahlep is a delicious milk drink made with the powdered root of the *sahlep* orchid, *Orchis mascula*. It is served in several Middle Eastern countries, but it is especially popular in Turkey, where, in the cold winter months, it is sold from large copper urns on street corners, at stations and cafes. *Sahlep* powder is available from Turkish or Middle Eastern grocery stores.

PREPARATION TIME: a few minutes
YIELD: 4 cups (1 litre)

4 cups (1 litre) cold milk
1½ tablespoons (30ml) sugar
1 tablespoon (20ml) sahlep powder
½ teaspoon (2ml) cinnamon powder

Combine the sugar and *sahlep* powder in a 2-litre/quart saucepan. Gradually add the cold milk, mixing to dissolve the sugar and *sahlep*. Bring the milk to the boil over moderate heat, stirring constantly to avoid scorching. Reduce to a simmer and cook for 1 or 2 minutes, or until it thickens slightly. Pour the *sahlep* into 4 individual cups, sprinkle each with ⅛ teaspoon (0.5ml) cinnamon powder, and serve hot.

FILIPINO GINGER TEA (SALABAT)

Ginger has been a well-known wonder tonic since the Vedic period. There are numerous references in the Vedic literature, and also in Chinese medical texts. In the *Ayurveda*, India's greatest medical treatise, ginger is described as *maha-aushadhi*, meaning "the great medicine". Ancient physicians used it as a carminative or anti-flatulent.

Galen, the great Greek physician, used ginger to "rectify the defective humours or fluids of the body". Ginger remains today a powerful treatment in digestive disorders, coughs and colds, respiratory disorders, impotence and general aches and pains.

This power-packed hot ginger tea is famous in the Philippines and is generally served very strong. You might prefer to add a little more water. Brown sugar is the preferred sweetener, but you may like to experiment with other sweeteners such as raw (turbinado) sugar, palm sugar, or maple sugar. For something quite different, chill the tea and serve over ice with a squirt of lime or lemon juice. Ginger sherbet!

PREPARATION TIME: about 30 minutes
YIELD: 4–6 small cups, or more according to taste

250g thinly-sliced fresh ginger
4 cups (1 litre) water
½ cup (125ml) brown sugar
pinch black pepper (optional)
squeeze of lemon (optional)
thin rings of lemon for garnish (optional)

1. Bring the ginger, water and sugar to the boil in a 2- or 3-litre/quart saucepan over moderate heat, stirring to dissolve the sugar. Cover with a lid and simmer for 30 minutes.

2. Strain the tea, adding the optional black pepper and lemon, and more water if required. Serve hot in small cups with an optional garnish of thinly-sliced rings of lemon.

CHILLED PAPAYA REFRESHER (REFRESCO DE PAPAYA)

Ripe papayas, whether red, orange or yellow fleshed are beautifully sweet. When choosing papayas, select fruits that are soft enough to hold an impression from gentle thumb or finger pressure. Their aroma should be pronounced and musky sweet. This refreshing drink from Guatemala is flavoured with lime and pure vanilla. Serve it icy cold. Refresco!

PREPARATION TIME: a few minutes
YIELD: 6 cups (1.5 litres)

1 large ripe papaya, about 700g
⅔ cup (165ml) very cold buttermilk or milk
½ cup (125ml) sugar
black seedy pulp scraped from 1 plump vanilla bean, or 1 teaspoon (5ml) vanilla sugar
2 cups (500ml) crushed ice
5 tablespoons (100ml) strained fresh lime juice
½ teaspoon (2ml) finely-grated lime zest
thin slices of lime for garnish (optional)

1. Peel the papaya, cut in half, remove the seeds and chop coarsely.

2. Place the fruit in a blender with the buttermilk or milk, sugar, vanilla and ice. Blend on high speed until the fruit is puréed. Add the lime juice, lime zest and process again until smooth and thick.

3. Pour into tall, chilled glasses and serve at once, garnished with lime slices.

MALTED PEANUT MILKSHAKE

This is an unusual but delicious drink.

PREPARATION AND COOKING TIME:
15 minutes
COOLING AND REFRIGERATION TIME:
at least 1 hour
YIELD: enough for 4 persons

3 cups (750ml) fresh milk
1 cup (250ml) water
¾ cup (185ml) smooth unsalted peanut butter
4 tablespoons (80ml) liquid barley malt, or more to taste
a few scoops vanilla ice cream (optional)
finely chopped, roasted peanuts for garnish

1. Combine the milk, water and peanut butter in a 2-litre/quart saucepan. Bring to the boil over moderate heat, then simmer for 5-10 minutes, or until smooth. Mix in the barley malt, remove from the heat, set aside to cool, then refrigerate for at least 1 hour.

2. Process the chilled drink in a blender with the optional ice cream until smooth and foamy. Serve in tall, chilled glasses, sprinkled with a garnish of chopped peanuts.

ICED VEGETABLE COCKTAIL

This is like a drinkable *gazpacho* salad.

PREPARATION TIME: a few minutes
YIELD: enough for 4 persons

1¾ cups (435ml) carrot juice
1¾ cups (435ml) tomato juice
⅓ cup (85ml) peeled and grated cucumber
½–1 teaspoon (2–5ml) salt
¼ teaspoon (1ml) freshly-ground black pepper
½–1 teaspoon (2–5ml) sugar, optional
2 tablespoons (40ml) finely-chopped fresh coriander leaves or continental parsley leaves
ice cubes
extra coriander or parsley leaves for garnish

Combine the juices in a large jug. Stir in the shredded cucumber, salt, pepper, the optional sugar and the chopped fresh herb. Refrigerate until chilled. Pour into glasses over ice, garnished with sprigs of your chosen herb.

MANGO NECTAR

Mango has been described as the king of fruits. It shows its royal colours in this nectarean drink. For best results, select the ripest, most fragrant mangoes at the peak of their season. Long live the king!

PREPARATION TIME: about 15 minutes
YIELD: 4 cups (1 litre)

¼ cup (60ml) sugar

1 cup (250ml) chilled water

2 medium-sized ripe fragrant mangoes, about 650g

1¾ cups (435ml) orange juice

juice from 1 lime

ice

long thin strips of the outer rind of an orange for garnish

1. Combine the sugar and ¼ cup (60ml) water in a small saucepan. Stir to dissolve over moderate heat. Bring to the boil, then set the syrup aside to cool.

2. Peel and cut up the mango flesh. Combine the mango, orange juice, lime juice and cooled syrup in a food processor or blender. Process until smooth. Add the remaining water and blend again. Serve with a strip of the orange rind in tall glasses over ice.

LEMON YOGURT SHAKE (NIMBU LASSI)

This is a refreshing and tangy drink.

PREPARATION TIME: a few minutes
YIELD: enough for 4 persons

2 cups (500ml) white grape juice
1 cup (250ml) plain yogurt
½ teaspoon (2ml) grated lemon zest
¼ cup (60ml) freshly squeezed lemon juice
extra water if required
crushed ice

Combine all the ingredients, except the ice, in a food processor or blender and process for 1 minute. Serve over ice in chilled glasses.

ICED TAMARIND SODA

This summer refresher makes an unusual change. Dark and tangy in flavour, tamarind drinks are popular wherever the tamarind tree grows. There are many varieties of tamarind in the shops. I have suggested tamarind concentrate for this recipe. It usually comes in small plastic jars — "Instam" and "Tamcon" are two common brands. You may wish to add extra water or sugar, and adjust the flavour of the drink according to your taste.

PREPARATION AND COOKING TIME:
15 minutes
YIELD: 6 cups (1.5 litres)

¾ cup (185ml) raw sugar
½ cup (125ml) water
3 tablespoons (60ml) tamarind concentrate
4 cups (1 litre) soda water
crushed ice

1. Stir to dissolve the sugar with the water in a small saucepan over moderate heat. Add the tamarind, mix well and bring the syrup to a boil for 1 minute, then remove from the heat and set aside to cool.

2. Place the crushed ice in your glasses, fill half with soda water, stir in 2 tablespoons (40ml) tamarind syrup per glass and mix well. Top up the glasses with soda and serve.

OLD FASHIONED HOMEMADE LEMONADE

Just like Mum used to make.

PREPARATION TIME: 10 minutes, plus cooling time
YIELD: enough for 6–8 persons

1½ cups (375ml) freshly-squeezed lemon juice
¾ cup (185ml) sugar
4 cups (1 litre) iced water
3–4 cups (750ml–1 litre) crushed ice
strips of lemon rind for garnish

1. Combine the lemon juice and sugar in a small saucepan and, stirring to dissolve the sugar, bring to the boil over moderate heat. Simmer for 10 minutes. Remove from the heat and set aside to cool.

2. Whisk together the cooled lemon syrup with the iced water in a large jug. Half fill each chilled glass with crushed ice, and fill the glass with lemonade, garnishing each with a strip of lemon rind.

GLOSSARY

AJOWAN SEEDS

Tiny, light-brown spice seeds closely related to caraway and cumin. They have a slightly hot, semi-bitter thyme-like flavour, and are used in many North Indian savoury dishes, especially in fried snacks. *Ajowan* seeds (*Carum ajowan*), also known as *omum* (bishop's weed) and *ajwain*, aid digestion and are used to relieve stomach problems. As well as being a culinary flavouring, they are cultivated for their essential oil, thymol. The seeds keep indefinitely and are available from Indian and Middle Eastern grocers.

AKHNIR JHOL

A traditional home-made spicy Bengali stock made by simmering dried and fresh spices, herbs and dal together until the liquid is reduced to about half. The liquid is then strained and used to cook fancy rice *pulaos*.

ALLSPICE

Also known as Jamaica pepper and myrtle pepper, the allspice tree (*Pimenta officinalis*), belongs to the myrtle family and has shiny, elongated, highly aromatic leaves. Allspice berries are mid- to dark-brown and vary in size, an average one being about 0.5 cm (¼ inch) in diameter. The berries are so named because their flavour suggests a combination of nutmeg, cinnamon and cloves with slightly peppery overtones. For the best flavour, purchase allspice berries whole, and grind them fresh in a mortar and pestle or pepper grinder. Allspice is used in pickles, savoury preserves and chutneys, and is available at all well-stocked grocers and supermarkets.

ANAHEIM CHILIES

(See CHILIES.)

ANISE SEEDS

The highly aromatic seeds of the annual herb *Pimpinella anisum*. These greenish-grey, slightly crescent-shaped seeds have a very strong licorice-like flavour and odour, although they are not related to the perennial plant of the pea family whose sweet roots are the source of true licorice. Anise is generally used as a flavouring for drinks, sweets, creams, and breads such as *Dense and Delicious Sourdough Bread (Pumpernickel)*. Anise seeds are available at supermarkets and specialty stores.

ANTIPASTO

A light starter or an appetiser, served before an Italian meal. It can also be used as a light snack. Vegetables and salads (served raw or lightly cooked) make delicious *antipasto*, as do simple hot dishes, fried breads (*crostini*), or miniature pizzas.

ARBORIO RICE

A short, highly-glutinous fat-grained variety of rice grown in Italy and classified as *superfino*. It is used in the preparation of *risotto*. Most rices absorb twice their weight in water during cooking. *Arborio* rice can absorb 4–5 times its weight in liquid and can therefore survive the long, slow stirring so characteristic of *risotto* cooking, resulting in a creamy, non-gluggy texture. *Arborio* rice is available at Italian grocers and well-stocked supermarkets.

ARUGULA

Also known as *roquette*, *ruccola*, rocket and *rughetta*. A small, green, leafy plant resembling radish tops that grows wild in the Mediterranean region. When purchasing or harvesting *arugula*, choose young plants with small, slender, dark green leaves. *Arugula* is related to mustard, and has a peppery, slightly bitter, slightly acidic flavour. It is used as one of the ingredients of *mesclun*, the traditional *Niçoise* mixture of tiny salad leaves.

ASAFETIDA

The aromatic resin from the root of the giant fennel, *Ferula asafoetida*. Asafetida, also known as *hing*, is extracted from the stems of these giant perennial plants that grow wild in Central Asia. In the spring, when the plant is about to bloom, the stems and roots are cut. Milky resin exudes from the cut surface and is scraped off. The gummy resin is sun-dried into a solid mass that is then sold in solid, wax-like pieces, or, more conveniently, in powdered form. Asafetida has been held in great esteem among indigenous medicines from the earliest times in India. It is highly reputed as a drug which expels wind from the stomach and counteracts spasmodic disorders. It is also a digestive agent and is used, among other things, for alleviating toothache and as a antidote for opium.

Due to the presence of sulphur compounds, raw asafetida has a distinctive pungent aroma. To cook with asafetida, small quantities of the powdered form are sautéed in a little slightly hot oil or ghee, before adding to a variety of savoury dishes, adding a delicious flavour reminiscent of a mixture of shallots and garlic.

I always use the mild Vandevi brand of yellow asafetida powder and not the grey variety. All recipes for this book using asafetida were tested using this yellow variety. If using other types, reduce the quantity to between a quarter and a half of the suggested amount. Asafetida is available at Indian grocers and specialty stores.

ATTA FLOUR

Also known as *chapati* flour, this low-gluten flour is derived from a strain of soft wheat popular throughout India. The entire wheat kernel, including the bran, germ and endosperm, is ground very finely, making a nutritious flour. *Atta* flour is suitable for all Indian flatbreads, such as *poories*, *chapatis*, and *parathas*. Doughs made from *atta* flour are velvety smooth, knead readily and respond easily to shaping and rolling. *Atta* flour is available from Indian and Asian grocery stores.

AYURVEDA

Ancient India's great medical treatise. The word *Ayurveda* literally means "the science of healthful living", and remains as the world's oldest known work on biology, botany, herbology, anatomy, hygiene, medicine, surgery and nutrition.

BAKING BLIND

To bake a pie or flan case while empty. In order to prevent the sides from falling in or the base bubbling up, the pastry is usually lined with paper and temporarily filled with raw, dried beans, rice or pasta.

BANGKWANG

(See YAM BEAN.)

BARLEY FLOUR

Coarsely ground barley flour is used as a bread ingredient in European cuisine, notably in German Pumpernickel. Wholegrain barley flour has a nutty flavour, with its colour darker and a texture coarser than wheat flour. You can replace up to one-third of the wheat flour in baked products with barley flour, although you will have to adjust the quantity of liquid as it absorbs more water than wheat flour. It is available from health food stores and many well-stocked supermarkets.

BASIL

The fragrant aromatic herb, *Ocimum basilicum*, known also as sweet basil. It is a small, profusely branched, bushy plant, whose tender green leaves are used worldwide, especially in Italian cuisine, where it is used mostly in dishes containing tomatoes and in salads and soups, on pizzas and in pasta dishes. There are many types of basil, which vary in size, colour and flavour, and all can be used for culinary purposes. Greek basil, purple ruffle, and dark opal are three useful varieties. (See also THAI BASIL.)

BASMATI RICE

A superb, light-textured, long-grained aromatic rice from North India and Pakistan, with a wonderful fragrance and flavour. Even served plain with a little ghee or butter, *basmati* rice is a treat. I have found Dehradun *basmati* to be most superior in taste and texture. *Basmati* rice is easy to cook and although more costly than other long-grained rices, it is well worth the extra expense. *Basmati* rice is available at Indian, Middle Eastern and Asian grocers.

BAY LEAVES

The leaves of the sweet bay or laurel tree, *Laurus nobilis*, an evergreen member of the laurel family native to the Mediterranean region and Asia Minor. The highly aromatic leaves are thick, dark green and glossy on the upper surface. Bay leaves used in their fresh or dried form are quite pungent with a slightly bitter, spicy flavour. They are popular in French cuisine.

BEAN CURD

(See TOFU.)

BESAN

(See CHICKPEA FLOUR.)

BITTER MELON

Also known as *karela*, balsam pear, bitter gourd and Chinese green melon (*Fak-keow*). The bitter melon has been cultivated in India for millennia. As well as being a popular delicacy from the Punjab east to Orissa, the melon is specifically used as folk medicine for diabetes. Recent studies by a team of British doctors have established that it contains a hypoglycaemic or insulin-like principle, designated as "plant insulin", which has been found highly beneficial in lowering blood and urine sugar levels.

Thick in the middle and tapering to pointy ends, with wrinkled green skin, bitter melon easily stands out at vegetable markets. Though bitter melon is an acquired taste, it is one worth exploring. It is available at Indian and Asian greengrocers.

BLACK BEANS

Shiny, black kidney-shaped beans, also known as Turtle beans, a variety of kidney beans, *Phaseolus vulgaris*. A good source of vegetable protein and exceptionally rich in dietary fibre. Available from Latin American and Asian grocers.

BLACK CUMIN SEEDS

Known as *shahi* or *siyah jeera*, it is the spice seed of a wild annual plant, *Cuminum nigrum*, which grows profusely in North India's mountainous regions. They are often confused with *nigella* or *kalonji*, which are tear-drop shaped. Black cumin seeds, however, are darker and thinner than cumin seeds. They are exclusively used in North Indian cuisine, especially in Kashmir. They're available at well-stocked Indian grocers.

BLACK PEPPER

(See PEPPER.)

BLACK SALT

A reddish-grey variety of salt with a distinct "hard-boiled egg" flavour. Black salt, or *kala namak* as it is known in Indian cuisine, is a major ingredient in the spice-blend *chat masala*. It is available at Indian grocers.

BOCCONCINI

A fresh, Italian mild-flavoured cheese, a little like mozzarella. It is hand-moulded into creamy white balls and sold swimming in whey. Ideally, it should be eaten as soon as possible after buying. If unavailable, fresh Italian mozzarella made from the milk of water buffaloes (*mozzarella di buffala*) is an excellent alternative.

BOK CHOY

The common Cantonese name for Chinese cabbage. These small cabbages used in Chinese cooking have dark green leaves and wide, white stalks joined near the base of the stem. They resemble a miniature Swiss chard (silverbeet). The smaller the individual cabbage, the more delicate the flavour. *Bok choy* is available at Chinese grocers.

BROAD BEANS

Also known as *fava* beans in Italy, *haba* in Spanish cuisines and *ful nabed* in the Middle East. Green broad bean pods can be picked young and the beans removed and cooked and eaten fresh. If left on the plant to ripen, the pods will dry out. Then the dried beans can be removed and stored until required. Whole dried beans must be soaked and the skins removed before cooking. Available at Continental, Spanish, or Middle Eastern grocers.

BUCKWHEAT

Buckwheat is not a grain in the botanic sense, as it is related to dock and rhubarb, although some cookbooks classify it as such. Native to China, Nepal and Siberia, buckwheat is rich in iron and contains 11 per cent protein and almost the entire range of B-complex vitamins. Buckwheat is available in the form of the whole seeds called groats, roasted whole groats called *kasha*, and flour. Buckwheat is popular in Russian and Jewish cooking. It is available at health food or specialty stores.

BULGUR WHEAT

A grain product made by par-boiling and drying whole wheat kernels and crushing them into various sizes. Bulgur is popular in Middle Eastern, Eastern European and Central Asian cuisine. It has a chewy texture and a pleasant nutty taste and is rich in protein, calcium, phosphorus and iron. Bulgur wheat is available at health food shops and Middle Eastern grocers.

BUSH TOMATOES

An indigenous fruit of the Australian outback. Whole bush tomatoes are about the diameter of a blueberry, earthy, red-brown in colour with a dry, wrinkled appearance. They have a firm, fleshy texture with small, soft edible seeds. Bush tomatoes have a caramel nutty aroma with an intense spicy flavour leaving hints of rich, caramelised sugar and a slight, but pleasant, bitterness on the finish. They have a dominant flavour and are generally used as an additive, especially marrying well with the flavour of tomatoes. Available whole or ground at well-stocked specialty food stores, especially those selling "bush tukka".

BUTTERMILK

Real buttermilk is the liquid residue after cream has been churned into butter. However, the buttermilk referred to here and used in this book is cultured buttermilk, which is low-fat milk cultured in a similar way to yogurt to produce a pleasant, mild-tasting dairy product, with the consistency of light cream. Available at most well-stocked supermarkets.

CANDLE NUTS

These tropical nuts are so oily they can be burned like a candle, hence the name. Under the name of *kemiri* or *burah keras*, they are used in Malay and Indonesian cooking, crushed in soups, and ground with other ingredients. Candle nuts are available from Asian grocers. If they're hard to track down, macadamia nuts are a good substitute.

CARAWAY

Caraway seeds are the fruits of the hardy biennial herb, *Carum carvi*, a native of Europe, Asia and North Africa. The brown seeds are curved and tapered at one end, and are sometimes mistaken for cumin seeds, although they taste quite different. Caraway seeds are warm, sweet, biting and pleasantly acrid. They are a favourite flavouring for many kinds of rye bread and are also widely used in cheese, cakes and biscuits.

CARDAMOM

The aromatic seeds of the fruit of the tropical plant *Elettaria cardamomum*, a member of the ginger family which grows in the moist, tropical regions of South India and Sri Lanka. Cardamom is the world's third-most costly spice, topped only by saffron and vanilla.

The odour and flavour of cardamom is quite pronounced—reminiscent of lemon rind and eucalyptus. Cardamom is popular in some Middle Eastern dishes. In Indian cuisine, cardamom is used in rice dishes, milk sweets and *halava*. It is also chewed as a breath freshener and digestive aid after a meal.

Cardamom is available in the pod (green or bleached) as decorticated seeds (the outer shell having been removed) or powdered. I would suggest you shun the latter forms and purchase whole pods, available at Indian and Middle Eastern grocery stores for the freshest and most flavoursome cardamom experience.

CAROB

The edible beans of the carob tree, a legume belonging to the locust family. The beans grown on this tall, evergreen tree are dried, ground into powder and used as one would use cocoa. Carob powder is rich in protein and is delicious in confectionery. It also contains pectin, which is an excellent tonic for the stomach. Carob powder is available at health food stores and specialty stores.

CASSIA

(See CINNAMON.)

CELTIC SALT

A natural, health-giving sea salt, obtained from the evaporation of the ocean's water, specifically near the Celtic Sea in Brittany, in the north-west of France. Unlike heavily refined salt, Celtic salt retains many valuable trace minerals.

CAPERS

The pickled flour buds of the wild Mediterranean bush *Capparis rupestris*. Capers have been used as a condiment for thousands of years, and they feature especially in French and Italian cuisine. They have a distinct sour, salty flavour and are featured in this book in *Sicilian Eggplant Appetiser (Caponata)*.

CAYENNE PEPPER

The orange-red to deep-red powder derived from small, sun-dried, pungent red chili peppers (*Capsicum frutescens*). This bitingly hot condiment should be used with restraint, for a small amount will add considerable zest and flavour to dishes. It is used in a number of hot dishes, notably in Mexican and Indian cuisine. Cayenne is available from supermarkets or well-stocked grocers.

CHANA DAL

Husked, split whole dried brown chickpeas (a relative of the common chickpea). They are very popular in Indian cuisine, especially in *dal* dishes and savories, being tasty, nutritious, and easy to digest. *Chana dal* is roasted and ground into chickpea flour (*besan*), and used throughout India for savories and sweets. *Chana dal* is featured in this book in *Maharastrian-style Sweet and Sour Chana Dal*, and *Chickpea Flour Dumplings in Creamy Karhi Sauce. Chana dal* is available at Indian grocery stores. (See also CHICKPEA FLOUR.)

CHAPATI FLOUR

(See ATTA.)

CHAT MASALA

A traditional companion to freshly-cut fruit in Indian cuisine. This light-brown spice blend contains a number of ingredients, notably black salt, mango powder and asafetida. Sprinkled on fruit with a few drops of fresh lime juice, it makes a deliciously different dessert. Available from Indian grocery stores.

CHICKPEA FLOUR

The finely milled, pale-yellow flour from ground, roasted *chana dal*. It is popular in Indian cuisine for making batter, as a binding agent, and in confectionery. It is also known as *besan* flour, gram flour and peas meal, and is available at Indian grocers. (See also CHANA DAL.)

CHICKPEAS

Known as *garbanzos* in Spanish-speaking countries or *ceci* in Italy, chickpeas are the peas from the pods of the plant *Cicer arietinum*. They are popular in India in their immature, green state, whereas they are commonly known outside of India in their dried state. These large, light-brown wrinkled peas must be soaked before use, then boiled until soft. They are used extensively in many cuisines around the world, especially Indian, Mexican and Middle Eastern. They are rich in protein — 100g (3 ½ ounces) of cooked chickpeas contain 20g of protein. Chickpeas provide nearly double the amount of iron and more vitamin C than most legumes. Chickpeas are available at Continental, Indian and Middle Eastern grocers and at well-stocked supermarkets.

CHILIES

Chilies, sweet and hot, are members of *Solanaceae*, a vast assemblage of plants to which potato, tomato and eggplant also belong. All chilies fall into the category of *Capsicum* and most of the readily available ones belong to the *annuum* species. There are hundreds of varieties of chilies, over 150 in Mexico alone, ranging in potency from sweet to fiery hot. The chemical in chilies that gives them heat and thera-peutic value is *capsacin*. The more *capsacin* a chili contains, the hotter it is. The seeds and the inner white ribs are the hottest part and often a recipe calls for removing both to tame the heat. Here's a description of some of the main varieties of chilies featured in this book:

ANAHEIM: 10–15cm (4–6 inches) long, and 2.5cm (1-inch) wide, smooth, medium-thick flesh with a mild sweet vegetable flavour. They are available green or red, are versatile and, like most chilies, their flavour improves on roasting.

CHIPOTLE: A smoked, dried red *jalepeño*, 2.5cm (1-inch) long and 1.5cm (3/4-inch) wide. Dark brick to coffee-colour with cream veins and ridges. Has a distinctive smoky hot flavour.

JALAPEÑO: One of the most well-known chilies outside of Mexico. There are many varieties, but their shape is unmistakable: like an elongated, blunt triangle. Their average size is 5–7cm (2–3 inches) long and 2.5cm (1-inch) wide. They are juicy, thick-fleshed, with a clean fresh vegetable flavour. They range from grass green to dark green or red, are fairly hot and are very versatile.

POBLANO: Averaging 12.5cm (5 ½ inches) long and 7.5cm (3 inches) wide, poblanos look like a triangle with a tapered point. They have a thick flesh with a mild but rich flavour. *Poblanos* are usually roasted, then skinned before using.

SERRANO: Small, bullet-shaped chilies with a rounded end. Measuring 3–5cm (1–2 inches) long, *serranos* have a thick, smooth flesh with a hard appearance. They are high in acidity with a pungent flavour. They are available bright green and scarlet red.

CHIPOTLE

(See CHILIES.)

CHIRA

(See FLAT RICE.)

CHOY SUM

Although this plant, also known as Rape, whose seeds are the source of Rapeseed oil, is grown in various parts of the world. It is used extensively in Chinese and Japanese cuisine as a vegetable. It is delicately flavoured, with yellow flowers, succulent green stalks, and small bright green leaves branching from a central stem. This attractive vegetable is available from Chinese grocers all year around.

CINNAMON

Cinnamomum zeylanicum is a moderate-sized, bushy evergreen tree of the laurel family, whose dried inner bark is true cinnamon. Native to Southern India and Sri Lanka, the thin, bark sheaths are sundried and packed, one inside the other, to produce "sticks" or "quills".

Confusion sometimes exists in distinguishing cinnamon from cassia. In some countries, what is sold as cinnamon is in fact cassia (*Cinnamomum cassia*). Cassia is a taller tree with smaller flowers and fruits than true cinnamon. In general, Cassia is prepared for the market in much the same way as cinnamon, and their flavours are similar, although cinnamon is less pungent and more delicate than cassia. Cassia powder is reddish-brown, while cinnamon powder is tan. Cinnamon or cassia sticks impart a sweet, aromatic flavour to fancy Indian rice dishes, vegetables and *dals*. Ground to a powder, cinnamon is an important ingredient in the North Indian spice blend *garam masala*. Cinnamon also features extensively in Middle Eastern and European cuisine. It is available at supermarkets and Indian and Middle Eastern grocers.

CLOVES

The dried nail-shaped buds from a neat evergreen tree with aromatic pink buds. These buds, when hand-picked and dried, turn a reddish-brown to become the cloves with which we are familiar.

Good cloves should have a strong, pungent, sweet aroma and flavour and should be well-formed, plump and oily. Cloves have diverse uses in different cuisines of the world, being used for cakes, tarts and pastries, fancy rice dishes, soup stocks, sweet cooked fruits and in various spice blends, including some North Indian *garam masalas*. Cloves are available at supermarkets and Indian grocery stores.

COCONUT

The coconut palm, *Cocos nucifera*, is grown on tropical coasts all over the world and is the source of many products. Most important are the nuts (technically called *drupes*). When coconuts are picked green, one can extract their sweet juice as a beverage. The pulp inside is used in many South Indian savoury dishes. When coconuts ripen on the tree, the picked fruits yield moist, white "meat", which is excellent in varieties of vegetable dishes, savouries, rice dishes, sweets, chutneys and beverages, especially in Indian and South-East Asian cuisine.

Dried coconut is desiccated and is familiar in Western cuisine as an ingredient in sweets and cakes. When a recipe calls for fresh coconut, however, dried desiccated coconut is a poor substitute. Fresh coconuts are easily available in tropical areas and can even be found for sale far from their place of origin. They will be suitable as long as they are still full of juice and have no cracks or signs of mould around their "eyes". Once cracked open, separated from their husk and peeled, fresh coconut can be sliced, grated, shredded, stored in the refrigerator for several days or frozen.

COCONUT MILK

Known as *santan* in Indonesian cooking, this creamy white liquid with a fresh coconut flavour is extracted from fresh coconut pulp and is used in varieties of South-East Asian and Indonesian dishes. It is available in cans from supermarkets and Asian grocers.

CONTINENTAL PARSLEY

(See PARSLEY.)

CORIANDER LEAVES

The fresh leaves of the hardy annual plant *Coriandrum sativum*, fresh coriander is one of the most commonly used flavouring herbs in the world, certainly on par with parsley. It is found in markets throughout the Middle East, China, South-East Asia, India and South and Central America. Bunches of coriander can be recognised by their smell and their fan-like lower leaves and feathery upper ones.

Also known as *cilantro*, Chinese parsley and *har dhania*, fresh coriander is a zesty and delicious addition to many of the world's cuisines. Its unique, warm-bodied taste is found in Indian vegetable dishes, *dals*, savories and fresh chutneys. (See *Green Mango, Mint and Coriander Chutney*.) It also makes a very beautiful garnish. Purchase fresh coriander from oriental and Latin American grocers or well-stocked produce markets and greengrocers.

CORIANDER SEEDS

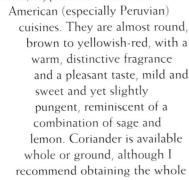

The seeds of the annual herb *Coriandrum sativum*. Coriander seeds are a favourite flavouring spice in Indian, Cypriot and some Latin American (especially Peruvian) cuisines. They are almost round, brown to yellowish-red, with a warm, distinctive fragrance and a pleasant taste, mild and sweet and yet slightly pungent, reminiscent of a combination of sage and lemon. Coriander is available whole or ground, although I recommend obtaining the whole seeds and grinding them yourself when you need the freshest coriander flavour. Known as *dhania* in Indian cuisine, coriander complements the flavour of many savoury dishes. Coriander seeds are available at Indian and Middle Eastern grocery stores and well-stocked supermarkets.

CORNFLOUR

When I mention cornflour in this book, I am referring to what Americans call "cornstarch", and not to the flour milled from corn. Cornflour, sometimes referred to as wheat starch, is the dry white powdered starch remaining when the proteins have been removed from wheat flour. It is used in many cuisines, especially Chinese, as a thickener for sauces. It is available from any grocer or supermarket.

CORN MEAL

(See POLENTA.)

COUSCOUS

A grain product made from semolina. It is also the name of the famous dish of which couscous is the main ingredient, being one of the most common and widely known North African Arab dishes. Available at well-stocked supermarkets and Middle Eastern grocers.

CRACKED WHEAT

(See BULGUR WHEAT.)

CUMIN SEEDS

The seeds of the small annual herb of the parsley family, *Cuminum cyminum*. Cumin seeds are oval and yellowish-brown, similar in appearance to the caraway seeds, but longer. They have a warm, strongly aromatic and slightly bitter flavour and are used extensively in Indian, Middle Eastern and Latin American cuisines (especially in Mexican dishes).

The flavour and aroma of cumin, like most spice seeds, emerges best after they have been dry-roasted or added to hot oil. In Indian cuisine, cumin is popular in vegetable dishes, yogurt-based salads, *raitas*, *dals*, and savouries. Cumin seeds can be obtained from any Indian or Middle Eastern grocer, or well-stocked supermarkets.

CURD CHEESE (PANIR)

The simplest type of unripened fresh cheese, produced by adding an acidic curdling agent to boiled raw milk. This versatile food ingredient is popular in all varieties of Indian cuisine, and it can also be used as a substitute for tofu, feta or farmer's cheese. It is high in protein, has a soft consistency, and is sweeter and creamier than tofu. It can be cubed and deep-fried, and added to moist vegetable dishes and rice dishes, crumbled into salads, kneaded and rolled into small balls, and made into confectionery.

(TO) CURDLE

When small amounts of acidic substances are added to hot milk, a protein known as casein coagulates and forms solid lumps known commonly as curd. Other proteins, principal among them lacto-globulin, remain suspended in the liquid, known as whey.

CURRY LEAVES

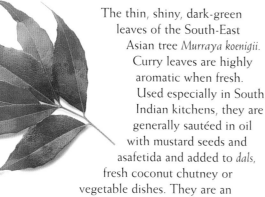

The thin, shiny, dark-green leaves of the South-East Asian tree *Murraya koenigii*. Curry leaves are highly aromatic when fresh. Used especially in South Indian kitchens, they are generally sautéed in oil with mustard seeds and asafetida and added to *dals*, fresh coconut chutney or vegetable dishes. They are an important ingredient in one variety of curry powder used in Tamil Nadu.

Dried leaves are inferior, but sometimes that is all that is available. Obtain curry leaves from Indian grocery stores.

DAIKON

A large, white winter radish, also known as Japanese radish, or *mooli* in Indian cuisine. It has a fresh, slightly peppery taste and a clean, crisp texture which makes it an ideal salad ingredient, although it can be steamed or stir-fried. It is available throughout the year, although it is at its peak of flavour during the winter months. Choose roots which are firm to the touch and slightly shiny. Daikon is available at well-stocked Asian foodstores or vegetable markets.

DAL

A generic name for all members of the dried pea and bean family, and also the name of the thick, gravy-like or thin soup-like dishes made from them. *Dal*, besides being a good source of iron and B vitamins, is an excellent source of vegetable protein. Examples of *dals* used in this book are yellow split peas, mung beans, *toor dal, chana dal*, and *urad dal.*

DAUN KESOM

(See VIETNAMESE MINT.)

DAUN LAKSA

(See VIETNAMESE MINT.)

DEHRADUN BASMATI

(See BASMATI RICE.)

DILL

A medium-sized herb with small feathery leaves and yellow flowers. Dill *(Anethum graveolens)* is related to anise, caraway, coriander, cumin, fennel and parsley. Dill seeds are oval, tan and light in weight with a clean odour faintly reminiscent of caraway, pungent and pleasantly aromatic. They are most frequently used as a condiment, either whole or ground, especially in pickling cucumbers and in breads. In France, dill seeds are used extensively in pastries and sauces, while in India they are used in traditional medicines.

The feathery fresh herb known as "dill weed" is excellent in potato salads. It can also be obtained dried. Fresh dill is available at quality produce markets or green-grocers, and dry dill weed and dill seeds can be obtained at health food stores, specialty shops or well-stocked supermarkets.

(TO) DRY ROAST

This technique refers to the process of slowly browning whole spice seeds, split *dal*, nuts and seeds and some types of flour. It is best done in a heavy pan or griddle that has been pre-warmed over low heat. The ingredients are stir-fried, without the addition of any oil or liquid, until lightly browned, releasing flavourful volatile oils and aromatic fragrances.

EKADASI

Literally "eleventh" in Sanskrit, it refers to the eleventh day after both the full and new moon. Strict followers of Vedic culture abstain from grains and beans on this day.

FENNEL

The tall, hardy, aromatic perennial of the parsley family native to southern Europe and the Mediterranean area. Fennel (*Foeniculum vulgare*) is distinguished by its finely divided, feathery green foliage and its golden-yellow flowers. It is used both as a herb and for its aromatic seeds. In Italian cuisine, the bulb of the Florence fennel, or *finocchio*, is used whole, sliced, or quartered as a vegetable and either braised or baked *au gratin*. It is also chopped raw in salads. Wild fennel stems and the frondy leaves, with a slightly bitter anise taste, are used in cooking, especially to flavour sauces.

Fennel seeds, although used to some extent in European cooking, are especially favoured in Indian cuisine. The oval, greenish or yellowish-brown seeds have an agreeable, warm, sweet fragrance, similar to that of anise. Fennel seeds appear in Kashmiri and Punjabi dishes and are one of the five spices in the Bengali spice blend called *panch puran*. They are used in a variety of vegetable dishes, *dals* and pastries. The most common use of fennel seeds in Indian cuisine is as an after-dinner digestive. They are dry-roasted, and chewed, freshening the breath and stimulating digestion. Fresh fennel bulbs are available seasonally at good greengrocer shops. The seeds are available at Indian grocers.

FENUGREEK

An erect annual herb of the bean family, indigenous to western Asia and south-eastern Europe. Fenugreek (*Trigonella foenum-graecum*) is cultivated for its seeds, which, although legumes, are used as a spice.

The seeds are small, hard, yellowish-brown, smooth and oblong, with a little groove across one corner. Fenugreek has a warm, slightly bitter taste, reminiscent of burnt sugar and maple. The seeds are used in Greece and Egypt and especially India, where they are lightly dry-roasted or fried to extract their characteristic flavour. One should note, however, that over-roasting or over-frying fenugreek results in an excessive bitter taste. The leaves of the fenugreek plant are also popular in Indian cuisine. Known as *methi*, they are used in vegetable dishes, breads and savories. Easily home-grown, fresh young fenugreek leaves are wonderful in salads, dressed with oil and lemon. Fenugreek seeds are available at Indian or Middle Eastern grocers. The fresh leaves (if you are shopping outside India), can occasionally be found in markets or can be home-grown.

FINOCCHIO

(See FENNEL.)

FIVE SPICE

Two varieties of five spice are prominent in the world of vegetarian cuisine: Chinese five spice powder and Indian *panch puran*, a blend of five whole spices. Chinese five spice powder is a combination of five dried, ground spices, generally cinnamon, cloves, fennel, star anise and sichuan peppercorns, the pungent, brown peppercorns native to the Sichuan province.

When used as a condiment for fried food, it is used in sparing quantities because it is very potent. Try making your own by grinding together two or three small sections of cinnamon stick, a dozen cloves, two teaspoons of fennel seeds, two teaspoons of sichuan peppercorns and three or four star anise. Keep the powder in a well-sealed jar in a cool, dry place. Obtain your ingredients at any Asian grocery store. You can also purchase Chinese five spice ready-made.

Panch puran is most often associated with Bengali cuisine. It is a combination of equal quantities of fenugreek seeds, cumin seeds, fennel seeds, black mustard seeds and *nigella* (*kalonji*) seeds. *Panch puran* is always fried in ghee or oil before use to release the dormant flavour in the seeds. Mix your own, or purchase it ready-made at Indian grocery stores.

FLAT RICE

Also known as *chira*, flaked rice, pressed rice or *poha*. It is a partially cooked rice product, popular in Indian cuisine. Unhusked rice is first soaked, boiled briefly, then drained, heated until it puffs, then flattened into thin flakes. It can be stored for months without deterioration, then simply reconstituted by soaking, rinsing in boiling water or deep-frying.

Flat rice is available from Indian grocers in two grades—

thick and thin. The thick variety, *poha,* is used for deep-frying, and the thin is suitable for dry *pulao*-type dishes. Flat rice is featured in this book in *Chira Pulao.*

FUL NABED

(See BROADBEANS.)

GALANGAL

There are two varieties of galangal greater and lesser. Both are closely related, although the lesser is more important. Greater galangal (*Alpinia galanga*), native to Indonesia, is related to ginger. Its large, knobby, spicy roots taste rather like ginger and are used in Indonesian cooking.

Lesser galangal (*Alpinia officinarum*) is the rhizome of a plant native to China. Its roots have a pepper-ginger flavour and are used in many Indonesian and Malaysian dishes. In Indonesia, it is also known as laos. Laos or galangal can occasionally be obtained fresh from Asian grocers. Peel and slice it before use. If unavailable, substitute fresh ginger, although the taste is not the same. Laos powder is also used, especially in Indonesian cooking. It is less hot and more bitter than fresh laos. Use very sparingly or substitute slices of fresh ginger.

GARAM MASALA

A blend of dry-roasted and ground spices well-used in Indian cuisine. The spices used for *garam masala* warm the body (*garam* means warm). Such spices include dried chilies, black pepper, cardamom, coriander, cinnamon, cloves and cumin. Other spices, such as *ajowan,* mace, nutmeg, fennel, bay leaves, ginger, and white and green pepper, as well as other ingredients such as sesame seeds, coconut and saffron, are also used according to the region, since Indian cooking styles vary immensely according to the geographical location. Generally, *garam masala* is added towards the end of cooking. Various recipes for home made *garam masala* appear in the *Special Ingredients* section. Various *garam masalas* can be purchased at Indian grocery stores.

GHEE

The oil produced by clarifying butter over gentle heat until all the moisture is driven off and the milk solids are fully separated from the clear butterfat. The essential difference between ghee and clarified butter, or butter oil, is that in the preparation of ghee, the solids (milk proteins and salts) are allowed to brown before being removed, thus imparting a nutty flavour. Ghee is an excellent choice for sautéeing and frying, and is much favoured in Indian cooking, as well as some French, Saudi Arabian and other Middle Eastern cuisines. Ghee can be purchased at Indian or Middle Eastern grocery stores or some well-stocked super-markets.

GINGER

The thick, white, tuberous underground stems or rhizomes of the plant *Zingiber officinale,* which thrives in the tropical areas of the world. Fresh ginger root has a spicy, sweet aroma and a hot, clean taste and is used in many cuisines, especially throughout China, Japan, Thailand and India. The young "green" ginger is especially appreciated for its fibre-free texture and mild flavour. Mature ginger root is more readily available at produce markets, Asian grocery stores and some supermarkets.

Fresh ginger should be peeled before use. It can be minced, sliced, puréed, shredded or cut into julienne strips and used in vegetable dishes, *dals* and soups, savouries, fried dishes, chutneys, rices, sweets and drinks.

Ginger powder is not a substitute for fresh ginger, for often it has lost its volatile essential oils and is sometimes stale or adulterated. Ginger powder is used mostly in European cooking, in puddings, creams, beverages, biscuits, breads and cakes. It is available at most grocery shops and supermarkets.

GINGER FLOWERS

These delicate red flowers are used like young ginger. The stalk needs to be peeled and the bottom few outer leaves removed. After being steeped in water for several minutes to dislodge any soil, they can be blanched before use. If ginger flowers are unavailable, used wild ginger or young ginger instead.

GREEN PEPPERCORNS

(See PEPPER.)

GLUTEN

A mixture of proteins which occur in wheat. Its two main protein constituents absorb water and form elastic strands when flour is kneaded with water. This is what makes possible the light structure of leavened bread.

A "strong" flour usually has a high gluten content and a high-rising, high water absorbing quality. It can make a large volume of dough with a light, open texture, such as needed in bread. A low-gluten, soft, starchy flour usually makes the best cakes and biscuits.

GLUTEN FLOUR

A flour made from the protein constituent of wheat flour. It creates an extra spongy texture when added to breads by virtue of the elastic network it forms in the dough when water is added.

HARICOT BEANS

A member of the *Phaseolus vulgaris* species, which includes not only haricot, but kidney beans, great Northern beans and pinto beans. These dried white beans are popular in soups, stews and casseroles. They are well-used in Italian cooking and are known as *fagiolo secco*. They are available at grocery stores and supermarkets.

HING

(See ASAFETIDA.)

(TO) INFUSE: To steep or heat gently to extract flavour.

JAGGERY

An unrefined sugar made from the juice crushed out of sugar cane stalks. The juice is boiled down to about a quarter of its original volume into a thick brown syrup. As the syrup thickens further and more liquid evaporates, it is scooped out and placed on palm leaves to harden. Jaggery is available in light to dark-brown lumps in Indian and Asian stores.

JALAPEÑO

(See CHILIES.)

JASMINE RICE

(See THAI RICE.)

JICAMA

(See YAM BEAN.)

(TO) JULIENNE

To cut firm ingredients like vegetables, fruits, citrus rind, chilies or ginger root, to name but a few into long, thin, matchstick strips, or very fine shreds.

KADAYIF

(see KATAIFI.)

KARELA

(See BITTER MELON.)

KARMA

This Sanskrit word means "action" or, more specifically, any material action that brings a reaction binding us to the material world. According to the law of *karma*, if we cause pain and suffering to other living beings, we must endure pain and suffering in return.

KATAIFI

A type of pastry resembling vermicelli, used throughout Greece, Turkey and the Middle East. Also known as *kadayif*, or *konafa*, the raw pastry is made by pouring and shaking flour and water batter through a sieve onto a hot metal plate. The pastry is the main ingredient in a syrupy sweet, also known as *kataifi*, or *kadayif*. The recipe appears in this book.

KALAMATA OLIVES

Large, ink-black olives with pointed ends and shiny skins, named after the seaside town of southern Greece where they are grown. Popular in Greek cuisine, they are flavoursome and full-bodied.

KALONJI SEEDS

Also known as *nigella* or black onion seeds (no relation to the onion). Very often these small, jet-black, teardrop seeds are confused with, or called, black cumin seeds, which they are not. *Kalonji* seeds, *Nigella sattiva*, have a peppery taste and, when heated, have a herbal aroma. They are an important ingredient in the Bengali spice blend called *panch puran*. They are available at Indian grocery stores.

KIDNEY BEANS

The popular kidney-shaped red bean from the plant *Phaseolus vulgaris*. Kidney beans can be used in many types of cuisine: as an alternative to borlotti beans in Italian cooking, as an alternative to pinto beans in Mexican style cooking, or in stews, soups and casseroles. Red kidney beans are known as *rajma* in India and are featured in this book in the spicy chili-style dish of the same name,

popular in the Punjab. They are available at Indian grocery stores or supermarkets.

KONAFA

(See KATAIFI.)

KRISHNA

The name for God given in the Sanskrit Vedic texts of India. Krishna is revered in the *Vedas* as the original form of the Godhead.

LAKSA LEAVES

(See VIETNAMESE MINT.)

LAOS

(See GALANGAL.)

LEMON GRASS

A tall, lemon-scented grass with narrow, sharp-edged leaves and a central rib. Lemon grass imparts a pleasant lemon fragrance to soups and curries, and is one of the most popular herbs of South East-Asia. Lemon grass can be usually purchased from the market in a bundle of three or four stems devoid of leaves. Look for firm, smooth stems, free from wrinkles. The bulbous lower stem, creamy-white to pale green, is the part to use.

The lower stem can either be sliced thinly cross-wise or bruised with a kitchen mallet and simmered whole in a dish, and discarded before serving. When preparing lemon grass for a spice paste or in a salad, peel off outer layers from the lower stem and use only the tender white portion, finely sliced. Lemon grass leaves may be used for infusions, to make a pleasant tea, but are not used much in cooking.

If lemon grass is not available, it is quite acceptable to substitute two or three strips of thinly peeled lemon zest for one stalk of lemon grass.

LEMON VERBENA

A small deciduous shrub with strongly perfumed, long, pointed, light-green, lemon-scented leaves. Lemon verbena leaves can be used fresh or dried to impart a pleasant lemon flavour to fresh fruit drinks.

LENTILS

Used extensively in many cuisines of the world. Brown lentils from the plant *Lens culinaris,* and red lentils (called *masoor dal* in India) are probably the most well-known. Lentils contain almost 25 per cent protein, 54 per cent carbohydrate and vitamin A, some of the B vitamins and good amounts of minerals, including iron and calcium. Brown and red lentils are available at almost any super-market or grocery store. Note that due to their very high protein content, red lentils are not consumed by strict followers of the Vedic culture.

MACE

The dried aril or fleshy cage that surrounds the seed of the nutmeg (*Myristica fragrans*). It is bright red when fresh, and creamy brown when dried. It has a taste something like nutmeg, but subtly different. (See also NUTMEG.)

MALT, BARLEY

A sweet, sticky extract made from barley that has been soaked, sprouted, heated, dried, then matured and mashed. The liquid filtered off the mash is sterilised and then boiled to evaporate into a thick syrup, rich in malt sugar, dextrins and flavour compounds. It is also known as malt extract.

(TO) MARINATE

A procedure during which foods are soaked in a liquid mixture (marinade) to either preserve the food, infuse them with flavour or tenderise them.

MARZIPAN

A confectionery consisting of powdered blanched almonds mixed with sugar.

MASALA

A combination of herbs, spices or seasonings used in Indian cuisine. Some *masalas,* like Bengali *panch puran,* contain whole spices. Others, like *chat masala, garam masala, sambar masala,* or *rasam* powder, contain numerous powdered spices combined together. For details on *masalas,* see individual entries.

MASOOR DAL

(See LENTILS.)

MESÇLUN

A traditional mixture of tiny salad leaves from the south of France.

METZUMA

Sometimes known as mizuna. A spikey-leaved salad green.

MINT

A widely used culinary herb. There are many species of mint and classification is difficult because the species easily cross and hybridise. Although spearmint (*Mentha spicata*) and peppermint (*Mentha piperata*) are the two most common mints, round-leaved varieties of apple mint, Bowles mint and pineapple mint (*Mentha rotundifolia*) are amongst the best mints for cooking.

Mint may be generally described as having a fresh, strong, sweet and tangy flavour, with a cool after-taste. Mint is better used fresh rather than dried. In Indian cuisine, mint is commonly used in fresh chutneys. (See *Green Mango, Mint and Coriander Chutney.*) Fresh mint also goes with many fruits and is excellent in fruit salad and fruit drinks.

MOOLI

(See DAIKON RADISH.)

MOZZARELLA CHEESE

This famous Italian cheese was traditionally made from buffalo's milk, but these days it is more frequently made from cow's milk. It is best eaten fresh, but when hung for some time it becomes a little dry and it is then specifically used for cooking. Mozzarella is a good melting cheese, making it a popular topping for pizzas. (See also BOCCONCINI.)

MUNG BEANS

The protein-rich, green-skinned, whole, oval beans, *Phaseolus aureus*, are commonly used for sprouting. Whole green mung beans are excellent for stews and soups, as well as for Indian dry bean dishes. They are available at Indian or Asian grocers or specialty stores.

When the beans are skinned and split, they are known as split mung beans, or mung *dal*. Split mung beans are a popular food item in Indian cuisine. Split mung beans are easy to digest and are high in protein and cook to a creamy purée in a short time. They are used extensively in soups, stews and sauces throughout India. Split mung beans are also used in Thai and Vietnamese cooking. They are available at Indian or Asian grocery stores.

MUSTARD SEEDS

Of the many varieties of mustard, the three most prominent are the tiny, round, brownish-black seeds from the plant known as *Brassica nigra*, commonly known as black mustard; the purple-brown seeds of *Brassica juncea*, commonly called brown mustard; and the yellow seeds from *Brassica alba*, known as white or yellow mustard.

Black and brown mustard seeds are often confused with one another. Brown mustard seeds, *Brassica juncea*, are commonly used as a spice seed in Indian cuisine where they are known as *rai*. In South Indian cuisine they are fried in hot oil or ghee to extract their nutty, pungent flavour before being added to soups, chutneys or vegetables dishes. In Bengali cuisine, mustard seeds are one of the five ingredients in the whole spice blend known as *panch puran*. Yellow mustard seeds (*Brassica alba*),

are less pungent than the darker varieties and are commonly used in European cuisine as a pickling spice. They are strongly preservative, discouraging moulds and bacteria, hence their inclusion in pickles.

When mustard seeds are pounded, they form the basis of immense varieties of commercial brands of the condiment known as mustard. Different varieties of mustard are made from different combinations of hulled and unhulled yellow or brown seeds. It is interesting to note that the pungency of mustard is due to an essential oil which is not present in the seed or the powder, but which forms when the crushed seed is mixed with water. An enzyme then causes a bitter substance in the seed to react with the water, and the hot taste of the mustard emerges. Yellow mustard seeds are available from supermarkets and grocers, and brown or black mustard seeds are available at Indian grocery stores.

NIÇOISE

A name given to many dishes consisting of ingredients common in the south of France.

NIGELLA SEEDS

(See KALONJI.)

NUTMEG

The fragrant nut found in the centre of the fruit of the densely foliated evergreen tree *Myristica fragrans*. The fleshy fruit of the nutmeg tree resembles an apricot. When it is ripe, it splits in half, revealing the beautiful, brilliant scarlet, net-like membrane, or avil, known as mace. It closely enwraps a brittle shell containing the glossy-brown oily nutmeg. Nutmeg is egg-shaped, and is about 2.5 cm (1 inch) in diameter, with a sweet, warm, and highly spicy flavour.

Nutmeg is used in many cuisines of the world. It is often an ingredient in the North Indian spice blend known as *garam masala*, and is used in cakes and sweet dishes. It is wonderful

with pumpkin, squash and sweet potato. In Italian cuisine, it is very popular in spinach dishes and combines well with cheese. Nutmeg is also a common flavouring in the Levant and in various spicy dishes of South-East Asia.

Whole nutmegs are best ground straight into the dish in which they are being used, as once grated nutmeg quickly loses its flavour. Whole nutmegs are available at specialty stores and well-stocked supermarkets and grocery stores.

OAT BRAN

The fibre-rich, coarse layer removed from under the outer husk of oats, during the early stages of milling. A good source of iron, thiamine and niacin. Available from health food stores and some supermarkets.

OATMEAL

The hulled oat grain that has been rolled or cut into flakes. There are three basic types: quick-cook or rolled oats, which generally has small flakes; hulled or gritted oatmeal; and steel-cut oatmeal. Oatmeal is among the most nutritious of all the grains. It is 16.7 per cent protein, and is rich in inositol (one of the B-complex vitamins), iron, phosphorus and thiamine. Oatmeal is generally used as porridge or muesli, but is also baked in breads and savoury dishes. It is available at any grocery store.

OLIVE OIL

The oil extracted from the fruits of the Mediterranean tree, *Olea europaea*. The finest olive oil is cold-pressed from fresh, ripe olives and has a pale-yellow or greenish colour and a very delicate flavour. Cruder versions of olive oil are second pressings made under heat. I prefer to have at least two grades of olive oil in the kitchen; mild, cold-pressed, extra-virgin olive oil for salads and uncooked dishes, and a pure, lighter grade olive oil with a high smoking-point for cooking.

Choosing olive oil is much a matter of personal taste and preference. Olive oil is used in many cuisines of the world, not only in Mediterranean cooking. Good quality olive oil is available at specialty and continental grocers and well-stocked supermarkets.

OREGANO

A piquant herb famous in Greek and Italian cuisine. Oregano is botanically confused with marjoram. In fact, for many years both marjoram and oregano were known as *Marjorana hortensis*. There is still confusion today— oregano is still sometimes known as "wild marjoram".

Generally, what is purchased as oregano today is most probably *Oreganum vulgare*, with a strong, piquant, sweet flavour and a pleasantly bitter, aromatic undertone.

Oregano is excellent with any tomato dish, especially pizza and varieties of tomato dishes that include pasta sauces. Its flavour marries well with basil. Oregano is available at any Continental grocer, supermarket or specialty shop. (See also RIGANI.)

PALM SUGAR

A dark brown sugar produced by boiling down the sap of various palm trees. Palm sugar has a rich, sweet taste and is an appropriate sweetener in various South-East Asian and Indonesian dishes. It is sold in thick, tubular sections or round lumps and is available from Asian grocers.

PANDAN LEAVES

Also known as *pandanus* leaves. These long, thin, green leaves are popular in Malaysia, Sri Lanka, Indonesia and Thailand as an important flavouring agent for savoury and sweet dishes. The flavour of *pandan* is aromatic and delicate, and it is as important to Asians as vanilla is to Westerners. Sometimes the leaves are pounded and strained to extract their flavour and colour for cakes and sweets. Their flavour can also be extracted by cooking whole sections of leaf in a dish and removing it after cooking. *Pandan* leaves are available frozen, from well-stocked Asian grocers. *Pandan* extract or flavouring is an acceptable, although inferior substitute.

(TO) PAN-FRY

The technique of frying any ingredient in a small amount of oil.

PANIR
(See CURD CHEESE.)

PAPRIKA

The bright red powder made from the dried, sweet chili-pepper pods of the many varieties of *Capsicum annuum*. Good paprika has a brilliant red colour and because it is not hot, it can be used in generous quantities, giving dishes a rich, red hue. It is also very nutritious, having a high vitamin C content.

Paprika is the national spice of Hungary, and is featured in Hungarian and Spanish, as well as North Indian cuisines, where it is used in *dals* and sauces. It is available at grocery stores.

PARMESAN

The most famous of the all the *grana* or matured, hard cheeses of Italy. Parmesan or parmigiano, takes at least two years to come to maturity, resulting in its traditional sharp flavour. Parmesan cheese should be bought in pieces, to be freshly grated over sauces, pasta or rice or added to cooked dishes.

PARSLEY

One of the best known and most extensively used culinary herbs in Western cuisine. There are numerous cultivated varieties of parsley, but the ornamental curled variety is most popular as a garnish, and the flat-leaved parsley is most favoured in Italian and other Mediterranean cuisines. Both are varieties of *Petroselinum crispum*. Healthful parsley leaves, with their familiar, mild, agreeable flavour, are an excellent source of vitamin C, iron, iodine and other minerals. Parsley is appealing to the eye, nose, and taste, will sweeten the breath, and is a natural herbal

deodoriser. It is a pleasant addition to an enormous variety of savoury dishes. It is available at produce markets, greengrocers and supermarkets.

PASTA

The finest pasta is made from durum wheat, which is one of the hardest varieties of wheat. When making pasta from durum wheat, only the endosperm of the grain kernel is milled into semolina, which is then mixed with water to make the dough.

When preparing pasta dishes, note that the completed pasta should be tender without being soft and sticky. This is called *al dente*. Pasta comes in many shapes and sizes. Notable varieties used in this cookbook are fettuccine, orecciette, cannelloni, lasagna, spaghetti and vermicelli.

PEPPER

The small, round berries of the woody, perennial, evergreen vine, *Piper nigrum*. Black pepper, white pepper and green pepper are also obtained from these same berries at different stages of maturity. For black pepper, the berries are picked while green, left in heaps to ferment, sundried and allowed to shrivel and turn dark brown or black. Thus the whole berry, including the dark outer hull, forms what we know as black pepper.

White pepper is produced from fully ripened berries, which are greenish-yellow when picked and at the point of turning red. Then they are soaked in water, the outer hull is rubbed off, and the grey inner berries are sundried until they turn creamy white, to become what is known as white pepper.

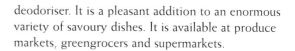

Green peppercorns are soft, immature berries that have been picked and preserved in brine or freeze-dried. Black pepper is characterised by a penetrating odour and a hot, biting, and extremely pungent flavour; milder flavoured white pepper is generally appreciated in European cuisine. Either way, black and white pepper are used in practically every cuisine in the world. Although available pre-ground, discerning cooks prefer the superior flavour of freshly ground peppercorns, for which a peppermill is an essential acquisition.

PESTO

Referred to as *pistou* in France, the famous pungent sauce made primarily of fresh basil leaves, parmesan cheese and toasted pine nuts. Three variations of this combination are all featured in this book: *Arugula Pesto* (served with *Hot Roasted Jacket-Baked Potatoes*), *Lemony Herb Pesto* (served with *Roasted Antipasti Vegetable Platter*) and *Fresh Coriander and Macadamia Nut Pistou.*

PILAF

(See PULAO.)

PINE NUTS

Also known as pine kernels, *pignolia* or *pinoli*. Pine nuts come from the Stone Pine, *Pineus pinea,* a beautiful Mediterranean pine tree. The pine cones are gathered, the seeds shaken out and cracked, and the small white or cream-coloured kernels are extracted. Their delicious, delicate nutty taste has made them a very popular ingredient in Italian, Spanish and Middle Eastern cuisine. They are available at specialty, Continental or Middle Eastern groceries.

PLANTAINS

A cooking banana, *Musa paradisiaca.* Plantains are larger than common eating bananas, with a thick green skin. Plantains are treated more like vegetables than fruit, and contain more starch than sugar, even when fully ripe. Plantains are available at Latin American stores and some Indian and Asian greengrocers.

POBLANO

(See CHILIES.)

POHA

(See FLAT RICE.)

POLENTA

A yellow maize or cornmeal grown in Northern Italy, where it is regarded as a staple food. Polenta is graded according to its texture and is available fine, medium or coarse-ground. It is available at most supermarkets and health food stores.

POPPY SEEDS

Two varieties of poppy seed are referred to here: black and white. Both are seeds of the poppy plant *Papaver somniferum.* The minute, kidney-shaped, bluish-black seeds have a pleasant nutty taste and crunchy texture. They are well-known in Middle Eastern and European cuisine as a topping for breads and cakes or ground up and sweetened as a pastry filling. White poppy seeds are much used in Indian cuisines. They are even smaller than black poppy seeds, have a similar flavour and are creamy-white. When ground, they add special flavours to Bengali dishes. They are especially used as a thickener for sauces or gravies. (Flours are generally not used in Indian cuisine for this purpose.) Obtain black poppy seeds from any grocer or supermarket. White poppy seeds can be purchased at Indian grocers.

PRASADAM

Food that has been offered to God before being eaten. *Prasadam* means "God's mercy". See the Introduction for more information.

PULAO

The terms *pulao* (*pilau*) and *pilaf* refer to classical rice dishes where dry rice is fried in oil or butter until it becomes translucent before liquid is added. The oil impregnates the outer layers of the grains and helps keep them separate while cooking.

QUINOA

(Pronounced *keen-wa*). Given the name "the mother grain" by ancient farmers in the South American Andes, *quinoa* has been cultivated for 5,000 years. Like buckwheat, it is called a grain but it is technically the fruit of a plant in the *Chenopodium* family. The most common variety of *quinoa* is pale yellow, and in both size and appearance is a cross between millet and yellow mustard seeds. It is highly nutritious and contains more protein than any other grain, an average of 16.2 per cent compared to 14 per cent for wheat.

It can be cooked like rice and yields a light, nutty flavoured result. For Vedic vegetarians, *quinoa* is a welcome food for Ekadasi grain fasting menus. *Quinoa* is available at health food and specialty stores.

RADICCHIO

A crunchy-textured salad green with a refreshingly bitter flavour. The most common variety has a spherical head and reddish-purple leaves with creamy-white ribs. When selecting radicchio, look for a compact head with fresh leaves without brown spots. Store in an upright container in the crisper section of the refrigerator.

RAITA

A name given to a wide range of raw or semi-cooked fruit and vegetable salads served on the Indian sub-continent.

RAU RAM

(See VIETNAMESE MINT.)

RICOTTA CHEESE

Crumbly, soft, white cheese made from the whey of cow's milk and popular in Italian cuisine. It is frequently used in cooking both sweet and savoury dishes in Italy, for like curd cheese or cottage cheese its mild, somewhat bland flavour combines well with other ingredients. It is available at selected supermarkets or grocers.

RIGANI

Greek or wild oregano is a stronger, sharper version of the familiar Italian herb. *Rigani* is sold dried in large bunches in Greek stores. It is worth seeking out to give an authentic flavour to Greek recipes. Italian oregano can be substituted, but the flavour will not be as authentic.

RISOTTO

The rice eaten throughout Northern Italy. Authentic *risotto* should be prepared only with an Italian *superfino* rice, such as *arborio* rice. In *risotto* cooking, the rice is first coated in butter, then cooked slowly with the gradual addition of stock, and stirred continuously until the stock is absorbed and the rice is soft, with a gentle coating of sauce.

ROCKET (See ARUGULA.)

ROSEMARY

The small, narrow, aromatic leaves of the evergreen shrub, *Rosmarinus officinalis*. This fragrant seasoning herb with its clean, woody odour reminiscent of pine, is popular in some European cuisines. Its strong, camphor-like taste is not always appreciated, however, and it is easily overused. Because whole leaves of dried rosemary are not pleasant to find in a dish, I find it useful to grind them to a powder before using. If fresh rosemary is available, whole sprigs can be added to a dish and removed at the completion of the cooking.

ROSE WATER

The diluted essence of rose petals, particularly from the highly scented species *Rosa damascena* and *Rosa centifolia*. It is widely used throughout the Middle East and India as a flavouring agent. It is available at Middle Eastern and Indian grocers.

RYE FLOUR

A flour made from milled rye, popular for bread making.

SAFFRON

The slender dried stigmas of the flowers of *Crocus sativus*, grown commercially in Spain, Kashmir and China. When the plants bloom, the brilliant stigmas, the flower parts that collect pollen, are hand-picked daily, just as the plants open in the early morning. About 210,000 dried stigmas, picked from about 70,000 flowers, yield half a kilo of saffron. Understandably, the cost of saffron production is very high, and saffron is the world's most expensive spice. Prices range from $3,000 to $5,000 per kilo.

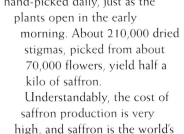

After picking, the saffron is dried in sieves over low heat, then stored immediately. The final product is a compressed, highly aromatic, matted mass of narrow, thread-like, dark-orange to reddish-brown strands, about 2.5 cm (1-inch) long.

Saffron has a pleasantly spicy, pungent, slightly bitter, honey-like taste, with such a potent colouring power that one part of its colouring component, known as crocin, is capable of colouring up to 150,000 parts of water unmistakably yellow.

Saffron has enjoyed immense popularity throughout the world for centuries. By the sixteenth century, for instance, saffron was being extensively cultivated in England as a culinary spice. Its popularity today is limited to mainly Indian, French, Middle Eastern and Spanish cuisines. Saffron strands should be soaked and ground or slightly dry-roasted and powdered before using. A big pinch of saffron is sufficient to colour a whole dish, but be sure to purchase the real thing — saffron is often adulterated. And remember, there is no such thing as cheap saffron! Saffron is available at Indian grocers, gourmet stores and large Chinese medical centres where it is known as *hoong fa* (ask for the more expensive variety).

SAHLEP

A powder derived from the *Sahlep* orchid, *Orchis mascula*. It makes a delicious hot drink when added to milk. *Sahlep* powder is available from Turkish or Middle Eastern grocery stores.

SALSA

The word *salsa* literally means "sauce" in Spanish. Outside of Spanish-speaking countries, it usually refers to a sauce or relish made with freshly chopped, uncooked ingredients, usually tomatoes, a herb, fresh chilies and sometimes a little lime or lemon juice.

SAMBAL OELEK

A hot condiment made from ground, fresh, hot red chilies, popular in Malay and Indonesian cuisine. It is often added to a dish for an extra hot chili dimension or served as an accompaniment. Available at Asian grocery stores.

To make 2 teaspoons (10 ml) of your own *sambal oelek*, pound together two hot red chilies and ½ teaspoon salt.

SAMBAR MASALA

A zesty South Indian spice combination, always added to the famous hot and sour *dal* dish called *sambar*. Varieties of *sambar* powder are available, each with different combinations of ingredients. To make your own *sambar masala*, refer to the *Special Ingredients* section of this book, or purchase *sambar masala* at Indian grocery stores.

SANTAN
(See COCONUT MILK.)

SEA SALT (See CELTIC SALT.)

SEMOLINA

The cream-coloured cereal obtained from hard durum wheat grains in the middle stages of flour milling, when the wheat germ, bran and endosperm are separated. The first millings of the endosperm are known as semolina. Semolina is ground fine, medium and coarse. Besides being used for making pasta in Italy, where semolina enjoys great popularity, it is also used in Indian cuisine, where it is known as *sooji*. It is simmered for fluffy, sweet *halava* puddings or savoury vegetable dishes called *upma*. I find that medium or coarse-ground semolina yields the best semolina *halava*. Semolina is available at Indian, Italian or specialty grocers and supermarkets.

SERRANO

(See CHILIES.)

SESAME SEEDS

The seeds of the cultivated annual plant, *Sesamum indicum*, grown predominantly in India and China. These flat, pear-shaped seeds are generally lightly roasted to bring out their nutty flavour and are popular in many cuisines of the world. In Western cuisine, they are scattered on breads and cakes before baking; they are ground into a delicious Middle Eastern confection called *halva* and a semi-liquid paste called tahini; in Japanese cuisine they are roasted with sea salt and ground to a fine powder called *gomashio*, a versatile condiment; and they are popular in many regional Indian cuisines.

STAR ANISE

The dried, hard, brown, star-shaped fruit of the small evergreen tree, *Illicium verum*. Star anise has a delicate, dry, spicy, woody, anise-like flavour and odour, and is an ingredient in the Chinese five-spice powder. It is delicious in chutneys, savoury dishes and in poached fruits. It is available at well-stocked gourmet or Indian grocers.

SNAKE BEANS

Known by various names, including asparagus bean, Chinese long bean and yard bean. These narrow, round-bodied beans are dark green, stringless and approximately 30 to 40 centimetres (12–16 inches) in length. They taste similar to green beans, but have a denser texture. Choose slender, crisp, bright-green beans, with no blemishes or signs of yellowing. They are best stored wrapped in plastic in the refrigerator. Available at Indian and Asian vegetable markets and well-stocked supermarkets.

SPLIT PEAS

Skinned and split, green or yellow dried peas. They cook to a hearty, creamy purée. Yellow split peas can replace *toor* or *chana dal* in a recipe. They are available at all supermarkets and grocery stores.

MUNG BEAN SPROUTS

Sprouted, whole green mung beans. In Chinese cooking, the mung beans are allowed to sprout until quite long. However, from a nutritional point of view, mung beans are best used when the beans have just sprouted and the shoot is less than 1 cm long. Sprouted mung beans are crisp in texture and bursting with nutrition. In Indian cuisine, (see *Sautéed Sprouted Mung Beans*), these barely-sprouted beans are favoured. They're rich in vitamins B, C and E. Sprouted mung beans are 37 per cent protein (their protein content is highly digestible). They are pleasantly sweet, low in calories and inexpensive.

SRILA PRABHUPADA

The Founder-Acarya (spiritual master) of the International Society for Krishna Consciousness (ISKCON). His Divine Grace A.C. Bhaktivedanta Swami Srila Prabhupada was the author of many spiritual texts and the world's most distinguished teacher of Vedic religion and thought. He guided his Society and saw it grow to a worldwide confederation of hundreds of *asramas*, schools, temples, institutes and farm communities.

SUNFLOWER SEEDS

The tightly packed core of sunflowers yields small oval-shaped off-white to grey-coloured kernels. They are firm in texture with a nutty crunch and are rich in protein (23 per cent). They are also a good source of zinc, iron, potassium and magnesium. Sunflower seeds are a versatile kitchen ingredient and are equally great in salads, pasta dishes, cereals and breads. Available at most super-markets or health food stores.

SUPERFINO RICE

(See ARBORIO RICE.)

TAHINI

A semi-liquid sesame butter used in Middle Eastern cuisine. This cream-grey paste has the consistency of runny peanut butter and is the basis of various salad dressings and *mezze* (entrées) throughout Greece, Cyprus, Lebanon, Jordan and Syria, where it is known as *tahina*.

TAMARIND

The pulp extracted from the brown pods of the tamarind tree, *Tamarindus indica*. The fresh pulp has a sour, fruity taste and is popular in Indian and Indonesian cooking. Tamarind is available in different forms commercially. The crudest consists of blocks of partly dried, unpitted, broken, sticky fibrous pods. They should be macerated in water to extract the sour, brown tamarind juice, as should blocks of seedless tamarind. The most convenient is tamarind concentrate, which can be used straight from the jar. Tamarind makes excellent sweet and sour chutneys or sauces and can be used in vegetable dishes and curries. Tamarind in its various forms is available at Indian and South-East Asian grocery stores.

TANDOOR OVEN

A barrel-shaped vertical standing oven for baking flatbreads, used by millions of people in north-west India, Pakistan and Central Asia, from Iran in the east to CIS countries in the west. Lined with clay and heated by either burning wood, dung, coal or gas, the fire burns fiercely at the bottom of the oven, preheating the oven walls. When the *tandoor* is sufficiently hot, the fire is dampened or lowered to maintain an even heat. The flatbreads are usually moistened, then slapped against the hot inside walls of the oven, then baked for a very short time. Baking on the hot walls gives the breads a firm, well-browned bottom crust. *Naan* is probably the most well-known *tandoor* baked bread. (See *Punjabi Baked Flatbread, Naan*.)

TARKARI

A textured, moist, braised vegetable combination, usually consisting of at least two vegetables cooked together with North Indian seasonings.

TAVA

A slightly concave iron griddle, 23–30cm (9–12 inches) in diameter, used for cooking flatbreads. A good quality *tava* should be at least 0.5cm (¼ inch) thick, with a smooth surface. Like all iron cookware, it must be seasoned with a little oil to avoid rusting. A *tava* is especially well-suited for cooking griddle-fried *parathas*, since its concave shape keeps the oil at the bottom of the pan where it is needed. *Tavas* are sold at Indian grocery stores.

TEMPE

Yellow-brown cakes of compressed, culture-inoculated, fermented whole soya beans. A soft white coating, similar to that which covers cheese like brie or camembert, forms over the cakes, holding the grains together. The texture of *tempe* is soft-crunchy, and nutritionally *tempe* is high in easily-assimilated proteins and low in cholesterol. *Tempe* is particularly popular in Indonesian cuisine. Obtain *tempe* from the chilled food compartment of Asian and health food stores. *Tempe* can be kept for several weeks in the refrigerator and freezes well.

THAI BASIL

Also known as *bai horapa*. It is a popular ingredient in Vietnamese, Thai and Chinese cookery. It is easily distinguished from sweet basil by its deep-purple stems and purple-tinged leaves, and has a more pungent, slightly anise flavour. Store it standing upright in a container of water at room temperature. Available at Asian greengrocers.

THAI RICE

A long-grained, aromatic white rice from Thailand. Sometimes called jasmine rice, it cooks to large, soft, fluffy grains.

THYME

This attractive herb is grown in Mediterranean regions and Asia Minor. There are more than 100 species of thyme, but common or garden thyme, *Thymus vulgaris*, is frequently used. Others include lemon, mint, orange, golden-lemon, caraway-scented, woolly-stemmed, and the silver thyme. Used fresh or dried, thyme imparts a distinctively warm, pleasant, aromatic flavour and is popular as one of the great European culinary herbs. It is used alongside bay and parsley in *bouquet garni*, and goes into many soups and vegetable dishes, especially potatoes, zucchini, eggplant and sweet peppers. It is available fresh at selected greengrocers and dried at grocery stores and supermarkets.

TOFU

Soy bean curd or tofu is used in Chinese, Japanese, Korean and Indonesian cooking. This white, almost tasteless and odourless substance is produced from soya beans that have been successively crushed, boiled in water, strained and pressed into a mould. Tofu is low in calories and is cholesterol-free. High in protein, tofu is becoming increasingly popular in Western kitchens. Standard Chinese tofu, which is lightly pressed, is sold fresh in most Chinese grocers. It has the consistency of firm custard. A firmer variety of tofu is also available in Chinese shops and health food stores. This variety is good for slicing, cubing and deep-frying.

TOOR DAL

Also known as *arhar dal, toovar dal* or pigeon peas, these cream-coloured split lentils, which are paler in colour, flatter and larger than yellow split peas, are widely used for cooking in northern and south-western India. They have a delightful, slightly sweet flavour and are easy to digest, especially in the famous South Indian soup-like dishes, *rasam* and *sambar*. *Toor dal* is available at Indian grocers.

TORTILLA

A thin, round flatbread made from white cornmeal, or *masa. Tortillas* are the national bread of Mexico and are cooked on a griddle. They're eaten fresh and are also the basis of Mexican dishes such as *enchiladas* and *tacos*. Wheat *tortillas* are used in Mexican cuisine as well. They are featured in this book in *Pan-warmed Wheat Turnovers Stuffed with Goat's Cheese and Sundried Tomatoes (Quesadilla)* and *Mexican Spicy Bean and Cheese Stuffed Flatbreads (Burras)*.

TREACLE

A sugar by-product produced from the liquid remaining after the refined sugar has been crystallised. It is a viscous, dark-brown to black syrup. Its colour and unique flavour make it suitable for baking.

TURMERIC

The rhizome or underground stem of the tropical herb *Curcuma longa*. The short, waxy, orange-yellow rhizomes are boiled, cleaned, sundried and then ground to a fine, aromatic, yellowish powder that is used as an essential ingredient in Asian and especially Indian cooking. Turmeric adds a brilliant yellow colour to cooked dishes and imparts a slightly bitter, pungent flavour.

Used in vegetable, legume, bean and *dal* dishes, it introduces colour and warmth to a dish, although overuse produces excessive colour and bitterness. Turmeric powder is available at Indian grocers and specialty stores. Fresh turmeric root is becoming more easily available in Asian stores. The most common is red turmeric (*Zingiber curcuma longa*). These small roots need to be scraped or carefully peeled to expose the deep burnt-orange flesh. Crushed in a mortar and pestle or grated, they form the basis of curry pastes, especially in Thai cuisine. I have used fresh turmeric root in rice with delicious results, as well as chopped finely in *dals* and soups. Fresh turmeric is available seasonally from well-stocked Asian grocers.

URAD DAL

The split dried beans from the plant *Phaseolus mungo*. Whole *urad* beans are blackish-grey. Split *urad dal* are cream-white. Their shape resembles their close relative, split mung *dal*. They are used to prepare protein-rich purées and soups in Indian cuisine, and when combined with grains and milk products, their protein value increases. In South Indian cooking, they are fried in ghee or oil for use as a nutty seasoning and soaked and ground into dumplings, pancakes and fried savouries. *Urad dal* is available at Indian grocery stores.

VAISNAVA

A devotee of the Supreme Lord.

VANILLA

The pod of the climbing tropical orchid, *Vanilla planifolia*. The vanilla flavouring material is obtained from the dried, cured, partially ripe pods. The white crystalline compound called vanillin, present only in the cured black pods, provides the delicately sweet, rich, spicy and persistent aroma which characterises vanilla.

Whole vanilla beans are cooked with creams, custards and sauces in French cuisine. The beans can be washed, dried and re-used. Vanilla sugar and pure vanilla essence are substitutes. Vanilla beans are available at specialty grocers.

VEDIC

The original culture of India, based on the tenets of the four original scriptures, the *Vedas*.

VIETNAMESE MINT

This pungent flavoured herb is not a true mint, but widely known by this common name. It is also known as Cambodian Mint, hot mint, *laksa* leaf, *daun laksa*, and *daun kesom*. It is easily available from Vietnamese grocers where it is known as *rau ram*. The leaves are narrow and pointed with distinctive dark markings in the centre. In Vietnamese cooking, the herb is not cooked but used in salads or eaten as a fresh accompaniment to the well-known Vietnamese spring rolls.

WATER CHESTNUTS

Fresh water chestnuts, with their crunchy, succulent texture and sweet, nutty taste, are a common delicacy in Asian cuisine. They are actually the edible root of an aquatic plant. The fresh water chestnut has a tight skin, and should be peeled and sliced as required. If unavailable at good Chinese produce markets, tinned Chinese water chestnuts sold at Chinese grocery stores are an acceptable although inferior-tasting substitute.

WHEY

The liquid by-product when milk is curdled in the curd-cheese making process, or from yogurt when it is allowed to drain in a cheesecloth. It can be used in bread-making, in soups or to cook vegetables. Allowed to sour, it can be used as an agent to curdle further batches of milk.

WHITE PEPPER

(See PEPPER.)

WILD RICE

Not an actual rice, wild rice (*Zizania aquatica*) is actually an aquatic grass. Since it cooks like rice, and is often mixed with real rice, cookbooks customarily include it in their rice recipe pages. Until recently, wild rice was grown mostly in the lakes and marshes of the northern Great Lakes region of the US and Canada. In 1992, wild rice production began in Australia. Wild rice takes longer to cook than regular rice, and when cooked doubles in size, unlike ordinary rice which quadruples in size. Although wild rice can be cooked for longer periods with extra water to form a very soft fluffy porridge of burst grains, it is traditionally cooked just short of bursting and should be fairly chewy.

WINGED BEANS

Also known as *goa* beans, these beans take their name from their flared appearance. They grow fast in tropical areas and in places where the soil is poor. The seeds, pods, shoots, flowers, leaves and roots are all edible. The seeds taste like a more starchy version of the green bean. Winged beans are available at well-stocked Asian grocers.

YAM BEANS

Known also as sweet turnip as well as by its Mexican name, *jicama* (pronounced *hee-kama*), a tuber native of tropical America as well as South-East Asia. The Asian variety of yam beans are disc-like with light brown skin and strongly marked segments. Their pleasantly crunchy, white flesh is slightly sweet and juicy and can be eaten raw, like a fruit. As such, yam beans are part of my *Indonesian Fruit Platter with Hot and Sweet Dipping Sauce*. Cooked as a vegetable in stir-fried dishes, yam beans make a good substitute for bamboo shoots or especially water chestnuts whose texture is similar. (See *Stir-fried Asian Vegetables*.)

When purchasing yam beans, choose tubers of moderate size with smooth, fine skin, indicating that they are young and fresh. To prepare yam beans, peel away the skin and slice or dice as required. While their flavour is delicate, they take on other flavours cooked with them. Obtain yam beans from Asian grocers or Latin American stores. Note the regional names for easy purchase: China, *saa got*; Indonesia and Malaysia, *bangkwang*; Philippines, *singkamas*; and Vietnam, *cu san*.

YEAST

Yeast is a single-celled fungus and works in bread by feeding upon the sugars in the dough. Later, it feeds on the maltose produced as starch granules are broken down by malt enzymes. As the yeast metabolises the sugars, it produces carbon dioxide and alcohol, a process in bread-making referred to as fermentation.

When the bread is placed in the oven to bake, the carbon dioxide expands in the heat and as it does it enlarges all the little air pockets by stretching the gluten.

Two types of yeast are available for baking bread: dry baking yeast, sometimes called dehydrated or dried yeast; and fresh yeast, sometimes called compressed yeast.

Brewer's and nutritional yeast are not suitable for bread-making, since neither have any rising properties.

Note that although dry yeast and fresh yeast are interchangeable in a recipe, you will need about twice the volume of fresh yeast as dried yeast. In other words, if a recipe calls for one teaspoon of dried yeast, you will need about two level teaspoons of fresh yeast.

YOGURT

This indispensable ingredient in the vegetarian kitchen can be easily made at home by adding a small amount of "starter" (which can be either previously prepared homemade yogurt or commercial plain yogurt) to warm milk. When incubated in a warm place for at least four hours, the live bacteria in the starter will transform the milk into yogurt, which can then be refrigerated and used as needed. Yogurt is called for in several recipes in this book, such as *Creamy Banana and Yogurt Salad*, *Chickpea Dumplings in Creamy Karhi Sauce* and *Lemon Yogurt Shake*.

ZEST

The thin, coloured skin of an orange or lemon, used to give flavour to various dishes. It is very thinly pared without any of the white bitter pith.

SUGGESTED MENUS

NORTH INDIAN BRUNCH
Green Papaya and Potato *Tarkari*
Super-flaky Wholemeal Griddle-fried Breads (*Parathas*)
Spicy Guava Jam
Fresh Fruits
Mango Nectar

INDONESIAN BRUNCH
Plain Boiled Rice
Indonesian Crispy Corn Fritters (*Perkedel Jagung*)
Hot Chili Relish (*Sambal Bajek*)
Indonesian Fruit Platter with Hot and Sweet Dipping Sauce (*Rujak Manis*)
Avocado Smoothie

ALFRESCO LUNCH I
Stuffed Baby Pumpkins
Spicy Cajun Cornbread
Sicilian Eggplant Appetiser (*Caponata*)
Fresh Peach Chutney
Gourmet Green Salad with Herbed French Dressing
Old Fashioned Homemade Lemonade

ALFRESCO LUNCH II
Simple Carrot and Ginger Soup
Rich and Tasty Lasagna with Grilled Vegetables and Sundried Tomatoes
Gourmet Green Salad with Herbed French Dressing
Herbed Bread Rolls
Poached Pear and Prune Tart

EAST-WEST LUNCH
Pecan and Orange Wild Rice *Pilaf*
Quick and Simple Snake Beans
Mauritian-style *Dal* Rissoles (*Gateaux-piments*) with Home-style Tomato Chutney
Cheesy Vegetable Tart
Kumquat and Passionfruit Refresher

GUJARATI LUNCH
Fragrant *Basmati* Rice
Sautèed Sprouted Mung Beans (*Vadu*)
Simple Gujarati Pumpkin
Steamed Semolina Bread (*Dhokla*)
Sweet and Sour Tamarind Chutney

CENTRAL INDIAN LUNCH
Hearty *Dal* with Vegetables (*Dalma*)
Fragrant *Basmati* Rice
Trinidad-style Flatbread (*Roti*)
Creamy Banana and Yogurt Salad (*Kela Raita*)
Tender Eggplant Pickles

ITALIAN SUMMER LUNCH
Chilled Avocado and Green Peppercorn Soup
Stuffed Baked Eggplant (*Melanzane Ripieni al Forno*)
Tender Pan-fried Asparagus
Stuffed Italian Flatbread (*Focaccia*)
Gourmet Green Salad with Herbed French Dressing

EAST-WEST PICNIC
Mayapur-style Stuffed Vegetable Pastries (*Samosas*)
Bush Tomato Chutney
Bavarian Potato Salad
Old English Saffron Bread
Iced Tamarind Soda

SOUTH INDIAN BUFFET
Hot and Spicy South Indian Tomato Rice
Buttermilk *Sambar*
Savoury Lentil Doughnuts (*Vadai*)
South Indian Coconut Chutney
South Indian Carrot Salad

CENTRAL AMERICAN BUFFET
Sweet Potato Soup with Corn and Chilies
Mexican Spicy Bean and Cheese Stuffed Flatbreads (*Burras*)
Mexican Green Chili Rice (*Arroz Verde*)
Spanish-style Curly Endive Salad (*Xato*)
Chilled Papaya Refresher (*Refresco de Papaya*)

INTERNATIONAL DINNER PARTY
Roasted Capsicum, Peanut and Tomato Soup
Turkish Pilaf with Currants and Pine Nuts
Spicy Bengali Potatoes
Spinach and Curd Cheese Patties (*Kofta*)
Fresh Coriander and Macadamia *Pistou*
Vegetable *Crudités* with Quick and Easy Cashew Chutney
Apricot and Walnut Crescents (*Rugelach*)

GREEK DINNER PARTY
Greek-style White Bean Vegetable Soup (*Fasoulada*)
Greek-style Eggplant Casserole (*Moussaka*)
Warm Vegetable Salad with Greek-style Oil and Lemon Dressing
Crusty Bread, Cheese and Olives
Greek-style Nut-filled Pastries in Fragrant Syrup (*Kataifi*)

NORTH INDIAN GOURMET DINNER
Punjabi Red Bean Curry (*Rajma*)
Seasoned Eggplant Rice
Punjabi Baked Flatbread (*Naan*)
Green Mango, Mint and Coriander Chutney
Creamy Banana and Yogurt Salad (*Kela Raita*)
Crispy Fried Batter Spirals in Saffron Syrup (*Jalebis*)

MEDITERRANEAN DINNER PARTY
Pumpkin Dumplings with Sage-scented Butter and Parmesan Cheese (*Gnocchi di zucca*)
Sicilian-style Roasted Sweet Peppers in Olive Oil (*Insalata di Peperoni Arrostiti*)
Tomato, Basil and Fresh *Mozzarella* Salad (*Insalata Caprese*)
Crusty Bread
Hot Roasted Jacket-baked Potatoes with *Arugula Pesto*
Spinach with Pine Nuts and Raisins
Rose-scented Marzipan Half-moon Pastries

CENTRAL INDIAN BANQUET
Festive Nine-Jewels Rice (*Navaratnam Pulao*)
Savoury Chickpeas in Tomato Glaze
Puffed Fried Sesame Bread (*Til Poories*)
Savoury Fresh Cheese Balls in Creamy Tomato Sauce (*Malai Kofta*)
Sautéed Potatoes with Cashews
Ginger, Saffron and Pistachio *Kulfi*
Lemon Yogurt Shake (*Nimbu Lassi*)

ASIAN BANQUET
Thai-style Fragrant Rice Balls
Crispy Fried Gluten with Sweet and Sour Sauce
Curried Malay Noodles (*Laksa*)
Spicy Javanese Eggplant (*Balado Terong*)
Stir-fried Asian Vegetables
Daikon Radish Salad

INDEX

ABOUT THE AUTHOR

Kurma dasa was born in England in 1952 and migrated with his parents to Australia in 1964. He attended Vaucluse Boys High School in Sydney and then went on to study at the University of New South Wales. It was in Sydney in the early '70s that he became a member of the International Society for Krishna consciousness, more popularly known as the Hare Krishna Movement.

Already embracing a healthy appreciation of good cooking, it was a natural sequence of events that led Kurma to the kitchens of the Movement. He started off, as most chefs do, cutting vegetables, grinding fresh herbs and spices and observing the experienced cooks at work.

He became a disciple of the Movement's founder in 1971 at the time of His Divine Grace A. C. Bhaktivedanta Swami Prabhupada's first visit to the temple in Sydney. It was from Prabhupada that Kurma first became inspired to follow his natural propensity as a cook, and at the same time satisfy his spiritual cravings.

Kurma has gained a wealth of culinary experience by travelling to India many times between 1974 and 1980, where he learned various regional cuisines. Across the massive sub-continent, he observed and assisted cooks in temples, restaurants and private homes.

In 1980 he became head chef at Gopal's Vegetarian Restaurant in Swanston Street, Melbourne. His cooking of over 1,800 meals a week propelled Gopal's to become one of Melbourne's, and indeed Australia's, most popular and best-known vegetarian eating places.

Desiring to share his experience with others, he first began teaching in 1981. It was not long before his cooking classes at the restaurant became booked out months ahead.

Kurma's presentation of healthy, delicious, attractive and innovative cuisine helped shake off the outdated notion that vegetarian food was dull, lack-lustre and bland.

It was at Gopal's that Kurma realised his full potential. Using his wealth of experience in various Indian cooking techniques, he was able to branch out into international vegetarian cuisine. He presented the best vegetarian items from the world's popular cuisines — Italian, French, Chinese, Mexican, to name but a few — and expertly blended them into innovative and tasty "East-West" combinations, much to the delight of his enthusiastic clientele.

The mid-eighties saw Kurma travel extensively across the world, simultaneously teaching and demonstrating his cooking in restaurants, schools and colleges of such places as London, Milan, Warsaw, Delhi, Stockholm and Beijing.

For Kurma, his teaching and travelling helped him gain an in-depth respect for international cuisine, although his passion for Indian cooking is still his primary sustaining force.

In 1987, he was contacted by his old friend David Shapiro, who was now head of ITV Productions in Los Angeles. With David, Kurma produced and directed a series of 13 television shows. *Cooking with Kurma* was screened across North America on PBS and throughout England and South Africa, receiving excellent viewer response.

As a natural consequence to his television shows, Kurma wrote his cookbook *Great Vegetarian Dishes*, receiving wide claim for its professional, clearly written and richly illustrated presentation of international vegetarian cuisine. The book, now in its sixth print run – 120,000 copies – continues to generate letters of appreciation from readers worldwide.

Perhaps Kurma's biggest success was his last TV series, based on *Great Vegetarian Dishes*. The 26-part series, also called *Great Vegetarian Dishes*, was screened in over 46 countries and seen by over 200 million viewers worldwide. It was broadcast across Asia and India via Star-Plus satellite TV.

Certainly Kurma has earned the epithet by which he is now known by among his closer friends and associates "The Gourmet's Guru". Kurma currently lives in Perth with his wife and son.

If you wish to correspond with the author, please write to him at:

PO Box 102, Bayswater, WA 6053 Australia

kurma@com.org